SUN, SEX, AND SOCIALISM

Cuba in the German Imaginary

GERMAN AND EUROPEAN STUDIES

General Editor: Rebecca Whitmann

JENNIFER RUTH HOSEK

Sun, Sex, and Socialism

Cuba in the German Imaginary

UNIVERSITY OF TORONTO PRESS
Toronto Buffalo London

ISBN 978-1-4426-4138-9

Library and Archives Canada Cataloguing in Publication

Hosek, Jennifer Ruth, 1969–
Sun, sex, and socialism : Cuba in the German imaginary / Jennifer Ruth Hosek.

(German and European studies)
Includes bibliographical references and index.
ISBN 978-1-4426-4138-9

1. Germany – Relations – Cuba.   2. Cuba – Relations – Germany.
3. Germany – Civilization – Cuban influences.   I. Title.   II. Series: German
and European studies

DD120.C9H68 2012   327.430729109'045.   C2012-901627-6

This book has been published with the help of a grant from the Canadian
Federation for the Humanities and Social Sciences, through the Aid to
Scholarly Publications Program, using funds provided by the Social
Sciences and Humanities Research Council of Canada.

University of Toronto Press acknowledges the financial assistance to its
publishing program of the Canada Council for the Arts and the Ontario
Arts Council.

Canada Council   Conseil des Arts
for the Arts   du Canada

ONTARIO ARTS COUNCIL
CONSEIL DES ARTS DE L'ONTARIO

University of Toronto Press acknowledges the financial support of the
Government of Canada through the Canada Book Fund for its publishing
activities.

To Ruth

For Rosie

In memory of Miguel Benavides

Contents

Figures

Acknowledgments

Portions of chapter three were previously published as '"Subaltern Nationalism" and the West Berlin Anti-authoritarians,' *German Politics and Society* 26.1 (Spring 2008), 57–81. An earlier version of chapter one was previously published as '*Buena Vista* Deutschland: Gender and Nation in Wenders, Gaulke and Eggert,' *German Politics and Society* 25.1 (Spring 2007), 46–69. I am grateful for permission to reuse that material here.

This project is the work of many. A tremendous thanks to the following persons and my apologies in advance for any omissions; so many have been so generous.

In North America: Julie Anderson, Barton Byg, Helen Cafferty, Belinda Davis, Karen Dubinsky, Max Friedman, Francisco García González, Veronika Garibotto, Gerd Gemünden, Kai Herklotz, Bob Holub, Young-Sun Hong, Marike Janzen, Tony Kaes, Cathie Krull, Sara Lennox, Susan Lord, Jacqueline Loss, Francine Masiello, Barbara Mennel, Matthew Miller, Dirk Moses, Christopher Nagle, Kerim Ousman, Walter Roberts, Miryam Sas, Christina Schwenkel, Jill Scott, Hinrich Seeba, Katrin Sieg, Irene Siegel, Quinn Slobodian, Nathalie Soini, Jim Spohrer, Anna Stenport, Frank Thompson, Jamie Trnka, and Kat Vester, as well as (members of) the UCB Comparative Literature Department, the UCB German Department, the Townsend Center Tourism Studies Working Group, the Beatrice Bain Research Group, the DEFA Film Library, the Coalition of Women in German, and the editorial staff at University of Toronto Press, especially my wise and kind editor Richard Ratzlaff.

In Germany: Roland Berbig, Peter Birle, Volker Braun, Ulrike Brodien, Jürgen Brüning, Nadja Bunke, Birgit Dahlke, Jeannette Eggert, Hans Magnus Enzensberger, Uli Gaulke, Mirko Gemmel, Tobias Hauser,

Ursula Heukenkamp, Frank Hoernigk, Bert Hoffmann, Gerlinde Irmscher, Günter Jordan, Ingo Juchler, Raimund Krämer, Wolfgang Kraushaar, Klaus Laabs, Bruce LaBruce, Christoph Links, Siegfried Lokatis, Siegward Lönnendonker, André Lüdtke, Kurt Maetzig, members of Cuba Sí, the Deutsch-Kubanische Gesellschaft, and El Caimán, Klaus Meschkat, Markus Mohr, Urs Müller-Plantenberg, Eberhard Panitz, Bernd Rabehl, Dieter Rauch, Christian Schertz, Hannelore Scholz, Arnold Schölzel, Rainer Schultz, Peter B. Schumann, seminar participants of the Berlin Program 2006–7, Christian Semler, Stefan Seum, Quinn Slobodian, Hasso Spode, Ute Woefel, and Michael Zeuske, as well as the archivists and staff at many institutions, including the Humboldt Universität, Staatsbibliothek zu Berlin, Deutsche Bibliothek, Ibero-Amerikanisches Institut, Institut für Sozialforschung, Bundesarchiv-Filmarchiv, APO-Archiv, Stiftung Archiv der Parteien und Massenorganisationen der DDR im Bundesarchiv, and especially the Hochschule für Film und Fernsehen.

In Cuba: Jorge Luis Acanda, Aurelio Alonzo Tejada, Miguel Benavides, Gabriel Benítez, Luisa Campuzano, María Caridad Cumaná González, Ulises Estrada Lescaille, Victor Fowler, Julio García Oliveras, Rafael Hernández, Marco Madrigal, Antonio Masón, Mario Naito, Rogelio Paris, Svend Plesch, Guillermo Rodríguez Rivera, Joaquín Santana Castillo, and Sander Zequeira García.

Institutional financial support came variously from the University of California, Berkeley; Stanford University; Queen's University; the Coalition of Women in German; the Berlin House of Parliament; the DAAD; the Humboldt Foundation; and the Mellon Foundation.

Finally, my deep gratitude to my early mentors Muriel Odel and Michael Palencia-Roth, family, and friends.

A Note on the Cover Images

The front image remakes Verena Kuzmany's original February 2008 snapshot: a postcard attached by one red and one green Ampelmännchen magnet to the brushed steel front of a sleek refrigerator in a Charlottenburg community living apartment. Its residents had moved to West Berlin in the 1960s as young, leftist artists when the Federal Republic was offering financial incentives and male city residents were not drafted. The Havana Hotel Nacional souvenir (original postcard sans automobile) hearkened to their post-1989 visit on the newly independent, intensely suffering, and fiercely socialist Cuba. Their traffic figure magnets of 'Save the Ampelmännchen' fame fondly and super-ficially remake East Germany as domesticated commodity. Kuzmany notes that the residents and their milieu 'were quite attached to the idea of their "old West," and a bit protective of it – that is, its subculture and arts scene, about which I heard lots of stories. They did not ven-ture much into former East Berlin, or the parts of town now considered young and hip … It had not occurred to me that people would feel nostalgia for … former West Berlin.'

The back image captures a metropolitan *camello* bus. While from afar, Cuba's 1950s U.S. automobiles seem cast-metal nostalgia and mystique; from up-close, their longevity testifies to their *chofers'* mechanical skill, inventiveness, and necessity. It is the camello that better emblematizes both Cubans' resilience and ingenuity during the Special Period after the Berlin Wall's opening, and also their suffering. In Havana, the last 'camel buses' – with their truck trailers, distinctive humps, and lurch-ing gaits – were replaced by modern buses from China in 2008. Camel-los continue to service passengers outside the capital city.

Abbreviations

BA-FA	Bundesarchiv-Filmarchiv (Federal Archive-Film Archive) at Fehrbellinerplatz, Berlin
BStU	Bundesbehörde für die Stasi-Unterlagen (Federal administrative agency of the Stasi documents)
DEFA	Deutsche Film-Aktiengesellschaft (German film corporation, GDR)
FDJ	Freie Deutsche Jugend (Free German Youth, GDR youth organization)
FRG	Federal Republic of Germany
GDR	German Democratic Republic
HFF	Hochschule für Film und Fernsehen (Technical University for Film and Television, 'Konrad Wolf') in Potsdam
HV	Hauptverwaltung (central administration, GDR)
ICAIC	Instituto Cubano de Arte e Industria Cinematográficos (Cuban Institute of Cinematographic Art and Industry)
KPD	Kommunistische Partei Deutschland (communist party of Germany, FRG)
MfK	Ministerium für Kultur (Ministry of Culture, GDR)
MfS	Ministerium für Staatsicherheit (Ministry for State Security, GDR)
RIAS	Radio in the American Sector (station founded by the US founded, based in West Berlin)
SAPMO-BArch	Stiftung Archiv der Parteien und Massenorganisationen der DDR im Bundesarchiv (The foundation of the archive of GDR parties and popular organiza-

	tions in the federal archive) in Lichterfelde (alternative title: SAPMO-DDR)
SDS	Sozialistischer Deutscher Studentenbund (Socialist German Student Union)
SED	Sozialistische Einheitspartei Deutschlands (Socialist Unity Party of Germany, GDR)
SPD	Social Democratic Party of Germany
VEB	Volkseigene Betrieb ('People's Enterprise' – a firm officially under public ownership)
ZK der SED	Zentralkomitee der SED (Central Committee of the SED)

SUN, SEX, AND SOCIALISM

Cuba in the German Imaginary

Introduction

Well beyond the multiple ways in which 'Che lives!' on,[1] Cuba has infatuated Germans. This study examines Germans' most important tales of revolutionary Cuba to learn more about these Northern tellers. It builds upon a contested insight: that utopias, dystopias, and partial visions offer particularly trenchant understandings of the social discourses in which they arise and that they shape.[2] It demonstrates, for instance, that as site of projection and possibility, Cuba furthered inter-German alliances and inspired attempts for change at home. This assessment of utopia builds on the related and variously expressed notion that 'creative misunderstandings' about others reveal most about the tellers.[3] By refracting the post–Second World War Germanies through Cuba, this study reveals rarely seen perspectives that prevailing geopolitical narratives pre and post 1989 obscure. Always tied to material and political relations, many of these ways of seeing and doing spring the bounds of specific actors into discursive realms of the imagination.

This triangulated study of the Germans through their Cubas intervenes in debates arising with and enabled by the official end of the Cold War. It demonstrates, for instance, that German-Cuban linkages exceeding the parameters established by the U.S. and Soviet blocs were more extensive and influential than dominant histories of peaceful coexistence show. A brief defining of terms will illustrate these debates. Words categorize, and therefore homogenize and reinscribe, yet they also articulate power disparities, convey resistance, and enable communication.[4] In this book, I express competing perspectives by alternating between contested expressions. For instance, I use the adjectives 'October' and 'missile' to describe the 1962 crisis and employ both primary descriptors for the period from 1947–89: 'Cold War' (coined in the United States) and 'peaceful coexistence' (favoured by the Soviet Union and

criticized by Cuba). This terminological practice may still risk overemphasizing the influence of the United States and the Soviets; the study
as a whole aims to unsettle this binary.[5] I employ local terms when
relating the perspectives under study, and analytic terms to highlight
power dynamics. Consider the naming of groups. From 1959 onward,
Cubans have preferred the terms 'imperialist'/'anti-imperialist' or
'revolutionary' and 'relatively more developed'/'underdeveloped.'
The GDR and the part of the student movement upon which I focus
used first/third world – with a gesture towards Third World Marxism –
rather than developed/underdeveloped, which gained currency in the
1970s. In contrast, critical discourses that oppose the first and second
worlds to the third world often include Eastern European bloc nations
as the first world.[6] The analytic designations North and South emphasize socio-economics and map onto geography.[7] Coined in 1980 by the
Independent Commission on International Development Issues under
former Chancellor of the Federal Republic of Germany Willy Brandt,
these terms are just as relevant in the post-1990 period.[8] I use North and
South analytically for the entire period of peaceful coexistence in an
attempt rethink its global relationships.

This case study of Cuba and the Germans helps us to understand
national identity more completely by revealing the unexpected influences of a Southern nation on Northern nations. As a projection and
idealized partner, Cuba shaped German self-understandings within
shifting and sometimes tenuous international relationships. This influence demonstrates that strong colonial, migrant, and politico-economic
ties are not necessary conditions for transnational connection. Moreover, Northern fantasies of Cuba change not only due to their dreamers,
but also due to real-world changes in this projection screen in the Caribbean. The Cuban-German example unsettles assumptions that nothing
of import for the North stems from the South or moves back and forth
across South-North borders. Its emphasis on the significance of extra-
national identifications and the constant work involved in shoring
up national alliances demonstrates that although national and citizen
identities co-constitute each other, domestic homogeneity is mythologi-
cal. The national is always already globally transnational.

Theorizing National Identity – Postcolonial, Minority,
and Transnational

This study contributes to lively debates about the formation of national identities. Benedict Anderson famously asks why citizens die for 'imagined communities' whose members they have not met and whose structures they have not chosen.[9] Cultural production furthers or undermines the 'daily plebiscite' necessary to re-create these enormous sociopolitical enterprises.[10] This book engages most intensely with conceptions of nation among German critical intellectuals and artists. It uncovers tensions and overlaps between these ideas, as well as demonstrates their influence on popular attitudes. It looks from above, below, and between at how the 'invention of tradition' intersects with grassroots ideas and practices to give rise to national entities.[11] It moves between specific and global perspectives to guard against the 'provincialism' – incisive specificity that remains inattentive to larger structures – that Lora Wildenthal bemoans.[12] It uniquely demonstrates how the South penetrates national borders and weaves the very fabric of the North, highlighting the hybridity and relationality that Edouard Glissant argues typifies nations.[13]

Not only do culture and nation-state articulate profoundly, artistic production can provide powerful alternatives to social structures. Similarly, disciplinary entities influence citizens and polities by legislating, sponsoring, and censoring such work. Narratives of Cuba both furthered German national policies and undermined them. For instance, in the early 1960s, GDR film-makers and writers thematized Cuba to express international solidarities that also engaged with their own fledgling nation. Frank Vogel's 1962 film *Und deine Liebe auch* (*And Your Love Too*) legitimates the GDR's construction of the Berlin Wall by paralleling it to revolutionary Cuba's shoreline defences. Kurt Maetzig's 1963 feature film *Preludio 11* attempts international solidarity against the West and illuminates inter-German debates through its representation of a U.S.-led mercenary invasion. More radically, Irmtraud Morgner's banned novel *Rumba auf einen Herbst* (*Rumba on an Autumn*, 1965) counters affirmative narratives and stereotypical gendering of the GDR by depicting Cuba as warning and hope for a new, fundamentally different generation of German socialists. These GDR tales ultimately sanction national borders although they unsettle national definitions. They reveal a fascination with reconciliation of individual and social goals that was also salient in the FRG at the time.

The sustained interrogation of German identity through Cuba undertaken here pushes the envelope of several contemporary debates on national identification. Postcolonial work examines the relationships between (post)colonized and (post)colonizing regions as processes of resistance and domination while emphasizing the constitutive agency of the other in such relationships. Widely cited Northern scholarship shows how the (de)colonized South shapes Northern conceptions of itself.[14] The end of colonialism proper and the concomitant destabilization of European nation-states have arguably precipitated the decline of the European modernist sentiment – that intimate core of the first-world psyche.[15] Anne McClintock has demonstrated the influence of the colonies on the British.[16] Gananath Obeyesekere has suggested that indigenous peoples performed 'nativeness' to meet the expectations of European visitors.[17] Analysis of Alexander von Humboldt's travels has shown how Latin Americans modulated reception of their culture.[18] Contact with and distance from colonies and the colonized shaped a particular Germanic 'imperial imagination.'[19] As Mary Louis Pratt puts it, 'the entity called Europe was constructed from the outside in as much as from the inside out.'[20]

This book suggests an expansion from postcolonial studies because focusing beyond paradigmatically colonial relations can illuminate understudied North-South connections. By triangulating national identity through an unstable third term – whose very instability suggests further multiplicity – it also moves from the binarism against which McClintock warns.[21] This study examines the complexity of instrumentalization and exoticization. For instance, although Cuba did (and does) not define the terms on which it functions as Northern role models, its influence sometimes promoted Cuban aims. Germans employed Cuba as utopian articulations of domestic desires that in turn recast domestic logics. 'Revolutionary fantasies' therefore had the potential to destabilize nationalist and imperialist tendencies in the North to the benefit of the South.[22] The effect on the ground is varied. At times, such revolutionary fantasies supported the peaceful coexistence of the Cold War on Soviet and U.S. terms, for instance by exposing the limits of global solidarian thinking. In other instances, they undermined domestic pruderies and international policies. Such fantasies helped Germans to rethink themselves and their place in the world. These visions primarily expressed first-world desires; yet attempts to learn from and with the third world both modulated North-South relationships and altered the North.

As these Cuban-German cases invite conceptual shifts in postcolonialism, they also engage thorny issues in minority studies. Such expansions are critical now, when assaults on both fields demonstrate both their relevance and their fragility. While these modes of inquiry work to unsettle notions of national homogeneity, recent debates seek to define the borders of minority discourse along a spectrum ranging from inclusivity that risks homogenization to exclusivity that risks obscurity. Leslie Adelson suggests employing a postcolonial lens for minority literature to increase its relevance; Claudia Breger uses notions such as mimicry to reveal orientalist assessments of 'multicultural' German writers.[23] Irene Kacandes considers German minority discourse distinct because most migrants in Germany live under unique material and cultural circumstances.[24] These debates have pressing strategic import. Yet must minority discourse respect ethnic boundaries, or can criteria such as common political goals provide cohesion?

Solidarian affinities between Cuba and the Germans suggest that minority cultures can bridge nationalities and ethnicities. Analytic classifications support this contention; for instance the postcolonial notion of 'oppositional discourse' has been employed to compare the aesthetics of both ethnic minority and GDR literature.[25] Such work resonates with the initially surprising thematic similarities I have found in texts by African-American and GDR women writers.[26] The study before you contends that German narratives of revolutionary Cuba function as oppositional discourse. This definition risks eliding power differentials. For instance, it could underplay distinctions in positioning between socialists of colour of the South and white radicals of the North. Yet, this perspective that defines oppositional discourses along strategic rather than ethnic standpoints opens up pathways as well. It destabilizes the potentially monolithic category of German by exploring the possibilities – and the problematics – of connections across ethnic, class, and national boundaries. Indeed, as I demonstrate in my analysis of the German intellectuals and writers Peter Weiss and Hans Magnus Enzensberger, when defined expansively, notions of oppositional discourse can expose connections between past imperialism and contemporary empire. In contrast, narrow historical focus on colonialism proper or on identity politics can elide study of how industrial nations may employ neocolonial globalization strategies for contemporary empire building.

Finally, the cultural history of Cuba and the Germans is also a transnational tale. Transnational studies emphasize interactions between members of various nations that take place beneath and beyond official exchange. For historian Young-Sun Hong, this perspective does not ignore the significance of national structures, nor does it discount the influence of foreign policy.[27] Instead, such work highlights that many types of connections shape the picture. Françoise Lionnet and Shu-mei Shih's 'minor transnationalism' emphasizes transnational participation 'from below' while keeping sight of all forms of connectivity across borders.[28] When practiced in these ways, such approaches decentre the nation-state and international policy and interrogate disciplinary practices.

Transnational analysis has overlooked many North-South and West-East influences. Such omission is typical in that work on Europe privileges the North and the West. Northern focus may seem particularly appropriate for the 'belated' colonizer Germany. Its imperial bonds may appear insignificant, especially when German fascism is mistakenly understood as a separate project. Writing the past is part of the 'forgetting' of certain histories that is critical for nation building, and so it may be expedient to forget this history insofar as political and social pressures do not dictate otherwise. Similarly, inventing tradition bonds the West. For instance, critical phases of European unification have seen emphasis on common histories for future goals. High-profile production in scholarship, media, cultural events, and educational exchange produce traditions of proto-federal identity. For the EU core nations Germany and France, such articulation includes in no small part the forgetting of potentially disruptive wartime pasts. This study bridges some of the gaps formed by hegemonic memory work. Its refracted approach means it can tease out influences of transhemispheric cultural imaginaries and ties between capitalist and socialist nations. Consider the German case from a different perspective. The emphasis on Western Europe is startling; do not the Germanies beg joint assessment?

This refracted examination of the Germanies through the prism of Cuba may be criticized for insufficient attention to Cuban perspectives. Does it reinscribe Northern privilege? The risk is exacerbated by geopolitics and my positioning as a North American scholar. An extended study of Cuba's influence on the Germanies from a Cuban perspective is overdue. Yet, the study at hand works to unsettle dominant paradigms by demonstrating the impact of diverse and underestimated extra-national influences on the North. Furthermore, in the spirit of Lionnet and Shih's work, I suggest that to engage with transpositional and transvaluational alignments and practices that are ideational, diffuse, and/or idealistic is to facilitate recognition of partial shifts and potentiations towards change. Especially in light of the significant material constraints involved in collaboration from below, we must find ways of seeing more than distinctly quantifiable successes. Such perspectives guard against a reflexive essentialism. Attempts matter;

we should attend to their varied array across national boundaries. Ideas are important; their transnational synergies create ripple effects and new materialities. My project contributes to transnational understandings of the Germanies in part by demonstrating that Cuba was and is influential in German cultural imaginaries in ways that surpass its material influences on, international relations with, or even diplomatic interest in these Northern nations.

Situating Nationalism and National Identity in the Germanies

As a singular colonizer and singular fascist with correspondingly unique post-war structures, Germany invites concentrated study of national identity. The Federal Republic of Germany (FRG) and the German Democratic Republic (GDR) variously 'worked through' the past while also strategically invoking it. The equally multilaterally embedded FRG of today has contended that its wartime histories and post-War responsibilities justify reserve in the international arena, yet it benefits from the more forceful actions of its allies.[29] Scholars are increasingly employing South-North perspectives to interrogate such positions. Katrin Sieg suggests that by identifying with subjects of oppression, a German can avoid consideration of historical complicity and cast himself as an 'outsider and moral arbiter.'[30] Sara Lennox, Sara Friedrichsmeyer, and Susanne Zantop argue that the focus of intellectuals and artists on neocolonialism risks eliding National Socialist pasts and presents.[31] Progressive FRG social movements are said to criticize contemporary globalization in lieu of examining German history.[32]

My own analysis of the post-War Germanies demonstrates continued attention to fascism as well as the global South in each. The above assessments that accurately describe paradigms common in official and mainstream discourse and among certain segments of the German left do not always apply. Critiques of imperialism and attempts at solidarian action are sometimes responses to both colonialism and fascism.[33] Discounting this possibility implies that national affiliations are fundamental and risks equating political identification and national affiliation. Arlene Teraoka has demonstrated how German writer in exile Peter Weiss's work on Vietnam attempted to prevent a repeat of Auschwitz.[34] I show how critical intellectuals, artists, and activists used Cuba to reinterpret German nationalism and to move towards transnational alignments. National pasts drive such transnationally inflected redefinitions whose sustained engagements are with global presents.

Reception of 'beyond' Germany has long shaped conceptions of 'within' Germany. Karl May's escapist travel literature of the U.S. Wild West expresses conflicts at home.[35] Germanic tales of 'The Orient' speak about Wilhelmine society.[36] 'Colonial fantasies' that circulated through Prussian material culture articulated and shaped domestic notions of nation.[37] 'Ethnic drag' performance of Native Americans and Turkish guest workers by white Germans has been shown to 'pivot' on the Holocaust as an obfuscated third element.[38]

My refractive viewing method situates German identities by attending to similar resonances and drawing on these ingenious reading traditions. Its apparently oblique strategy circumvents the entrenched positions of bloc politics that recent changes have only exacerbated. Capitalist and socialist 'sibling' nations invite comparison, yet years of divisiveness pre and post 1989 have made innovative direct evaluation impossible. Similarly, this study gives voice to national narratives silenced in popular and political spheres because they counter dominant explanations of growth. For these reasons, looking across the North-South axis enables richer understandings even of nations as intimately related as the FRG and the GDR. Indeed, my work on German-Southern relations invites further study of the international impacts of different socio-economic systems on the Germanies by highlighting that their many similarities allow for an unprecedented isolation of variables. Finally, there is a dearth of FRG-Southern analysis, and such work on the GDR is even rarer. This study demonstrates that understanding the FRG, the GDR, and also the larger FRG transnationally is necessary for comprehending national and global constellations.

A cultural studies approach is equally necessary. This investigation takes every genre seriously in order to consider the most important examples of German cultural production about Cuba. It recognizes that the island holds the attention of many Germans who did and do not engage significantly with what is often called high culture. Moreover, Cuba's exotic attraction is manifested in commerce as well as in what is commonly understood as art. This project accounts for the material and foreign relations between the Germanies and Cuba, while its primary aim is to reveal how 'revolutionary fantasies' of Cuba shaped German national understandings.

Germinal Tropes – Cubas, Islands, Utopias

In one of the few studies of Cuba and the Germans from a cultural perspective, Charlotte Melin and Cecile Zorach suggest multifaceted

connections to the island: 'Despite the pronounced and enticing differences between Cuba and the Germanies, the vulnerability of the
one seems to awaken feelings of affinity in writers from the other. In
German writing about Cuba, Berlin in particular, a small and isolated
entity caught between the superpowers, appears as a parallel to the
Caribbean island.'[39]

Cuba was compelling as a site of refraction for many Germans for
many reasons. While propinquity between the 'islands' of West Berlin
and the GDR cooled mutual admiration, remote Cuba gave impulses
for global futures. It was an alternative for left-leaning thinkers on both
sides of the Wall who were dissatisfied with Eastern bloc socialism
because the Southern nation seemed to offer a model of populist, non-
aligned governance. Although many Germans were sceptical of Cuban
concessions to the USSR, these compromises were sometimes seen as
born of necessity, not of ideology. Some Germans even identified with
the Cuban situation because they saw themselves as similarly dependent on the superpowers.

The fledgling country also recast the post-war problem of German
nationalism that National Socialism had contaminated. Many deemed
the Federal Republic's denazification to have been flawed at best.
Although the official GDR ideology represented its 'new' Germany as
explicitly and adamantly anti-fascist, many Germans questioned such
assertions as well. The Cuban model embodied an untainted nationalism that German leftists valued. Its socialist internationalism even
comfortingly maintained national structures while circumventing
imperialist aims.

Moreover, Cuba represented abrupt change inspired by revolutionary
thinkers of Latin America and revolutionary Marxism. This immediacy
was attractive for leftists who were not satisfied with rule from above
or with slow change from within. During the 1960s in particular, Cuba
seemed to concretize revolutionary, grassroots socialism, offering hope
that such radical shifts were possible on an international scale. In the
larger FRG, narratives of Cuba continue to express contested perspectives on the desired shape and positioning of contemporary Germany.

Finally, Germans longed to have that which they perceived to be
Cuban culture at home. Some fantasized the unification of individual
and social goals. Others envisioned a loosely organized and ever-
changing grassroots project. Many were attracted to this 'socialism
under the palms' where citizens expressed political support through
song and dance. Gender roles that were under intense scrutiny in Ger-

many seemed unproblematic in Cuba. Healthy, ethical sensuality and pleasure within a socialist paradigm was a welcome change from the ascetic, cerebral, and often embittered traditions of the established German left. Cuba had something for many a one.

For many Germans, Cuba is distinct from Latin America. A few recent historical, political, and cultural analyses have looked at German relationships with Latin America, yet no extensive study has focused on the island. Sigrid Bauschinger and Susan Cocalis categorize by region to express the homogenization of Latin America in mainstream German perceptions.[40] Susanne Zantop's work explores proto-German national identity through fantasies of generalized Latin American liaison, while Arlene Teraoka uses Latin American themes in German literature and drama to understand post-war national identity formation. Indebted to these examinations, my book focuses on revolutionary Cuba to gain specificity and depth in the German context and to enable a clearer vocalization of the 'other' partner in intercultural discourse.

Although in many ways unique, these German Cubas draw upon familiar themes. Islands have long held special places in cultural imaginaries. Cuba and the islands of the post-war Germanies participate in this rich history. As early as the Nibelungen saga, Brunhild's isle has contained within it seemingly uncontrollable forces of nature and magic. Its boundedness both magnifies its power and makes its conquest by the heroic Siegfried more absolute. In sixteenth-century Europe, islands are Edenic evidence of the post-lapsarian world. *Robinson Crusoe* (1719) and its many rewritings explore society by means of society's obverse: island exile. In contrast, as enlightenment narratives of progress, colonial travel, and industrialization gain in popularity, the island becomes an escape from the alienation and complexity of modern life through the possibility of social utopia. By the late 1700s, the period of the colonial 'discovery' of the South Sea Islands, fictional island time becomes explicitly anterior to European time, justifying colonization of 'underdeveloped' societies. In texts ranging from the travelogues of George Forster to romantic works by Ludwig Tieck, islands are utopian spaces that counter quotidian European stresses.[41]

Today, Northern 'escapes to the island' are shaped by tourism and tradition. The rise of jet travel in the 1960s first offered masses of Europeans temporary respite from the industrial world in locations billed as paradise experiences par excellence. The island tourism industry banks on qualities that artistic representations have made familiar. It maintains that the delimited character of islands increases their attractiveness due to tourist desire for controlled variance in leisure, climate, environment, and culture. Where political separation accompanies physical separation, the appeal is even greater.[42] Idyllic, hazy visions of manageable tropical paradises such as Madeira, Tahiti, Capri, and most recently Mallorca[43] contrast with quotidian experiences of complex and overwhelming urbanized life.

These fantasies incorporate notions of liberal sexuality and indulgent sensuality that have been part of German recreational consumerism from at least the earliest post–Second World War period.[44] The well-worn expression 'Ready/Mature enough for the Island?' (*Reif für die Insel?*), as used in a youth travel campaign, markets relaxation and sexual adventure.[45] This question resonates with long-standing unease about and yearnings for seductive hedonism promised by warm, exotic settings.[46] Such island fantasies have been made available to consumers on every budget. East and West German policies competitively oriented towards citizen satisfaction translated into domestically accessible, tropicalized adventure concretized in swim and recreational resorts. As public funding dwindles post 1990, state subsidized private investors are stepping in, betting on the sustainability of such desires. In a former dirigible hangar on a windswept Brandenburg plain near Berlin, Tropical Islands offers nearby residents an accessible exotic retreat (see fig. E.1, page 181). From Caribbean dancers at poolside to a manufactured rainforest, this resort with multiple Southern travel themes is a consumption-oriented reinterpretation of the promised 'flourishing landscapes' of prosperity that have yet to materialize in most Eastern regions. Enabled by fantasies of vast separation, this budget escape is literally confined to the national landscape.[47]

Within commodity paradigms, island life remains mythologically distinct from the productive world; other narratives seek to subjectify and integrate it. Island natives understand their nations as part of larger entities – archipelagos or insular seas.[48] GDR texts harness the energy of islands into larger frameworks. Getaway fantasies conclude that every citizen must participate in society in order to escape its constraints.[49] For instance, Joachim Hasler's popular youth film *Heisser Sommer* (*Hot Summer*, 1968) reorganizes the wanderlust of youth on a vacation island at the GDR border by channelling their sexual journeys into monogamous pairing and community service. This study shows in more detail how, in the 1970s and 1980s, the island of Cuba contributed to discussions about consumption and bureaucratization within socialism. Fritz Rudolf Fries's travel narrative 'Kubanische Kalenderblätter' (Cuban

Calendar Pages, 1976) and Frank Beyer's *Bockshorn* (*Ram's Horn*, 1983) employ Cuba to inspire a critical gaze among disillusioned GDR citizens largely fascinated with capitalism. *Venceremos* (we will overcome) brigades and the 'revolutionary tourism' of solidarity organizations seek to diminish the distinction between work and pleasure that mass tourism emphasizes.

Intersections between Cuba, West Berlin, and the GDR incorporate such island rhetoric. Whether Cuba is understood as a dangerously quixotic 'island of dreams,' or as an island 'that is not satisfied with playing the role of an island,' German reception of revolutionary Cuba traces and reinterprets such roles.[50] As a utopian site, Cuba avoids stasis and anachronism and often appears to lead the march of history into a better future. Paradoxically, exactly here Cuba simultaneously gains historical specificity and risks being flattened into a singular progress narrative. The physical distance between Cuba and Europe intensifies these romantic and revolutionary visions; I explore how this separation and its symbolic overcoming through cultural texts such as eyewitness reports influence how Germans think themselves through Cuba.

This insular history infuses understandings of West Berlin and the GDR. By at least the Weimar period, the cosmopolitan metropolis of Berlin held island status in the popular imaginary. The well-known West Berlin political cabaret that broadcast on the U.S. supported radio station RIAS, 'the free voice of the free world,' called itself Die Insulaner (The Islanders). Die Insulaner and the West Berlin blockade of 1948–9 underscored the isolation of the city. By the 1960s, Cold War political discourses cast West Berlin as an island in a sea of communist influence.

The GDR was also an island of sorts, an interpretation that does not belie the semi-permeability of some of its national borders and its international relations and exchange. Former citizens conceptualize the GDR as peninsular and emphasize its relationships to the Eastern bloc. This understanding is anachronistic in that in the 1950s and 1960s in particular, travel played smaller roles in the Germanies. Yet travel did function differently in real-existing socialism, where for ideological and economic reasons even restrictions on the tourism between socialist countries were only gradually relaxed. Cuban actor Miguel Benavides recalled anecdotally that during his visit to the GDR in the early 1960s, movement within the country itself was controlled – creating, as it were, islands within the island, policed by paperwork.[51]

These examples suggest some of the many ways in which islands invoke utopia. Understood as a force for social betterment, utopia functions as critique because to articulate future possibilities is to unsettle contemporary norms.[52] Understood as a threat to the status quo, utopia works to prescribe change. The struggle over definitions is critical because if utopias are understood to be unattainable, they risk losing their critical purchase and their ability to potentiate transformation.

Left-leaning thinkers have dealt variously with this definitional challenge, notably by characterizing utopias as possible in a particular space or time.[53] Karl Mannheim distinguishes between ideological states of mind that are 'incongruent with reality,' yet cannot alter this reality, and utopian states of mind. While utopian states are also incongruent with reality, 'when they pass over into conduct, [they] tend to shatter, either partially or wholly, the order of things prevailing at the time.' Many critical thinkers in the 1960s imagined such shattering possible by democratic means. Yet, as Mannheim admits, and as this project variously demonstrates, the distinction between ideology and utopia is tenuous.[54]

Poststructuralist post-mortems of definitions such as Mannheim's and of the rebellious activity of the 1960s, 1970s, and 1980s highlight the totalizing potential of utopianism.[55] More recent discussions seek to avoid this pitfall. Michel Foucault's 'heterotopia' emphasizes utopias as sites of difference,[56] while Ernesto Laclau and Chantal Mouffe insert difference through 'agonistic' debate among citizens.[57] The geographer David Harvey focuses on spatio-temporal change to imagine a continuously developing utopia,[58] while Immanuel Wallerstein's 'utopistics' emphasize rationality to dissipate the zealotry that the combination of emotionalism and intellectualism risks.[59]

Mannheim envisions utopia as dialectically moving that which is conceived of as reality towards change. Two aspects of his paradigm are deeply relevant to the Cubas of the Germans. First, because particular circumstances engender particular utopias, historicizing is instructive. For instance, pejorative classification of utopia as quixotic should be interrogated as symptom rather than ground. For instance, the specific utopias employed by 1960s social projects implied possibility. Second, utopias become intelligible by understanding the groups that espouse them.[60] It follows that study of utopian models enables insights into social discourses within which they arise; this hermeneutic is axiomatic to my project.

Historically linked to socialist thought, utopias abound in art. It may be unsurprising therefore that the relationship between utopianism and GDR cultural production is particularly rich. Mainstream audiences interpreted socialist realism against its objectives, however; narratives seemed to assert impossible rather than future utopias. Some of the films considered here were also criticized for the disjunction between their purported verisimilitude and GDR lived experience. The official denial of this tension frustrated many. Under circumstances of limited public debate, socialist realist-style art subverted its formal pedagogical project by, in effect, highlighting social shortcomings. In intriguingly similar fashion, mainstream audiences of today criticize the overt politics of engaged artistic production. Might their discomfort signal desires to avert comparisons between screen and reality that would expose shortcomings in dominant ideologies? Such issues are key to understanding utopia and art.

Much German cultural production about Cuba engages utopia. Particularly in the 1960s, the island appeared to be transforming into an 'active' revolutionary idea. Irmtraud Morgner's 'partial visions' of Cuba in a particular time and space emphasize the liberatory potential of feminine values for the GDR,[61] while the West Berlin anti-authoritarians' revolutionary praxis of the same decade valued what it read as its masculinist tendencies.[62] Post 1968, Enzensberger's documentary-style play *Das Verhör von Habana* (*The Havana Inquiry*, 1970) depicts the triumphant sublimation of violence into courtroom justice. Eight years later, in his epic poem *Der Untergang der Titanic* (*The Sinking of the Titanic*) Cuba is party to senseless violence, a dystopia 'exactly as at home and as everywhere else as well.' On the other side of the Wall, Volker Braun's *Guevara oder der Sonnenstaat* (Guevara or El Dorado) (performed in 1977 in the FRG, 1984 in the GDR) employs Guevara's futile quest in Bolivia to illuminate tensions between citizen, state, and revolution. The play addresses the core problem of conflict and utopia, suggesting that if contradictory desires mean violence at home, the socialist project has failed. In a near inversion of the anti-authoritarian model, socialist utopia here reaches its limit in the structural violence of third-world revolution and in the overt violence of the first world. Some of these texts primarily about Germany were little noted in Cuba. Yet as solidarian, critical engagements with the Caribbean site, they decreased the potentially isolating effect of utopian thinking on Cuba's global positioning.

Cuba in the German Imaginary

The Cuban scholar Roberto Fernández Retamar calls Cuba's extraordinary ideational meaning relative to its geographic size the 'enormity' of Cuba.[63] One of the heights of this enormity formed in the early years of the struggle against Batista. As the British historian Eric Hobsbawm writes: 'The Cuban revolution had everything: romance, heroism in the mountains, ex-student leaders with the selfless generosity of their youth – the eldest were barely past thirty – a jubilant people, in a tropical tourist paradise pulsing with rumba rhythms. What is more, it could be hailed by all Left revolutionaries.'[64]

Hobsbawm's assessment here alludes to Northern fantasies about Cuba and to Southern entities, events, and practices that moor these fantasies. My study takes as axiomatic that fantasies and their 'real world' referents are both distinct and mutually constituting. Fantasies are representations largely unconcerned with their referents and very much shaped by their producers. While fantasies are by definition ideational and subjective, entities, events, and practices are contested by so few and accepted by so many voiced subjects that the term 'fact' is commonly used to describe them. Yet, not only fantasies, but also entities, events, and practices are apprehensible only within language/culture.[65] The ontological status of fact is contested; this project understands fact as contingent and distanced from – at perspectival remove from – the always inaccessible thing-in-itself (*Ding an sich*).

The relationship between language/culture and 'reality' has been debated and theorized extensively in many different fields using many different vocabularies. My project recognizes the fraught and contested distinctions between representations of fantasy and representations of the 'real world' while highlighting the mutually constituting, necessary, and necessarily charged relationships between them. What are understood as fantasies engender shifts in what are understood as entities, events, and practices, and vice versa. Projections require 'real world' screening surfaces in order to manifest. All of these actors, their contact zones, and the ensuing refractions engage in continuous revision. Most generally, then, this study engages with the mutually informing ontologies of projections, screens, and the dialectical negotiations between them over space-time.

More concretely, this book engages this theory using as a case study the meaning of revolutionary Cuba for the Germans. It demonstrates how German visions of this kaleidoscopic Caribbean screen express German self-understandings and how these identities are altered through such transnational projections. It treats the most important themes in the most significant cultural genres at precise spatio-temporal moments and over space-time. This synchronic and diachronic

approach highlights how conceptions of Cuba change according to differing concerns of the Germans. It also accounts for how Cuban self-
representations and politico-cultural landscapes influence(d) German
visions of the island.

Stated more generally, this analysis demonstrates that the other influences its own representation in the eyes of the 'self' and also shapes this
self and its own self over time. The book tracks differences and power
differentials that inhere, while revealing how other and self mutually
inform. In North-South terms, the Northern representation and appre-
hension of what is understood as the Southern other thus not only represents this other on Northern terms, but also in the parlance of the
South. The self-understandings of the North and the South *become* in
the Heideggerian sense through ever-shifting relationships over space-
time. This conceptualization engages common understandings of the
Hegelian master-slave narrative by insisting, furthermore, that neither
actor is subsumed within the power dialectic. Rather, they shape each
other while retaining excesses and resisting synthesis.

This conceptualization has specific relevance in postcolonial German
studies, where scholars have expanded upon the work associated with
Edward Said that correlates orientalism with imperialism.[66] German
colonialism is often deemed peripheral in comparison to other national
building blocks and to the historical legacies of Germany's neighbours. Nevertheless, work such as Zantop's, Pratt's, and Todd Kontje's
shows the deep imbrication of the other in Germanness. For instance,
Kontje has shown the orientalist weave of the traditionally canonical
in German culture.[67] In that my project demonstrates how a putatively
marginal Caribbean other shapes German identity, it establishes that
influence can take the form of utopia, dystopia, beacon, imagined ally,
to name a few examples. Ways of seeing are expanded by highlighting
how representations of the other shape the self while attending to the
ways in which this relationship moves on contested ground. One effect
is to underscore the porousness and fragility of German national identity, radically modifiable by phenomena such as solidarity and transnational affinities.

My examination offers historically situated, robust treatments of the
primary meanings of Cuba for the Germans. I have outlined its primary themes in relation to specific texts above; the narrative structure
is as follows. My study begins near the present, a place that sets the
stage for understanding the past. Chapter one considers the *Kuba Welle*
– an ongoing, diversely manifested wave of popular interest – in rela-

tion to the possibilities that it suggests for German (re)unification and the direction of the new nation. A constellation of examples illustrate the most salient threads: the marketing of Cuban rum in the island of formerly socialist East Berlin; the quasi-documentary film *Buena Vista Social Club* (1999) by West German–Hollywood film-maker Wim Wenders; the documentary films *Havanna mi amor* (Havana, My Love, 2000) and *Heirate mich!* (Marry Me, 2003) by Eastern German film-makers Uli Gaulke and Jeannette Eggert; and the narrative travelogue *Cuba libre bittersüß* (Free Cuba, Bittersweet, 2000) written by West German radical and writer Inge Viett. Each of these cultural artefacts envisions Cuba according to particular concerns for the new Germany. Chapter two focuses on the GDR of the early 1960s and Cuba as political inspiration in foreign and domestic policy. Chapter three treats the West Berlin student movement. Chapter four explores the disillusionment of the 1970s in the Democratic Republic and the Federal Republic. The last chapter considers tourism, travel freedoms, and the youth generation with a focus on the heroic and subversive figures of Cuban/Argentinean Che Guevara and East German/Argentinean Tamara 'La Guerrillera' Bunke. Each chapter highlights particular narrative threads that re-emerge variously in other sections. This networked structure resists the thought habit of a teleological arc, reminding that specific places and spaces mutually inform.

Chapter One

Contesting the New Berlin Republic through Germany's Cubas

'They didn't know the first thing about socialism, they didn't know the first thing about the GDR and they didn't care. They just wanted to go "help the poor Cubans." It was an adventure for them,' recalled the Eastern German André about his Western German fellow passengers, with whom he had flown from Düsseldorf to Cuba in 1991.[1]

This comment is particularly intriguing because the Western Germans were on their way to a solidarity brigade, while the Eastern German was on his way to a large beach resort. André identified as a tourist, yet he supported his analysis by presuming superior understanding of Cuba due to his socialist background. He understood the attitudes of the Western Germans towards the GDR as of a piece with their attitudes towards Cuba, implying that their ignorance and condescension towards the one mapped onto and indeed exacerbated their ignorance and condescension towards the other.

Inspired by his visit, André and one of his travelling companions returned to Eastern Berlin and opened a bar with a Cuban theme in the Prenzlauer Berg district. The decor includes a section of a boat with benches and a table cut into it. I read this fragmented hull as an escape vessel that could not reach Miami. For the bar owner, the ship represents Cuba's fishing culture. Our different interpretations reveal a lot about us. Raised in an overseas U.S. military environment, in which the government provides for U.S. personnel who remain loyal in word and deed, I saw the boat according to a U.S. account of Cuba. In contrast, André's reading combines a narrative of island fishing culture with his own GDR understanding of life in a 'society of scarcity' (*Mangelgesellschaft*). He sees the boat as a means of self-sufficiency. Indeed, his reuse of the boat itself enacts this practice; he and his colleague moved the old dinghy from a nearby lake to the Yolanda Bar themselves.

1.1 Yolanda Bar.

This anecdote exemplifies Cuba's overdetermination in the Germanies, where tales of Cuba express German relationships to the GDR, the FRG, and the larger FRG.[2] Contests around dissemination of each narrative of Cuba are also contests around the cultural capital that each narrative of Germany can leverage. I demonstrate in this chapter that post-1989 cultural artefacts involving Cuba reveal a bristling landscape of rival perspectives on German pasts, presents, and futures. These generically diverse exemplars that feature varied means and ends speak to, with, and against each other; taken together they illuminate the key concerns in German-identity debates.

My analysis treats the following constellation. I consider the Berlin Kuba Welle (wave of interest in Cuba) as a particular cultural phenomenon and a ground that engenders and is expressed by the other instances that I examine, namely rum advertising, film, and travel literature. Havana Club employs the GDR past and the post-GDR present within the now capitalist island of Eastern Berlin to reach and enlarge its demographic of German consumers. Film and prose also involve commodity, but foreground polities and politics. I read Wim Wenders's *Buena Vista Social Club* (1999) against two other documentary-style films, Uli Gaulke and Jennette Eggert's *Havanna mi amor* (2000) and *Heirate mich!* (2003), and in relation to a written travelogue, Inge Viett's *Cuba libre bittersüß* (2000). Their very different versions of Cuba function as oppositional commentaries on the merger of the Germanies.[3] Taken together, each artefact represents distinct perspectives on Germany post 1989. To take a good look at the Kuba Welle, a sketch of the discursive landscape around German identity and particularities of post-1990 Cuba is first in order.

Each of these cultural artefacts that thematize Cuba responds to the question 'What is post-1989 Germany?' Defining nation has been a thorny task since at least the Second World War. Progressive thinkers in the Federal Republic often emphasized the post-national. They also placed great store in the international, in the first decades by turning towards the United States, later by focusing on Europe.[4] These attitudes strengthened the FRG's economic and political health as they facilitated U.S.-FRG relations and European unification efforts. In contrast, many in the GDR sought to form a new national identity based on the understanding of a socialist German nation distinct from its predecessor. A mythology of wartime anti-fascist resistance and a pacifist agenda, as well as a more thorough denazification than that in the FRG, fostered this identity. Focus on a socialist national project within a socialist international imaginary and polity built citizen support for the GDR.

The merger of the FRG and the GDR provoked renewed debate about German identity. Theories ranged from the hope that post-1990 Germany had for the first time birthed itself as a democracy to fears that this larger Germany could again birth fascism. For many, most publicly the FRG Chancellor Helmut Kohl, the reunification offered return to 'normalcy.' By this logic, the GDR embodied the last vestige of the fascist past. The GDR's close thus reopened the possibility of (again) defining Germany as a *Kulturnation*, a nation based in a common cultural tradition, a notion that had been considered problematic because it smacked of fascist sensibilities.[5] The controversy over Kulturnation was in essence a Western German debate. The incorporation of the GDR canon or Eastern German positions was not at issue, although the GDR had increasingly assimilated pre-GDR German literary and philosophical texts into its cultural heritage and in this sense had a similar discourse underway.

The public debate around Kulturnation elided other efforts to reform national structures.[6] This situation is one of the many examples in which the FRG set the terms of reunification.[7] Although the only democratically elected GDR parliament voted for a quick merger into the FRG political structure, many public figures, perhaps most famously Jürgen Habermas, contended that the FRG had used its economic and political dominance to force reunification on these terms.[8] The Western German writer and intellectual Günter Grass argued that the opening of the border and the quick merger were meant to halt the development of a 'third way' of nationhood: democratic socialism – in the GDR and, by extension, in any resultant Germany.[9] Many Eastern German intellectuals agreed.

The Kulturnation paradigm eased the integration of certain populations, such as Eastern Germans and the so-called ethnic Germans who had been living in the Eastern bloc. It also supported dominant groups, such as men and the Christian-bred, and weakened 1980s efforts to integrate so-called multicultural Germans, women, and socialists. Coupled with intoxicating – although often short-lived – personal material gain, the collapse of the Soviet Union, the political stability of the 1990s, and the comparative global economic upswing, the concept of Kulturnation invited the embrace of many Eastern Germans.

These particular concerns around German national identity post 1989 resonate with particularities of post-1990 Cuba that may further its allure as a projection screen. Unlike the larger FRG, the newly independent Cuba is not a potential Goliath. Unlike Germany's pre-1945 past, Cuba's pre-1959 history is seen as politically unproblematic, for some because Cuba's people rose up against their dictators, for others because their rulers did not take over other nations. Cuba is untouched by German colonialism and German fascism and thus summons no guilty spectres. Cuba currently resists neoimperialism and capitalism; its socialist-style independence suggests something of a third way. Moreover, its class and ethnic tensions pale in comparison to those of the larger FRG. Such favoured attributes are both oft cited and exaggerated in German reception. For example, while projections that represent Cuba as free of racism are gently shaped by the contemporary situation on the island, they articulate liberal and socialist ideals and concern about the increasing disenfranchisement of people of colour in the larger FRG.

Cuba's attraction is ultimately in the eyes of its beholders, yet certain changes that the government made post 1990 also facilitated the Kuba Welle. When the end of Soviet support precipitated a collapse of the Cuban economy, the island quickly began developing joint ventures between the state and private Northern investors, particularly in international tourism.[10] Economic reliance on tourism increased from less than 5 per cent in 1989 to about 75 per cent in 1998. By the mid-1990s, large travel agencies in cooperation with Cuba had launched major advertising campaigns in Canada, Spain, Germany, and elsewhere in Europe.[11] Celebrated by many Cuba sympathizers on and off the island was the fact that the centralized Cuban state generally holds 51 per cent control of these ventures, which circumvents the usual Northward flow of capital and profit. Feisty, resourceful, and determined, Cuba seemed once again to be beating the titans. These terms may be unsustainable, for since 1995 some joint venture companies hold 100 per cent ownership and garner the corresponding profits.[12] Cuban tourism and Cuban society show the negative impacts, despite/including efforts such as the well-publicized revitalization of Old Havana under Cuban Eusebio Leal Spengler.[13] Yet capitulations notwithstanding, Cuba maintains a special status in the popular imaginary because of its attempts to maximize profit sharing among the populace in its post-1990 negotiations and because the negotiations themselves brought many foreigners into contact with the island.

The Kuba Welle

The dissolution and subsequent unification of the islands of West Berlin and the GDR facilitated German projections of domestic identity issues

onto the geographically faraway, suddenly independent, still socialist island of Cuba. The Kuba Welle manifested itself diversely with
increases in tourism to Cuba, writings concerning the island, solidarity
groups, cocktail bars, cigars, rum, and salsa.[14]

Tourism means differently for every visitor. The majority come to
Cuba for sun, sea, and/or sex tourism, flavoured with a bit of sight-
seeing, while a minority are interested in socialism. For instance,
approximately 75 per cent of the international tourists remain in
the isolated megaresort Varadero, and make short visits to nearby
Havana.[15] Perhaps unsurprisingly, Cuba experts believe that mainstream Western German tourists consider Cuba's socialist touch
intriguing but not vital, while Western and Eastern German left-leaning tourists have deeper political and social interest in Cuba.[16] The
latter is historically based. For left-leaning Western Germans, post-
1990 travel continues the brigade tradition. For Eastern Germans, the
former socialist brother nation has long been a favoured part of public
discourse, yet few saw it in person as GDR citizens. Such expensive
international travel was shaped by many factors. Some GDR citizens
travelled to Cuba in professional capacities as technical experts or
political envoys. A few went on brigades, or more commonly in delegations for work, sports events, or cultural festivals. Others obtained
slots through their workplace or volunteer organizations. For instance,
by the seventies, the writer's organization was allotted a number of
trips each year. In later decades, individual citizens could also purchase travel. In the case of Cuba, however, airplane travel involved
a stopover, which meant that the political backgrounds of the travellers had to be beyond reproach, their West connections minimal, and
their GDR family ties strong. Ship travel remained slow and the fleet
was small. The February 1967 arrival of 489 tourists on the Völkerfre-
undschaft (Friendship between Peoples) luxury passenger liner was
noteworthy enough to be mentioned by the GDR news correspondent
(ADN) in Cuba.[17] Post-1990 visits to Cuba by Eastern Germans often
fulfil desires long in the making.

The Kuba Welle is also expressed by an increase in the number of
German prose works about Cuba published since the early 1990s: non-
fiction, belles-lettres, and travel guides.[18] In his study of post-1989 German scholarship on Cuba, Cuban historian Joaquin Santana Castillo
finds that both Eastern and Western authors are interested in the island
as a real-existing socialist nation. He detects a focus on the socialism
of daily life in texts by Eastern German authors, while more Western

German studies consider causes for the general demise of organized socialism and its future possibilities on the island.[19]

German solidarity efforts towards Cuba have become more extensive and more grassroots. This phenomenon is due Eastern Germans in particular.[20] In the GDR, many citizens identified with official third-world solidarity in ways that far exceeded social requirements. They also sometimes aligned themselves with the third world in symbolic opposition to their own system.[21] Solidarity efforts in the Democratic Republic represented both an egalitarian ideal and an oppositional stance. It is telling that the independent 1989–90 GDR government spent large amounts of money on solidarity projects.

An important player in the post-1989 solidarity landscape, Cuba Sí, incorporates several of these impulses translated into the larger FRG. Consisting primarily of Eastern Germans, this non-profit that educates and fundraises in Germany and supports work projects in Cuba has organizational ties and a stormy relationship with the German socialist party (Partei des Demokratischen Sozialismus [PDS]) – many of whose members were in the Eastern German SED party. Cuba Sí was founded out of keen desires to continue support for the newly independent and struggling Cuba after the Soviet collapse. As a social phenomenon, Cuba Sí expresses *Ostalgie*, nostalgia for the East (*Ost*), in a manner that incorporates sober assessments of material and communitarian losses post 1989.[22] Its case proves a point. The mainstream definition of Ostalgie delegitimizes Eastern Germans by implicating them in naive attachment to a glorified past unmarked by authoritarian state structures. As Dominic Boyer has pointed out, this concept coined by the West simultaneously 'allows those Germans gendered western to claim a future free from the burden of history.'[23] I reclaim Ostalgie here to mean an idealized and critical attitude towards the past that speaks to the present and the future. Romantic Ostalgie would denote an affirmative stance to all elements of this past. The former describes Cuba Sí. Numerous members were critical of GDR structures then and are critical of FRG governmental and socio-economic structures today; their Cuba solidarity expresses a third way scepticism. Many are underemployed thirty-somethings; in the larger FRG, this activist work functions as self-actualization as well as multifaceted political statement.[24]

Conversely, Western German solidarity efforts and brigade visits have decreased somewhat since 1989. This trend may be related to the disarray of the Western German left and a disenchantment with socialism after what many see as its failure as a large-scale project.[25] That Eastern and Western German solidarity groups have only recently begun to combine their efforts also suggests that their international solidarity is inflected by divergent attitudes towards their respective pasts.[26] Despite many differences, however, for both Easterners and Westerners, these practices of solidarity express hopes that global equity can become a 'peace dividend' and discontent with current circumstances.

Practices of German solidarity groups suggest that politically and socially specific interest in Cuba reflects dissatisfaction with conditions in the larger FRG. In his study of U.S. political tourism to Cuba, Paul Hollander argues similarly: 'The propensity to visit countries boasting of superior social institutions almost invariably arises at times when social, economic, or cultural conditions in the tourists' countries become problematic or unsatisfactory.'[27] In post-1990 Germany, then, interest in Cuba may express desires for some version of socialism, of previous Germanies, or of a third way. It may manifest in desires to live temporarily within a socialist-style structure, to discover how socialist Cuba and Cuban socialism is shifting post 1990, or to help the island nation survive.[28]

These examples show that German domestic understandings and experiences inflect cultural manifestations of interest in Cuba. The marketing of Havana Club rum in the larger FRG is another particularly intriguing case that merits longer discussion. Havana Club's campaign uses precisely these commodifiable relationships between Cuba and the Germanies.

Havana Club Rum: Marketing with German Spaces and Travel Fantasies

Havana Club's success in Germany is based on and is an expression of German interest in Cuba and German understandings of itself. I will consider the three primary elements of its advertising campaigns during the height of the Kuba Welle: marketing and distribution in Eastern Berlin, the Web world of Havana Club Cuba, and the island as socialist travel site. Havana Club was a completely Cuban product until the collapse of the Soviet Union and was available in the GDR directly from its socialist brother country and preferred trading partner. The joint venture Havana Club was founded in late 2004 between the French firm Pernod Ricard and government-guided Cuban companies, first Cubaexport, today Cuba Ron S.A. Pernod Ricard's marketing in Germany from the mid-1990s to the mid-2000s used the historical

relationship between pre-1989 socialist Germany and pre-1990 socialist Cuba to its full advantage. At the same time, this German-language
publicity campaign sought and seeks to reach Western Germans with
a pro-Cuba attitude and, increasingly, younger Eastern and Western consumers who came to drinking age post 1989. Havana Club's
distribution and promotional strategies in Germany attempt to reconcile Eastern and Western histories, identities, and proclivities in order
to engender similar consumption patterns in these historically diverse
groups. Upon the international launch of Havana Club, the company
focused its European marketing efforts on the new German states
and Eastern Berlin in order to leverage the existing brand name recognition of its product among former GDR citizens.[29] Its marketing reach
on the Web in particular has expanded and diversified over the years;[30]
of interest here is its advertising in Germany as part of the Kuba Welle.

In Eastern Berlin, Havana Club capitalized on the demographic and
architectural changes of the area. Post 1989, the central Eastern Berlin
neighbourhoods (Mitte, Prenzlauer Berg, more recently also Friedrich-
shain and Neukölln) developed as hip nightlife and living areas. Their
visitors are a mixture of post-1990 arrivals from Eastern and Western
Germany and Eastern Europe, some Eastern Berlin residents from the
GDR period, Western Berlin residents from the Schöneberg and Kreuzberg neighbourhoods, and tourists. Residents are largely white, Christian-bred, socially liberal students, and white-collar and blue-collar
workers from Eastern and Western Germany. Unlike in the hip areas of
Western Berlin (Schöneberg and Kreuzberg), there are few non-white
ethnic minorities, particularly those of Turkish descent. As in national accounts of the merger, the story of Eastern Berlin is largely that of
Western white meeting Eastern white. However, in this city space, the
East has maintained a unique profile that is also uniquely marketable.

Shortly after 1989, many underground nightspots, galleries, and
theatre spaces ran on private initiative opened in these districts. The
accompanying makeshift, underground aesthetic often consisted of little more than bright paint over crumbling walls and second-hand sofas.
Gradually, licenses were granted or enforced, and the underground
aesthetic was commercialized into an urban feel that cites its makeshift
predecessors with the skill of a professional interior designer. The popularity of these establishments evidences the romantic appeal of this
retro aura that cites both the semi-anarchy of the immediate post-Wall
Eastern Berlin and the legendary Prenzlauer Berg artist scene of the
GDR.

Havana Club reaches out to this clientele by marketing its rum in these trendy locales, rather than in a cross-section of establishment types. With this strategy, the company has been attempting to attract Eastern German consumers who recognize Havana Club as a GDR luxury good that is again accessible. Crucial here is that, unlike most *Ost Produkte* (commodities that were produced in the East that survive primarily on commercialized romantic Ostalgie, cult, or most recently retro value),[31] Havana Club is marketed as a luxury good in the post-1989 context and on post-1989 terms. While Ost Produkte are often considered inferior, Havana Club has 'made it' on its own merits in the larger FRG. The message of quality is underscored by this spatial product placement: trendy Eastern Berlin neighbourhoods whose GDR past is a basis for their popularity. This strategy also speaks to Western German, younger, and out-of-town visitors frequenting what to them has the taste of the exotic: inner Eastern Berlin. An unfamiliar, chic, direct import from Cuba adds to the mystique. Pernod Ricard's marketing of Havana Club as a fashionable, quality product in this particular geographical and temporal context thus both relies on the positive surplus value of the GDR past and helps to create this surplus value.

Havana Club's billboard marketing also used and increased the GDR's and Eastern Berlin's cultural capital. One of the first and largest Havana Club billboards was hung on construction scaffolding placed over the walls of a large shopping centre on Eastern Berlin's premiere commercial square, Alexanderplatz. The advertising image consisted of a brightly coloured, peeling wall less reminiscent of contemporary Havana than of Eastern Berlin nightspots, and with no suggestion of the newly rehabilitated Old Havana facades that the Cuban tourism industry promotes.[32] The colour of the wall, a yellow of rum and of no particular politics, matched the colour so ubiquitous in trendy Eastern Berlin bars as to have been dubbed 'Prenzlauer Berg Baroque' by Berlin interior designers and architects.[33] Placed on the crumbling walls of what was East Berlin's most important public commercial space during the reclamation of this space for private enterprise, this image overtly conjured an 'authentic, nostalgic' Havana. It also conjured an 'authentic, Ostalgic' GDR reclaimed in Eastern Berlin by grassroots entrepreneurship. The mapping of this exotic, luxury Havana rum with a revitalizing, gentrifying, and commercializing Eastern Berlin shores up and capitalizes on a particular Eastern German present that draws on its GDR past for profits in the larger FRG future.

Relative to the specificity of its Eastern Berlin advertising, the first

German-language Havana Club website launched in 2001 reached out to a more demographically and geographically diffuse target audience that is 'young, sporty, upwardly mobile' (*jung, sportlich, dynamisch*). Here, domesticated island themes are legible for a broad cross-section of visitors; its funky, tongue-in-cheek cartoon style references familiar tropes and abstains from discomfiting verisimilitude. While core thematic elements present an accessible, sensual, fun-filled Caribbean fantasy, subtexts offer a socialist and sexual utopia. Accessible for many, its hip, light-hearted, aesthetic, and inclusionary social narrative primarily interpolates a youngish, well-educated, heterosexual male target group of Germans. They are constructed as independent travellers who hold left-leaning ideas, are Cuba sympathizers, and seek to 'get to know the natives.' Havana Club's island is formed of wide-spread tourist fantasies of egalitarianism, as well as narratives of a socialist society with few governmental controls, robust distribution of wealth, little commerce and commercialism, and plentiful goods and services.

The website offers individualized activities in a Havana of egalitarian intercultural exchange. The guest is welcomed by Cuban characters speaking Spanish, with German translations in speech balloons. The e-traveller participates in quotidian festival as a foreigner without advantage for whom, however, all possibilities are open. A myth of economic and social parity enables this positioning. For instance, the Cuban characters all drink Havana Club, that is, an export product purchased in dollars, although most Cubans can only afford products produced for domestic consumption, subsidized by the state, and sold in non-convertible Cuban pesos. The Cuban characters also frequent the same establishments as the tourist, although on the island, regulations and cost considerations often segregate foreign visitors.

Other inequities between the natives and the guest are also elided. Not only does the ubiquitous presence of the well-known 1950s-style U.S.-make taxis belie Cuba's well-publicized transport situation, the visitor symbolically ameliorates it. In a video game–style site component, an inebriated Cuban cab driver asks the visitor turned drinking partner to chauffeur the two of them in his taxi. This request initiates a travel fantasy of solidarity, competency, and superiority. While manoeuvring the car past various obstacles, the visitor enters a shared daily struggle in which he provides solicited aid as an honorary member of the native social group and leaves the traditionally infantilizing role of the tourist behind. Even the guilty touristic desire to drive the legendary car of the U.S. neocolonial period is recast in this act of soli-

1.2 Image from the Havana Club website: HavanaCuba hintergrundbild intro 1. Used with permission.

1.3 Image from the Havana Club website: HavanaCuba hintergrundbild kurs b. Used with permission.

darity. By successfully alleviating this particular transportation concern at the behest of a Cuban compatriot, the website visitor also symbolically overcomes the more generalized Cuban transportation problem. The freedom of association and movement in the narrative belies the contemporary situation wherein, until very recently, Cubans who transported foreigners with these taxis risked legal consequences. Not only is this Cuba sans governmental controls, it is precisely the controls most visible to tourists that are elided. In sum, the website visitor enjoys a Havana free of any discomfiting reminder of global inequity and infused with a concomitant potential for solidarian transnational relationships. Lovable and capable, he is welcomed in a panacea of community living where everyone is on equal economic and social footing, open to social interaction, fun loving and content. This electronic Cuba is a perfect utopian socialism and a perfect socialist utopia that speaks to German visitors with East and West socialist sensibilities and desires for solidarian global exchange.

This virtual environment also offers an idealized narrative of sexual relations between tourist and native. Cuba is increasingly well known for sex tourism and it is a destination of choice for Germans, although precise information about the attitudes of these particular visitors is limited. Prevailing discourses link historical mythologies about the hypersexuality of the Cuban *mulatta* – embodiment of both a specifically Cuban sexuality and a sexually enticing 'miscegenation' – with mythologies (perpetuated by sources including the Cuban government) that Cubans engage in sex work purely for economic enrichment, not out of need.[34] These narratives of desire and choice are shored up by the widespread Cuban practice of performing sex work part-time and sometimes independently as *jinteras* (literally: riders), by the fact that many practitioners have significant formal education, and because both men and women are involved.[35] Evidence suggests that sex tourists fantasize that they can enter into communicative and non-coercive relationships with Cuban sex workers.[36] This fantasy is particularly relevant for a Havana Club clientele with solidarian attitudes towards the island. The sexual subtext of this version of the website works with these clichés and contexts. The visitor is desirable based on personal characteristics rather than privilege. The singularly beautiful, friendly, and available female Cuban characters instigate sincere romances with fluttering eyelashes, shy gazes, and smiles. The friendly, unattractive, and usually middle-aged male Cuban characters present no threat to the visitor, as competitors or as chaperones.

A sequence in the segment of the Spanish/German webpages for Havana Club entitled 'Cuban for Beginners' exemplifies how these sexual fantasies work. The overt aim of this segment is to share with the male website visitor the vocabulary necessary to have his needs serviced while in Cuba. Less overtly, this sequence promises him sexual companionship on acceptable sociopolitical terms. The narrative uniquely presents a male foreign visitor: a white thirty-something with an angular blonde beard. The bookish, bespectacled character reads simultaneously as a Western German intellectual and as an Eastern German of Prussian background. He is a manifestation of the target audience whose presence buffers this audience from the events by moving the story into the third person. This one-time alteration in the narrative structure allows the visitor to avoid identifying with commodified sex; the inclusion of the theme expresses its selling power. The unattractive German character is shown in profile on the right of the screen, looking at a beautiful, bikini-clad mulatta beach companion positioned in the primary space of specularization on the left, midway between the top and bottom of the frame. Her status as sexualized object for both the character and the website visitor is further emphasized with a nearly full figure presentation in a three-quarter angle to the viewer and an open body posture.

A femme fatale subtext in the sequences furthers the dominant logic, according to which the visited is desirable and the characters have parity. Leaning back on one arm and blinking while maintaining eye contact with the character, she makes the advances: 'I like your swimsuit; can we see each other again tonight?' The innocent responses of the male tourist suggest domesticity and friendship: he asks if she would like to build a sandcastle or drink a beverage. 'You can go ahead and go into the water, I'll follow in a moment,' she says in Spanish; if the translation button is clicked, menacing motives are revealed: two circling sharks appear in the water alongside the German rendition of her utterances. The subsequent frames articulate other dangers: the reddening visitor asks whether the visited knows a skin doctor. Because in Germany a *Hautarzt* (dermatologist) generally treats sexually transmitted diseases, a double valence maps this health risk onto the exchange between the characters. The danger reads in reverse through the bumbling innocence of the German and the aggressiveness of the Cuban. Belying epidemiological statistics that demonstrate tenfold higher infection risk for females, the narrative casts the sex worker as a source of contagion as well as a predator. The humour of the scenes and their reliance on double entendre – for instance, infection represented as sunburn –

facilitates the transport of the larger message: the availability of willing sexual partners and the desirability of the Havana Club consumer.

The website offers the German visitor a range of interactions that complement his self-fashioning as a traveller in Cuba; in this scenario, the offer is sexual. Whether he identifies with or judges himself against the easily bested cartoon character, the visitor garners the libidinal interest of the female without overtly demonstrating financial or citizenship privilege and without instigating the exchange. In this manner, the unequal power dynamics of Cuban sexual tourism are also reconfigured to conform to the overt values of the target market: the commercial transaction is represented as a non-coerced offer based on sexual desire, not economic interests. Whether the visitor is driving a car or impressing a woman, the site furthers a comfortable mythology of free choice for the Southern visited that simultaneously reinforces the myth of a socialism that meets the needs of its citizens. These myths in turn validate the primary target group that identifies around North-South solidarity, authentic interaction, and mutual positive regard.

This eminently visitor-friendly e-island that references post-1990 Cuba harnesses particular German identifications and uniquely profiles Havana Club. Its advertising draws on lived relationships between the GDR/Eastern Germans and Cuba and between the West(ern) German left and Cuba. For these German groups, post-1959 Cuba was and is of interest and travel there played and plays longstanding roles in their lives. While the Cuban joint venture Havana Club is located primarily on the island, its main competitor Bacardi left for the United States and Puerto Rico during the Cuban revolution. Continuing legal battles allow Bacardi to sell under the name Havana Club in the United States, while more recently Spain has upheld Pernod Ricard–Cuba Ron S.A.'s sole right to the trademark in Europe.[37] Distanced from today's Cuba, Bacardi has traditionally marketed with colonial images and more recently employs generalized Caribbean 'high life' beach tourism.

These rival advertising campaigns reflect and intervene in contests around defining Cuba post 1990 and defining Germany post 1989.[38] Considered schematically, Havana Club aligns with the GDR and Eastern Germany, while Bacardi is positioned alongside the FRG and mainstream Western Germany with their links to the United States, U.S. products, and Western versions of history. Havana Club and Bacardi's struggles for market share in the larger FRG parallel the struggle to position and define the GDR and Eastern Germany, and the FRG and Western Germany, post 1989. For those consumers in the know, choice of rum is a question of allegiance to East or West. This rudimentary

mapping also makes the Bacardi boycott intelligible. Although Western Germans spearhead it, the campaign has not led to significantly
increased Havana Club purchase among Western Germans. For them,
the Bacardi boycott may be more about anti-U.S. government stances
and anti-imperialism than pro-Cuba sentiment. In turn, this attitude is
symptomatic of the general hesitancy among the Western German left
to engage with the culture and citizens of the new German states.

Especially from the mid-1990s to the mid-2000s, but still today,
Pernod Ricard's marketing campaign employs particular consumer
understandings of and relationships to both Cuba and the Germanies.
Perhaps German critique of the United States is increasing the status
of the rum, contemporary Cuba, the GDR, and/or Eastern Germany.
What is clear is that Havana Club, Cuba, and Eastern Germany all draw
advantage from historical transnational relationships. The joint venture
retains Havana Club's traditional German customer base while reaching out to its Western buyers. Because Pernod Ricard's profit-driven
motives are nevertheless functionally solidarian, Cuba increases its
economic and cultural capital and resists colonial-style representations
such as those of Bacardi. Incarnated as Eastern Berlin, Eastern Germany
benefits from its alignment with a high-end product – practically a sin-
gularity in the Eastern-Western German relationship, where all truly
good things putatively come from the West. Havana Club's deployment of Eastern German culture and history manifests as an Eastern
German resistance to Western German cultural hegemony. At the same
time, Pernod Ricard's sales objectives translate into marketing that uni-
fies German communities into consumers. Indeed, as Havana Club has
established itself, its marketing scope has broadened. Its website version launched in 2007 visualizes a metropolitan Havana reminiscent
of recent feature film co-productions and *Beuna Vista Social Club*, with
linguistically specific aural tailoring. Its current version interpolates a
normative audience of shiny, happy, moneyed Northern consumers.

Buena Vista Social Club as Reunification Narrative

While Havana Club employed East and Eastern German specificities
to interpolate a consumer audience in the 1990s, *Buena Vista Social Club*
elided them to reunite a larger FRG on Western terms. This analysis will
focus on Western German audiences; big-budget films are transnational
in production and distribution.[39] *Buena Vista Social Club*'s West German–
Hollywood director Wim Wenders has long thematized German identity. Aligned as he was with the 68ers (the 1945 generation that came of

age in the universities of the 1960s) his post-1989 national project might privilege constitutional rights and heterogeneity. That it is inspired by Kulturnation traditions reflects shifts in political allegiances; Wenders now seeks to fill the 'vacuum' of Germany by rediscovering authenticity.[40] Films such as *In weiter Ferne, so nah!* (*Faraway, so close!*, 1993) and *Viel passiert – Der BAP-Film* (*Ode to Cologne*, 2000–1) laud explicitly German narratives, others such as *Bis ans Ende der Welt* (*Until the End of the World*, 1991), *Lisbon Story* (1994), and *Don't Come Knocking* (2004) seek the authentic beyond the border. Wenders's transnational films are not generally understood as commentaries on Germany,[41] yet *Buena Vista Social Club* participates in this search for national authenticity. Cast as a foreign, primitive nation, Cuba refigures a dubious pre-war Germany and shores up often unspeakable attitudes about the appropriate future of the larger FRG. Through the logic of a common culture, an imaginary, innocent past is reunited with a market-based present while alternatives are eradicated.

Buena Vista's vision is strikingly illustrated in its very premise: the rediscovery of the premier Cuban musicians who played in the Batista-era Buena Vista Social Club vicariously living in an idealized version of that past. The fond reminiscences of the musician Compay Segundo and the former neighbours of the club belie the social inequities of the period – as a black-only establishment, the Social Club emblematized the apartheid system.[42] The secret to health in contemporary Cuba remains not modern healthcare but folk remedies – in Segundo's case, cigars and consommé made from a bloody goat neck; Afro-Cuban deities assure personal well-being – in Ibrahim Ferrer's case, St Lazaro. The elderly Cuban musicians and their community possess elements 'lost' to the industrialized world: a spirit of cooperation, non-materialism, a 'natural' oneness with place and time. In the street scenes the musicians interact with the people as part of one singing community. The film implies that irrespective of everyday circumstances or political regime, the Cuban people retain this sort of joyful, musical social interaction. It is part of their nature: 'I didn't only have music in my blood, I was also surrounded by music day and night,' Eliades Ochoa says of himself. In the German context, such communalism resonates with traditional notions of *Heimat* that Nazi ideology favoured. This celebration of unity also resists attempts to define a heterogeneous Germany beyond mere tolerance of multiculturalism.

Ochoa's telling statement expresses common culture in biological terms. The interrelationship between cultural and racial identity is generally disavowed in mainstream German discourse.[43] When familial ties metonymically represent the German merger, Eastern and Western relationships are naturalized and trump former political affiliations.[44] Yet, discourse based in blood ties risks conjuring unwelcome spectres. The Cuba of *Buena Vista Social Club* offers a welcome solution. The narrative homogenizes differences under the sign of communal unity even as the camera exposes a racially heterogeneous culture. Under these circumstances, the reunification of a people across a common culture raises no spectre of racial supremacy.

Buena Vista Social Club's reunification of Cubans expresses and shores up mainstream U.S. and Western German discourses about the reunification of Germans. It is thus all the more significant that Wenders draws an intellectual, artistic, and generally left-leaning crowd; as German tale, these audiences would overtly disagree with *Buena Vista*'s message. The climax of the film is the arrival of these premiere musicians of pre-revolutionary Cuba in the United States and their reunification with the U.S.-Cuban community during their concert at Carnegie Hall. This mutual embrace is most overt during the ovation, when an audience member identified excitedly by the Cuban singer Omara Portuondo as 'una cubana' hurries to the stage to present the beaming musicians with an unfurled Cuban flag. The middle-aged matron wearing a traditional Cuban-style outfit embodies an ur-Cuba. Indeed, she resembles the motherly incarnation of the island featured in the post–*Buena Vista* Cuban film *Miel para Oshún* (*Honey for Ochun*, 2001) by Humberto Solás. During the performance a teary-eyed Ferrer calls the audience 'his family.' In the next scene, Ferrer caresses the head of the walking stick carved as a santería deity that belonged to his mother, displaying its phallic matriarchal power. Such scenes employ myth, emotion, and familial narrative to naturalize the fusion of ur-Cuba and contemporary diasporic Cuba.

The film works formally in several ways to intensify the dramatic effect of this reunification scene in the form of a concert sequence. Perhaps most interesting is the use of colour, one of Wenders's trademarks; indeed, much of *Buena Vista Social Club* is digitally remastered.[45] Throughout the film, the scenes of Cuba are brilliantly coloured, while the juxtaposed concert scenes in Amsterdam are muted, with a palette heavy in browns, beiges, blacks, whites, and greys. In contrast to these almost sombre concert sequences off of the island, the later scenes in Carnegie Hall and on the streets of New York also employ a supersaturated colour palette. This ascription of colour registers suggests that the fullness of traditional Cuban life as embodied in these Cuban artists has achieved its apotheosis in the United States at this moment of reunification. This message is underscored by the camera work. For instance, a continuous low-to-high angle shot from the stage first focuses on the concentric circles of lights in the ceiling, then pans down to the musicians on stage, effectively encircling them with stars. This visual crowning cites an earlier statement by Rubén González in which he recalls the Statue of Liberty's crown, seen when he was first in New York on a visit that the viewer must assume was prior to 1959. Here, stardom, success, capitalism, and freedom are united through the coronation in lights that Wenders's camera undertakes and his project enables.

The reunification shown here is not the merging of one state system with another state system, but the reuniting of members of a Kulturnation with members of the same Kulturnation. Their common identity is revitalized precisely through the performance and celebration of this common musical heritage.[46] Yet, this reunification is enabled by the embrace of the capitalist state system and the abandonment of the socialist state system. The triumphant scenes in the opulence of Carnegie Hall and the sequences of the wonderment over New York are juxtaposed with angled, moving shots of the dismal life of average Cubans that these musicians have left behind: the vacuous stare of an impoverished, disoriented lost soul; a healthy young man deftly and pointlessly spinning an empty oil drum on a city street at midday; the faded official slogans 'Esta revolución es eternal' (This revolution is eternal) and 'Creemos en los sueños' (We believe in dreams) on Havana's walls. These glimpses of socialist Cuba suggest a past without a present or a future. Such depictions justify the triumphant Cuba of Buena Vista's denouement: a happily reunified Kulturnation that had been separated by a doomed socialist experiment.[47]

In typical Wenders fashion, Buena Vista also seeks to garner the emotive cultural capital evoked by alternatives to mainstream capitalist lifestyles, even as the film explicitly critiques these alternatives. Many of the aforementioned scenes permit more sympathetic readings of contemporary Cuba. These particular images are reminiscent of an amateur tourist video in their choice of subject matter (stereotypical images of Havana) and in their style (bright natural lighting and scenes shot as if from a slow-moving vehicle). Such images have the potential to evoke a nostalgic sentiment common among those whom Hans Magnus Enzensberger might call revolutionary tourists, and among GDR supporters.

Yet, the limits of the revolution are always underscored. In the slow

right-to-left pan over the state-sponsored political slogans, the gaze
of the viewer is held briefly on the word 'sueños,' freezing this direct
object as if it were a subject, before the camera reads backward along
the sentence to the inflected verb 'creemos,' the actual acting subject of
the phrase. In the most literal sense, this 'metonymic freezing' apprehends the visited according to the interests of the visiting gaze.[48] It
holds these dreams as state inscribed and undercuts the agency of citizen supporters.

Indeed, it is the camera that most frequently belies Cuba's post-
revolutionary successes. Ferrer recalls that life prior to the revolution
'was ... harder, one had to take it into one's hands oneself.' Yet, Ferrer's statement comes as a voice-over to a contemporary scene in which
a cluster of people must take things into their own hands simply to
move an ancient refrigerator. The tension between the aural and the
visual messages here implies that Ferrer's words are shaped by the self-
censorship common in real-existing socialist states, censorship that was
widely disparaged in German and international debates in the 1990s.
Such scenes of apparent inefficiency also suggest that self-sufficiency
is not fully lived in contemporary Cuba. This message is most strikingly evidenced by the Cuban musicians themselves, who live in relative poverty and seemingly have not performed since the end of Cuba's
relationship with the United States.

The mythic nation conceived through this reunification shores up the
global status quo. Contained within the arms of the United States, the
resultant Cuba runs no risk of challenging other nations. Cuba's Southern status further legitimates its national aspirations insofar as subaltern nationalism is sometimes understood as a necessity and therefore
as an acceptable means of gaining cohesion and leverage. Finally, elision of revolutionary Cuba also elides aspirations for global change. In
these ways, Buena Vista Social Club offers validating fantasies of benign
re-creation for citizens of a larger FRG who have increasingly turned
from the post-national to the national, despite discomfiting historical
spectres. In response to a fraught political climate, the Cuban reunification narrative in Buena Vista Social Club details a vicarious return to a
nationalism free of a problematic past.

In mainstream Western German reunification narratives, the FRG
with the help of its Cold War partner, the United States, is frequently
cast as the land where dreams come true, while the GDR, with its partner in peaceful coexistence, the Soviet Union, is a fantasy turned nightmare. Easterners are deemed fortunate to be permitted to profit from

the FRG system built up through the hard work and ingenuity of their Western German brothers.[49] New FRG citizens are to leave GDR values and culture, as well as criticisms of the FRG, behind them. As I have shown above, each of the primary elements of reunification – rejection of socialism, endorsement of market logics, and return to the national – is celebrated in *Buena Vista Social Club*. The FRG embrace is to be as enthusiastic as the embrace of the audience in Carnegie Hall, as long as these tenets of reunification are accepted.

Especially insofar as the film takes such great pains to render reunification as positive, it is telling that *Buena Vista Social Club* also seeks to redefine the U.S.-German relationship. On one hand, the United States, in the form of the market-driven film and music industry, is the enabler of a very American Dream that becomes a reality for the Cuban musicians through the film project itself. Here Wenders continues to pay tribute to what he sees as one of the prime sources of his creativity – the United States. On the other hand, *Buena Vista Social Club* also reclaims a position of authority for Germany vis-à-vis the United States in that it constructs a familial national account of healing between the United States and Cuba, a narrative that the United States has been unwilling and unable to produce. Indeed, because the United States has officially discouraged any positive representations of Cuba, Wenders's film and Ry Cooder's CD prior to it are unusual in that they make the island intriguing not only for the mainstream Western German public but for U.S. audiences as well. The Bush administration's suspension of Cooder's travel permit suggests that this result remained unwelcome.[50] Post 1989, Wenders has become more critical of U.S. influence on Germany and other nations; *Buena Vista Social Club* rewrites the film-maker's well-known statement 'my life was saved by rock 'n' roll' to something like 'my life was saved by reclaiming Cuban *son* music for German mainstream culture.' This rewriting suggests not only reclamation of Eastern Germany on Western German terms, but an attempt to regain status for the larger FRG relative to the United States.

Havanna mi amor and *Heirate mich!* – The GDR and Eastern Germans in the Larger FRG

I have argued above that Western German discourses have strongly shaped definitions of the larger FRG, while Eastern perspectives have garnered less interest and influence. To make this broad distinction between Western and Eastern Germany risks reinscribing the binary, yet also highlights significant power differentials. The dissimilar reception of the films in question here demonstrates how this disparity plays out. A product of an internationally known film-maker with ties to the renowned New German Cinema movement, *Buena Vista Social Club* attracts canonical capital. Critics regularly foreground the aesthetics of such art and suggest the broad relevance of what are read as transcendent and universal themes. Such high art is cultural glue that binds the nation. Indeed, to examine *Buena Vista Social Club* for its politico-cultural content may seem to some an act of violence that completely misses the point.

In contrast, 'minority' films frequently inspire socio-historical, even ethnographic, scrutiny rather than aesthetic analysis. Works outside of the traditional canon are conventionally understood to articulate the specific rather than the general. Of interest as expressions of particular experiences, they tend to elicit attention among a limited demographic. In our examples, audiences and critics alike grant *Buena Vista Social Club* license to speak as if objectively about conditions on the island, the transcendence of music, about futures lost, and dreams fulfilled. Indeed, *Buena Vista*'s putative omniscience articulated as aesthetic sensitivity heightens its fame. This is not the case with *Havanna mi amor* and *Heirate mich!* As independently produced films by Eastern German film-makers, their perspectives are always already understood as situated. This situatedness both generates and limits interest in the films. Audiences and critics alike authorize them to speak about a specific Cuba and a specific GDR. Indeed, in this case, it is the oscillation between the two, coupled with the exotic of Cuba, that generates openness for GDR and Eastern German narratives that have such limited resonance in the new Germany. The German stories articulated in the films augment their cultural capital by refraction through temporally and locally specific narratives of Cuba.

In distinct contrast to *Buena Vista Social Club*, both the film-makers and media reception characterize *Havanna mi amor* and *Heirate mich!* as Cuban narratives that are also about Germany. Eggert and Gaulke overtly reposition themselves in the larger FRG through Cuba, stating that their knowledge of the GDR gives them unique insights and that they feel drawn to a socialist Cuba that seems 'very familiar.'[51] The film title itself binds the German spelling of 'Havana' and the Spanish of 'my love.' Eggert explicitly parallels the Cuban protagonist Gladys's move to Hamburg in *Heirate mich!* to her own entrance into the larger FRG itself in a manner that bespeaks GDR Marxist formation.[52] Eastern Germans often cast themselves as inhabiting positions similar to those of people of colour.[53] Whether sincere, strategic, or both, Gaulke and Eggert's conceptions of Cuba as GDR/Eastern allegory were taken up by a majority of film reviews.[54]

I contend that through participation in the Kuba Welle, Eggert and Gaulke's 'minority' documentaries draw a larger audience than a serious and direct treatment of the merger and of the GDR from an Eastern German perspective would allow. Bettina Bremme of the activist-oriented, historically Western German journal *Lateinamerika Nachrichten* calls attention precisely to this dynamic. Her analysis grants Gaulke's claim to some expertise in things Cuban due to his biography, then remarks that a similar film about the Eastern German suburb Marzahn or the town of Gera would not have interested him or his critics.[55] Bremme's commentary highlights the increasing indifference towards Eastern Germany in mainstream culture. Moreover, qualitative aspects of daily life in the East have proven difficult to thematize in serious ways.[56] An important draw of Gaulke and Eggert's films is their implicit pact to deliver a street-level perspective of life in the real-existing socialism of the GDR and its legacy in the larger FRG through their construction of the real-existing socialism of Cuba.

Havanna mi amor opens with the repair of a television at a shop. Lifelines to the *telenovela* soap operas, all televisions seem be in need of repair, under repair, or functioning briefly in the meanwhile. Escapism, scarcity, and struggle are embodied in this metonymy of post-1990 Cuba. The owners of these TVs are the narrative focus. The lives of characters such as the matron hairdresser Silai, lovers Juana and Felix, single mother Gladys, unemployed Marino, and gifted TV mechanic José are recounted in plots that are overtly about love and encompass life on the island. These daily lives offer few opportunities and lack many necessities. They are 'waited out' with the pleasures and aggravations of TV soap operas, romance, and rum. In Havana, stagnation has superseded revolution.

The formal structure of *Havanna* is indebted to styles of artistic production common in the GDR. Its focus on quotidian life is one example, while its analysis of intimate relationships is marked by historical materialism and by the production of the personal as socio-political. The centrality of female characters is characteristic of socialist art. Although the results were often ambivalent, the mere existence of genres such as the *Frauenfilme* (women's films) testifies to cultural efforts to centre women in public life.[57] The films also stand in the tradition of GDR documentary, for instance through their narrative focus on the everyday and on the depiction of subjects over extended periods.[58] These themes and practices are rooted in the socialist realist focus on the working class, a perspective that gradually shifted to more realistic representations of average people. In the 1980s in particular, documentary films about the daily lives of small groups and individuals accompanied the move of many GDR citizens away from public life into more private niches of society. Younger film-makers of this period often engaged with social problems by representing tensions between the ideal and the norm, or by indirectly critiquing public discourses through analysis of private circumstances.[59] Artists with GDR background commonly consider 'simple stories' best able to illuminate important issues. Grand narratives are easily manipulated and self-censorship makes direct discussion of public debates improbable. It is in everyday conversation that political insights can be best articulated.[60]

Havanna mi amor and *Heirate mich!* employ just such filmic strategies in representing the Cuban protagonists.[61] For instance, takes are generally long and the camera often remains on the faces of the characters after they have finished speaking, as if inviting more information. Scenes are shot indoors or in secluded outdoor venues, as if to gain privacy in which the protagonists can speak. Questions focus on relative banalities such as lovers' quarrels and television sets, and on assessments of the verisimilitude of the soap opera that is meant to represent contemporary Cuban life. The responses move beyond these topics to oblique commentary about social structures such as gender relations as well as job situations and lacks of goods and services. Direct discussion of politics, however, is noticeably absent. For example, when Marino and his ex-wife reminisce about their relationship, they recall their marriage date in 1960 by recollecting that they met in 1958. The political events of those years receive no mention, seemingly because of their irrelevance and their relevance.

Havanna mi amor's focus on daily activities evidences an Ostalgic gloss on GDR life. The characters lack necessities, have few opportunities, and have an overabundance of time. This is the tenor of the GDR in the 1980s, at least for many of those in their twenties and thirties in those years.[62] Simultaneously, the bittersweet vision of a small, delimited, intelligible nation of citizens with simple, delimited, honest lives stands in for a fantasy of what the GDR may have become if it had survived the Soviet Union's dissolution and for what the GDR remains in idealized cultural memory.

The entwined plots of television repair, soap opera, and romantic relationships illustrate this vision. For instance, televisions are depicted solely in relation to Cuba's past as a Soviet partner and to its present as an insular nation. They recall the decades during which Cuba received Soviet aid and each marriage meant governmental bestowal of a TV and a refrigerator. The film suggests that with Cuba's sudden independence, citizens struggle to retain their living standards through barter, skill, and cooperation despite the constant decrease in the availability of resources from the pre-1990 period. They accept this seemingly inalterable situation, in part by retaining a value system not based primarily on material goods, in part by escape into simple pleasures and niche societies.

This emphasis on the insular belies Cuba's international ties, especially those developed in the post-Soviet era. For instance, while Cuban-U.S. borders are not as porous as the GDR-FRG borders were, U.S. programming remains accessible via satellite and video. This elision might be a sign of the Cubans' reticence to discuss such topics; the filmic effect is to emphasize the hermetic quality of island life and to link Cuba solely to an international socialism of the past. The perspectival omission gives a romantic sheen to the Ostalgic gaze and overemphasizes the naivety of the Cubans. In the GDR context, such a depiction finds its parallel in presenting as normative those few whose valley location blocked their access to West German television (the so-called *Tal der Ahnungslosen* [valley of the ignorant] around Dresden). The film virtually disavows the availability of luxury Western goods (including televisions) in Cuba, the dollar economy, and the legal and shadow commerce that enables access to these goods. The camera accompanies young and attractive Gladys to a cigar factory where she inquires in vain about work, then heads off down the street. Her libidinal relationships are related as solely personal. In the sequel to *Havanna mi amor* (*Heirate mich!*) however, Gladys grasps the economic advantage of marriage with a Western German tourist and moves to Hamburg.

The interpersonal interactions that *Havanna* depicts are open, tender, and characterized by an often familial solidarity. There is no mention of other relationships, such as informal sex work or the citizen groups organized by the government to control illegal activities. The selective, delicate, respectful representation of these Cuban citizens is a function of the close relationship that the film team believes itself to have developed with the Cuban protagonists. Their conviction of solidarity, in turn, correlates to their desires to reclaim their own GDR history. The value of this history rests in its ability to enable noninstrumental relationships between the visitors and the visited on the basis of a common background, as well as in its ability to render this contemporary real-existing socialism intelligible. Moreover, the value of the filmic present that also represents the GDR past impacts the contemporary value of the GDR. This representation of real-existing socialism works to undercut post-1989 narratives of East Germany that characterize it as a hypocritical society in which individualistic materialism was the overriding – if concealed – value, corruption was rampant, and interpersonal relationships were systematically betrayed for personal gain.

The gender messages about this Cuba also reconstruct an idealized GDR. A film about people, *Havanna* is ultimately a film about women and their strength under a socialist system. The documentary closes with the matriarch Silai on her apartment balcony and with a pan down the street below. How will life in Cuba go on? The narrative suggests that strong women will be the prime determiners. Eggert sees the focus on Silai and her employees as a tribute to the generation of her mother who held the GDR together. Indeed, the hair salon run by the middle-aged, single woman is the only fully functional establishment in *Havanna*. Unlike the dreary, tension-ridden television repair shops run by men, the salon builds community. Here people meet, communicate, support each other, and do excellent work with inadequate tools – as evidenced by Silai's skill at cutting hair with ancient shears. Here the state has some positive impact on daily life – as evidenced by the uniforms Silai distributes among her employees, work clothes provided by the government to acknowledge their service. These scenes recall GDR workplaces that functioned as places of social life as well as employment. In this idealized structure, the social and professional status of women is commensurate with their workload and machismo has been vanquished. This depiction downplays and even belies labour concerns common to Cuba and the GDR: excessive governmental influence, lack of supplies, difficult working conditions, poor morale, and the sometimes overwhelming additional duties attached to employment. The filmic focus on womanism is intrinsic to *Havanna mi amor*'s construction of an ideal GDR by means of an ideal Cuba.[63]

To sharpen this perspective, compare it to Wenders's film. The Cuban fantasy of *Buena Vista Social Club* is a man's world – women are nearly absent except as topics of and audiences for love songs. Omara Portuondo, the only female musician, merits a short interview but func-

1.4 Scene from *Havanna mi amor*. Used with permission.

tions primarily to enable a performance of sexual play during concerts. In addition to Cuban women, who create local colour, the viewers may once glimpse Cooder's unnamed wife during one of the recording sessions, and the voice of one unseen translator is female. What was normative for the FRG's 68er generation remains here: men make history; men make narratives.

The dynamics of racialization in Gaulke and Eggert's films problematize the larger FRG, while socialist Cuba and by extension the socialist GDR embrace difference as part of a harmonious society. Racism is represented for the first time in the Germany of *Heirate mich!* Western German children of various ethnic backgrounds pick fights with Gladys's Cuban son and mock him with racial epithets. Gladys's position in the family of her husband Erik is paralleled with that of a pet bird of Erik's mother that has been trained to speak German. The inhabitants of Hamburg are represented as intolerant of difference: of people of colour and, by implication, of Eastern Germans as well.

In contrast, in Cuba citizens of all backgrounds live in harmony. Gladys's desirability resonates somewhat uncomfortably with stereotypes of the hypersexualized mulatta. Yet, in these narratives Gladys primarily embodies the diversity on the island. The film actively perpetuates this idealized representation of Cuba. One narrative plotline that was cut from *Havanna* depicts a Marxist Cuban father who forbids the intimate relationship between his white daughter and a brown man. Such editing upholds the non-racist mythology of socialist Cuba and by extension the GDR. Interestingly, both the Western and the Eastern German films emphasize race blindness. This accentuation suggests commonalities across capitalist and socialist mythologies that resonate loudly in a larger FRG increasingly hostile to underprivileged people of colour.

Heirate mich! participates in the tendency to cast the merger of the Germanies as a marriage between a masculine FRG and a feminine GDR.[64] Gladys's journey begins in Cuba with her suitor Erik as a great white hero who magnanimously rescues the third-world maiden with a white wedding. His self-fashioning leverages the economic privilege of the Northern tourist into masculine prowess, promising a lifestyle that Gladys must unquestioningly embrace. This econo-sexual transaction across national boundaries is apparent in Erik's preparations of the German domestic sphere: goods in exchange for marital possession. Erik shops for a bed with his parents. His foreign wife is to share in the generational capital of the nuclear Western German family in exchange for her fidelity to the system, represented by her dependence and monogamy.

In Havana, couples share in amassing and dispensing resources; in the larger FRG, Gladys is not to earn or spend, instead she is to be a recipient. Only her skills of seduction – upon which wives in capitalist nations have long relied – are marketable. Gladys's journey into the larger FRG is disempowering. While on her island, Gladys had access to most social realms; in the new Germany's 'flourishing landscape,' her horizon is a domestic enclosure. The intolerance that she and her son encounter is not the German life she was expecting. Her tearful complaints recall the cliché of the eternally complaining Eastern German (*Jammer-Ossi*). Its similarly stereotypical counterpoint is Western German Erik's response that highlights his sacrifices and her ingratitude, particularly in considering her lack of capital and marketable skills in this new economy.

Cuba libre bittersüß – Searching for Revolutionary Home

Cuba libre bittersüß offers another competing perspective on larger Germany. The prosaic, short travelogue tells a story of revolutionary consciousness and global change that many Germans polarized by a post–Second World War history of political violence and contemporary discourses of international 'terror' would be loath to entertain directly. Its author Inge Viett was born in 1944 in Germany and became politically active in the extra-parliamentary opposition before joining the 2 June Movement, later named the Red Army Faction (RAF). Having gone underground in the GDR, she was arrested in 1990 and imprisoned until 1997. While incarcerated she wrote political letters and her autobiography, the latter of which is the basis of Volker Schlöndorff's 2000 melodrama *Die Stille nach dem Schuss* (*The Legend of Rita*). Viett remains politically active in the radical left and has most recently published *Morengas Erben: Eine Reise durch Namibia* (Morenga's Heirs: A Journey through Namibia, 2004). *Cuba libre bittersüß* is based on her experiences immediately after having been released from prison. In this first travelogue, the narrator seeks political abode in contemporary Cuba among the post-national community of 'us humans' of socialist consciousness. The opening lines juxtapose her experience in the German penitentiary with this alternative space:

> Now I must get away from here, now I must go,
> before I become a small, hard concrete block,
> pressed together by the Nothing after a hundred thousand
> Words.
> Now I must get away from here, now I must go,
> before I become a small, cold ice block,
> frozen after the only, constant question:
> How to go further?
> So I pack the backpack and walk off on the search for us humans.
> So I travel to Cuba. There where the International is sung with swaying
> hips. My warmest thanks to Helene and Karl, who had already given me
> this prospect when I was still in prison.[65]

The narrator does not seek home in the larger Germany; instead, this industrial, modern society alienates and debilitates as did her prison cell. Actions seem impossible and words – even the words of her prison writings – lead only to the threat of knowledge that these words will move nothing. It is a nation without opportunity where the tension between the desire for change and the impossibility of creating change threatens to freeze life and emotion. As a still-existing socialist system, Cuba represents the most likely sanctuary for the narrator; yet the belonging that she seeks is elusive. 'Would you want to stay here?' muses this metaphorically stateless former RAF member in this would-be Caribbean homeland situated beyond the German correctional institution – tangible embodiment of her national estrangement – and the post-1990 FRG of which she has never been a fully enfranchised part.

The narrator Viett's concern with the possibility and impossibility of larger Germany as home and hope for political space motivates the shape of Cuba in the text. The circumstances of everyday Cubans and Cuba are repeatedly juxtaposed with the circumstances of the narrator Viett and Germany. In contrast to her symbolic – that is, subjectively felt – statelessness, the Cuban characters she meets have arrived at what seem non-coerced grounded conclusions about their identity and their nation. The wife of the German-Cuban Friendship Society representative in Pinar del Rio, Elena, returned to Cuba from the FRG after only three months; she could not imagine raising her child in such an individualistic and racist nation. The openly homosexual electrician and dance instructor, Benito, chooses to remain in Santiago de Cuba with the support of the entire community and against the wishes of his emigrant father. The cab driver in Havana complains about the current state of affairs, but also decided to return to Cuba from the Soviet Union in 1990, although he had the opportunity to move to Canada; 'I am Cuban,' he says. In these characteristic examples, the text weaves a mythology of choice – choice of location, lifestyle, and citizenship – while also suggesting that national identity is deeply embedded in Cuba's citizens.

Their commitment is critical for the grassroots revolution and is anchored in more than the socialist structure. It is part of a long and particular national history. The narrator compares the attitudes of workers in a publicly owned dairy (*vaquería*) with her own in the following terms:

> If it does come, capitalism, they will remain Cubans and not give up that which the Revolution has given them in human dignity, freedom and solidarity … I feel very good among the *compañeros*, their optimism is without pathos and is like balsam on my historical optimism, which has been attacked by defeats.

But I cannot measure how strong and confident the Revolution has made the Cubans, how deeply anchored their individual and collective sovereignty is. I only have the experience of one who is historically defeated. The coup-like victory of capitalism over the socialist East and the disturbing, courtly humility of the defeated have perhaps made me too timid, too mistrustful and have made me uncertain in my optimism. Cuba has different experiences. Cuba's revolution grew from the people, they undertook it out of self-respect, and it is the result of a five hundred year history of oppression and liberation. Why am I constantly worrying? The *compañeros* don't do it. Their optimism fascinates me. It is often not even formed by politics, rather it is an attitude that is contagious, that makes one happy.[66]

In contrast to these Cubans whose national trajectory is cast as successful and unbroken, the narrator Viett and those Germans who supported state and other German socialisms do not identify as citizens of their post-1990 nation. Their political and social values have no place in the new Germany. They find themselves estranged both from their past, their present, and likely futures. The search of this revolutionary tourist for belonging in transnational political community located in Cuba is thwarted by differences in national experiences. The opposition between the political unfoldings of a failed revolution in the Germanies and the continuing grassroots revolution of Cuba is not the only difference; rather, the optimism of the Cubans 'is often not even formed by politics.' This surplus is a national identity that moves beyond material conditions to maintain a division that cannot be overcome by solidarian politics and practices. From one perspective, these explanations for the different ontologies of the Cubans and the Germans work to absolve the narrator for failing in her own national struggle. Yet, the admiring narrator considers herself abject and unworthy of insider status in the political community situated in Cuba. In this way, she also maintains a division between Northern subject and real-existing revolutionary Southern nation.

This ever-present disjuncture notwithstanding, the narrator identifies emancipatory remnants and weaves them into a form that she can recognize as a political home. The text didactically employs what are presented as manifestations of revolutionary consciousness in contemporary Cuba to criticize manifestations of capitalist consciousness in the larger FRG. The freedoms of everyday life in Cuba contrast with the constraints of everyday life in Germany. Women travel with more ease on the island despite material difficulties than women in Europe who experience the public sphere as dangerous despite their putative travel freedoms. Cuban men respect the personal boundaries set by women whom they do not know; in capitalist nations, in contrast, such interactions are organized around the objectification of women. In Cuba, citizens are intrinsically linked by their socialist mentality; Germans are individuals who cannot find community. Racism is not pronounced in Cuba, while in Germany, onlookers do not even intervene in the beating of foreigners. The old, the weak, and the 'unproductive' are respected in Cuba because they are human.

The 'society of scarcity' in Cuba expresses cultural specificity and values that oppose consumerism and otherwise signify differently than they do in the North. In Cuba, human relations are not reified and material possessions are not fetishized; thus, poverty is not humiliating. Shortages are symptoms of a continued struggle against global capitalism and people solve problems together. Such practices are revolutionary acts in themselves. Herein lies the most important distinction between revolutionary Cuba and Germany. In the FRG, poverty is a result of national and international imperialism, of disregard for humankind. Thus, mitigating problems only upholds global oppression. In the larger FRG, as in the FRG before it, the only revolutionary actions are those that alter the status quo, which is the cause of global inequity and its miseries. In addition to sketching an ideal political home, these comparisons in which the island is the obverse of the FRG also serve to quietly articulate and explain the reasons for the radical political actions of the author Viett in Germany.

A scene in the Museum of the Revolution reveals this function of narrative comparison most clearly. Perhaps more than any other, it reads as a pedagogical explication of revolutionary violence. In articulating motivations and standpoints as well as links across national boundaries, the narrator works through her past and opens it to her readers. The narrative of real-existing Cuba gives impetus to and space for multiple trajectories of articulation. Viewing the exhibit on the 1959 governmental takeover, the narrator identifies with Castro's forces, asserting that the success of the guerrilla fighters in Cuba and Africa inspired the German 'guerrilla fighters of the cities' (*Stadtguerilla*). Yet, she continues, while in Cuba these actions catalysed a new regime and were legitimized by popular support, in Germany such actions failed and were delegitimized by popular rejection. While the Cubans embraced change, the Germans feared the actions and aims of the

2 June Movement and the Red Army Faction. The German public did not gain what the narrator calls (writing of the Cubans and citing Guevara) the revolutionary consciousness of the new human. Thus, those who sought change through violence came to be defined as terrorists not revolutionaries. This comparative rehearsal of the violent past of which Viett was a part elucidates it, as well as explaining her fascination with the political community of the island.

Scenes such as this one highlight that the divergent histories shaping current structural realities also shape individual subjectivity. For this reason as well, political convictions are insufficient conditions for full assimilation. Despite her enthusiasm about aspects of contemporary Cuba, the narrator herself sometimes furthers continued differentiation from it. Her actions in these cases are not politically principled, but rather embrace the privilege engendered by her distinct global positioning. Consider the hitchhiking scene: 'It cannot be hidden that we are foreigners and have dollars. My bad conscience relative to those who have been waiting so much longer calms itself quickly in the comfort of the POV and in the prospect of being in Pinar del Rio in two hours. In the final analysis, I am innocent for not having been born in Cuba.'[67]

This passage casts the narrator's exercise of privilege as an inevitable role. Even were Northernness only written on the body, its manifestations trump political alignments. From this basis, the passage proclaims her innocence at living her privilege. Related instances intimate that its use is necessary because she is feebler than the Cubans.

The rejection of guilt that organizes this passage articulates the Cuban situation most overtly, while the transnational sensibility of the text invites further comparison. For her German readership, guilt resonates with understandings of political violence. The uncommon phrasing 'I am innocent for' (*ich bin unschuldig daran*) rather than the more usual expression 'I am not guilty for' (*ich bin nicht schuld daran*) highlights the possibility of moral innocence even where a state juridical system has passed a guilty verdict. Had the West German been born in Cuba, her actions undertaken with the aim of revolutionary change would not have been understood as voluntaristic and seditious, but would have been endorsed.

In the global context of functioning state actors and governmental monopoly on violence, the transnational propinquities articulated throughout the travelogue do not unite the narrator with Cubans, Germans, or a world community. Indeed, the Cuban state also enforces division between the narrator and Cuba. Concerned that her sojourn will negatively impact Cuban-U.S. relations, the government rejects her visa renewal application. Economic and foreign policy trump transnational political solidarity. Despite her internationalist agenda, the narrator remains bound to her Northern and national past and present, a foreigner separated from the Cuba that, for her, contains traces of political home. Simultaneously, in contrast to the returned cab driver who states 'I am a Cuban,' this German is estranged from the current iteration of her country of birth. Its values condemn her prior actions and clash with her convictions. In the final analysis, her only potentially recognizable home is a utopian revolution that can continue independently of a particular nation. Traced lightly in the interstices of *Cuba libre bittersüß*'s narrative Cuba, this is an abode that the radical German can just imagine.

Conclusion

Each of these cultural artefacts of the Kuba Welle represents the island according to its own concerns for Germany. Havana Club began its German marketing of contemporary Cuba through the GDR, increasing the value of Cuba, the GDR, and Eastern Germany in the process. Increasingly, it also conjures a successful merger through mutual commerce. *Buena Vista Social Club*'s Cuba transports a subtext of Western-led reunification. *Buena Vista*'s Cubans – and the new members of the larger FRG – happily buy into the flourishing landscapes of capitalism, while middle-aged 68ers symbolically reclaim centre stage, directing reclamation of the East and the global South as well as besting the loved and hated United States. *Havanna mi amor* and *Heirate mich!* articulate positions on the GDR and the larger FRG that would garner little attention were they not refracted through Cuba. Narrated by a German who feels a stranger in her nation and everywhere else as well, *Cuba libre bittersüß* envisions a revolutionary Cuba located beyond real-existing bounds. The promulgation of these German visions of Cuba is enabled by, expresses, and seeks to strengthen the cultural capital of each contested national design. Moreover, the voice that each perspective can garner delimits the influence of these visions in the new Germany. Significant today, the role of the island as inspiration and justification was perhaps never stronger than in the first decade after the Cuban revolution. This is the period to which we next turn.

Chapter Two

Extending Solidarian *Heimat*: Cuba and the 1960s Democratic Republic

By the early 1960s, the German Democratic Republic liberally deployed old concepts to ground its new polity. Defined according to Marxist-Leninism, familiar notions such as *Vaterland* (fatherland) and nation were now understood as originating from and serving citizen workers. Even the traditionally anti-modern, locally focused *Heimat* (homeland) was being rehabilitated for this expansive project as early as the mid-1950s.[1] Socialist Heimat was imagined in a dialectical relationship with its inhabitants. Lyrics from a youth-group song emphasize the ties between affective relationship to, duty towards, and common ownership of the homeland: 'And we love the Heimat, the beautiful, and we protect it, because it belongs to the people, because it belongs to our people.'[2] While socialist Heimat foregrounded the cultural and geographical diversity of the GDR,[3] this broad vision extended to socialist brother nations.[4] Complementary spheres nested seamlessly to form a local, national, and international organization of socialism.

In theory and practice, extended socialist Heimat encouraged domestic support for the foreign relations critical to nation building; the putatively insular GDR was no exception. Cultural production from newsreels to travelogues, from feature films to literary texts, demonstrated the internationalist solidarity of socialism. The political struggles of Southern nations proved capitalist imperialism and legitimated Northern socialism. Documentaries such as those by Heynowski and Scheumann emphasized U.S. involvement in global oppression.[5] Brother nations and transnational exchange were highlighted in ways that furthered the national project. For instance, the GDR was represented more favourably than its partner nations.

Extended Heimat represented travel in distinct ways, making international sites familiarly *heimisch* while recasting tradition. Against the common understanding of international travel as a journey backward to a previous iteration of the self, it reconfigured the relationship between time, movement, and change. Travel was to the familiar, not to the (previously) known. Forward-looking, it might lead to a future being made elsewhere.[6] Extended socialist Heimat referenced traditional notions of domesticating the other, but focused on the possibility of learning from exchange. The weighting shifted according to the partner; unsurprisingly visits to the Soviet Union were exemplary occasions for edification.

Such representations built support for the GDR's national project precisely as travel for its citizens was being abridged, notably by the building of the Berlin Wall. They offset confinement by depicting the Democratic Republic as part of an expansive socialist geography that included nations as exotic and distant as Cuba.[7] Cultural difference showed the diversity of the extended Heimat of socialism, while socialist commonality demonstrated its familiarity. Depictions of international exchange through small-scale travel made the foreign heimisch, in part through identification with the travelling protagonists. In contrast to early cultural production whose international themes highlighted 'Western imperialists,' later works treated socialist brother nations.[8]

My examination of extended Heimat, focusing on the 1960s, complicates established views that in the decade following 13 August 1961, GDR public discourse shifted to domestic issues.[9] Border closure to the West indeed diffused immediate concerns for national survival by stemming the loss of workers and subsidized goods. The ensuing cautious optimism of the early 1960s engendered constructive sociopolitical critique of the newly sheltered Germany. Under the cultural program of the *Bitterfelder Weg* (Bitterfeld Way), art that foregrounded domestic production was meant to extol the 'Workers and Farmers' state. Yet could a largely sceptical general populace be so easily convinced to reject the allure of the West and the wider world and embrace this circumscribed domestic production? Introspection did not suffice; GDR Heimat was marketed by justifying, configuring, and extending it through international socialist community. Refracted through the extranational in popular and political discourse, the national was to become more desirable at home.

Extended Heimat also furthered GDR foreign policy. It suggested homeland expansion by coalition, rather than usurpation, strengthening the nation whose relatively weak global positioning necessitated international alliances. In the 1960s, relations between the GDR and other socialist nations became all the more critical, due to enforcement of the Hallstein Doctrine, according to which the FRG would break ties with any nation, except the Soviet Union, who recognized the other Germany. The GDR hoped that the politically unruly Cuba would take up relations despite the Doctrine and shaped their foreign and cultural policy accordingly. While Cuba did recognize the GDR in January 1963, it did not show as much interest as the GDR had hoped. Reports from GDR correspondents on the island bemoan Cuba's trade agenda, its enthusiastic relations with certain Western nations including the FRG, and its criticism of the GDR's agreements with various socialist nations including the Soviet Union.[10]

Because of its unique positioning, Cuba was a choice embodiment of extended Heimat and a refraction point through which GDR domestic conflicts were articulated. Cuba fit imperfectly with bloc practice and theory. Despite its success against capitalist oppressors, 1960s Cuba did not practice pure Soviet Marxist theory. Its revolution had not sprung from the urban proletariat or a party; moreover, Castro decreed Cuba's revolution socialist under the duress of threatened U.S. invasion. Nevertheless, this socialist-style tropical island nation had significant cultural capital, a situation attested to anecdotally, yet forcefully, in that cosmonauts, those supreme icons of socialist prowess, basked in their glory on Rest and Recreation visits to a Cuban beachfront mansion built specially for this purpose. Such contradictions invited multiple interpretations.

Mainstream GDR cultural production often underplays potentially divisive specifics to cast the island as a spirited part of a unified internationalist movement. As we will see in more detail later, after the highly touted rapprochement between the GDR and Cuba under Erich Honecker in the early 1970s, GDR news reporting on Cuba increased, with a focus on economic and cultural ties.[11] Official communications between the GDR and Cuba emphasize national similarities.[12] Travel narratives present idealized visions of a revolutionary, courageous, exotic island.[13] The well-known adventure television series of the 1980s, *Das grüne Ungeheur* (*The Green Monster*), casts the island as a socialist haven, a beacon of hope for Southern nations such as Guatemala, but avoids any explicit mention of Cuban military and political strategy.

Generally speaking, travel narratives and fiction of the Democratic
Republic present a more multifaceted picture of Cuba than mainstream
FRG texts of any given period, while nevertheless creating the island
according to their own agenda.

To return to the 1960s, three exemplary GDR texts variously extend
and interrogate Heimat through revolutionary Cuba. In the feature film
Und deine Liebe auch (*And Your Love Too*, 1962) Cuba furthers the political
project of the Wall through reinterpretation of international solidarity,
travel, consumption, and production under an international socialism. The GDR/Cuban co-production *Preludio 11* (1963) is a fictional-
ized account of a U.S.-led invasion of Cuba that shores up the GDR's
position against the United States and the FRG. The Cuban film *Carlos*
(1966) that was produced and directed in the GDR makes similar connections. Yet, importantly, it also criticizes the privileged position of the
Germans relative to the Cubans, to which, the film suggests, the GDR
public insufficiently attends. Irmtraud Morgner's banned novel *Rumba
auf einen Herbst* (*Rumba on an Autumn*, written ca 1962–5) depicts Cuba
as a site of danger and hope for leftist youth whose national example
challenges the staid first generation of GDR socialism. In contrast to
the Cuba of the West Berlin anti-authoritarians, in which the resultant
national model seeks ultimately to spring national borders, these GDR
texts envision bounded, solidarian, populist brother islands in common
cause for national protection.

Und deine Liebe auch: 'Drinking in the Light of the Revolution'

Und deine Liebe auch was planned as an introspective film meant 'to
poetically shape the love and morals of young people in the GDR.'
Three months prior to the building of the Berlin Wall, discussions in
the film-makers' working group included determining whether the
FRG should even play a role.[14] This singular focus was to encourage
a new national identification by rewriting the larger German historical narrative into a specifically German Democratic Republic narrative
expressed by the working title, *Bei uns…* (*Among us…*).[15] Yet the sealing
of the border drew the film ever further from this hermetic perspective.
The final version of *Und deine Liebe auch* seeks to justify and reconfigure
the new domestic Heimat primarily by extending beyond GDR borders, especially towards Cuba.

Available files reveal no evidence that the GDR film studio, DEFA,
knew of plans to seal the border. Indeed, the building of the Wall inter-

rupted filming and engendered alterations in the plot. The filmic style leant itself to such changes, for in a citation of the European avant-garde, *Bei uns...* sought to blur the lines between fiction and reality. The small crew used only an outline of the plot between the three main protagonists as the basis for filming and interwove the gradually developing interpersonal narrative with current events by working on-site, sometimes with hidden cameras, and by inserting documentary footage. This study of the GDR national project set in Berlin incorporated more and more international elements as the film-makers continued their work of capturing the essence of contemporary GDR politics while the border was closing.

Circumstances of production and politics that encouraged this increasingly international scope increased Cuba's role in this film, as well as engendering the production of *Preludio 11*, in which Armin Mueller-Stahl also stars. Interdepartmental correspondences suggest that he surprised the film team with the news that he planned to attend the first DEFA film weeks in Havana in November 1961. He broke the news at a meeting on October 18, less than a month before he arrived in Cuba, and months after filming for *Und deine Liebe auch* had begun.[16] The prospect of Mueller-Stahl's absence led to debates between the Ministerium für Kultur and some members of DEFA; the ministry of culture wanted the established actor to represent the GDR in Havana, the latter wanted timely completion of the film. Mueller-Stahl's trip was important to the GDR government; a compromise altered the script to include scenes in which Mueller-Stahl's character Ulli visits Cuba. Other alterations were made as well. In early versions, Ulli is also a ham radio operator; however, these communications are peripheral to the narrative – the final version emphasizes transnational, interpersonal communications between the GDR and Cuba. Ulli's Cuban short-wave radio contact Alfredo even visits Berlin. Mueller-Stahl may have been instrumental in this change and in casting Alonzo Arau as Alfredo, for he became acquainted with the work of the Mexican actor while in Cuba.[17] Arau was popular on the island, and this cameo appearance may have aimed to increase Cuban interest in the film. Such marketing would have been useful. Although journals such as *Cine Cubano* and *Deutsche Filmkunst* regularly covered the subsequent series of reciprocal ICAIC and DEFA film weeks in the GDR and Cuba, respectively, *Liebe* screened on the island in 1963 with only brief mention.[18]

In the Democratic Republic, the stated mission of *Liebe* became to train the embrace of the new national configuration.[19] Promotional materials avowed emotive relationships between the state and citizenry. The filmic narrative allegorizes the Wall as a romance; publicity calls the film 'a declaration of love to the people of Berlin ... for true love is not the all-tolerating, the all-forgiving, rather [it is] the upright, the demanding, the love that also knows that a border must be set when it is necessary.'[20] Beyond this domestic affective relationship, advertising highlighted the Cuban elements of exotic pleasure and parallel danger. Documentary footage of hot struggle in the global South and Berlin's Checkpoint Charlie 'proved' the international threat against which the Wall putatively stood. Such marketing attests to the significance assigned to the international aspects of the film. Nevertheless, even the Cuban connection could not convince viewers to embrace it. Newspapers bemoaned poor attendance and negative viewer response.[21] The license of the film was not extended in 1967, officially because the treatment of the subject matter was outdated, yet certainly also due to public opinion.[22]

Let us consider the final version of the film in more detail. *Und deine Liebe auch* depicts Berlin as a node of socialist Heimat extending as far as Cuba. The narrative centres on a love triangle between the main protagonists Ulli, the socialist hero; Klaus, his capitalistic, thrill-seeking brother of sorts (Ulrich Thein); and Eva, the politically disinterested, small town girl (she is frequently even called a *Mädchen*), a young postal carrier who has been drawn to the excitement of the big city (Kati Székely). On 12 August 1961 the two young men meet at the grave of Klaus's mother, who brought both of them up during the Second World War after Ulli lost his own mother in the Berlin air raids. Klaus invites Ulli to accompany him on a first date with Eva, who had delivered a winning West lottery ticket to him earlier that day. The three dance the cha-cha and drink at a crowded downtown nightspot, while the young men vie for Eva's attentions. Klaus shows off by buying expensive Russian sparkling wine using his West German mark salary. Seemingly unconcerned that Klaus's wealth will give him an upper hand with Eva, Ulli admonishes him to stop undermining the GDR. Klaus is a *Grenzgänger*, a frequent border crosser who profits from both systems by working in the West and living in the East on subsidized housing and goods. His labour power does not help build the new socialism. Later, the three head to Ulli's apartment where Ulli attempts unsuccessfully to make radio contact with the Cuban Alfredo at their scheduled appointment time. A further scene of rivalry that includes a guitar ballad by Ulli is interrupted by the electrical engineer being called away to the light-bulb factory where he works, located just across the Warsaw railway bridge. His citizen-soldier brigade is to guard the closing border at the continuation of the railway overpass, the Oberbaum Bridge spanning the Spree River. Ulli's voice-over emphasizes that this action is necessary to maintain the GDR's peace and the safety. Guard duty becomes all-consuming and by the time Ulli sees Eva again, the young woman is living with Klaus, who, frustrated that he cannot continue working as a cab driver in the West, remains jobless in the East, despite labour shortages. The relationship of the couple is problematic, primarily because Klaus is self-centred, chauvinistic, and choleric. Thus, Eva does not tell him that she is carrying his child, although she does find him a job as an auto mechanic through Ulli. After much vacillation, Eva finally breaks up with Klaus and begins a relationship with Ulli. She is about to tell him of her pregnancy when he excitedly tells her of his imminent trip to Cuba on a friendship and technology exchange. The plot now shifts between Ulli in Cuba and events in Berlin. Eva decides to carry the child to term, defying her fear of war and nuclear catastrophe, while the aimless and cowardly Klaus plans his escape through the very cemetery in which his mother is buried. Ulli returns in time to thwart Klaus and is shot in the shoulder as he does so by a border guard whose national affiliation is unclear. After hard labour in a work camp, Klaus repents insofar as his underdeveloped personality allows. Ulli and Eva continue their tentative relationship; Eva's child will grow up in the family of socialism, whether or not the two remain together. Thus, the personal desires of the protagonists move towards being reconciled with the new demands placed on the citizens of the new socialist island formed within the archipelago of international socialism.

In *Und deine Liebe auch* extended Heimat is personal and political. A voice-over by Ulli narrates documentary footage of the GDR-FRG border; the position of his fully developed socialist personality aligns with official policy. Indeed, Ulli's use of the third-person plural to describe the citizenry as actors in the Wall's construction situates the new GDR as the will of the people. Documentary footage of West Berlin residents deriding the provisional barrier near Checkpoint Charlie suggests that average citizens clashed in the German contest. The voice-over parallels the GDR situation with revolutionary struggles worldwide, including those in Vietnam, Algeria, and particularly Cuba. These brief comparisons set the scene for the more in-depth interpersonal exchange between the Cuban citizen-soldier Alfredo and the GDR citizen-soldier Ulli. On an unspecified, apparently surprise delegation visit, Alfredo seeks out his ham radio contact at the German border on the Warsaw/ Oberbaum Bridge where Ulli's militia is stationed. This mise en scène on the Spree river, an uncharacteristic section of a mostly land border, invokes the thin strip of ocean dividing Cuba and the United States. The interactions between the men further parallel the situations of the GDR and Cuban militias. Both militias highlight the exigencies of defending against stronger aggressors and the key roles that their respective citizenry play in national defence. They see their nations as aligned. When Ulli asks Alfredo why he does not wear a revolutionary beard, Alfredo responds by asking Ulli why he does not wear such a beard himself.

Although the GDR and Cuba are depicted as similarly positioned, their national characters are presented as distinct, with Ulli and Alfredo as the primary embodiments of this difference. Far more effusive than the thoughtful Ulli and his quiet compatriots, Alfredo brings the enthusiasm, rhythm, and sensuality of the Cuban revolution to the Germans while affirming the filmic message of international solidarity. Drumming on the clip of a GDR machine gun, Alfredo sings to communicate that socialists across national boundaries share interpersonal affinities. The lyrics in Cuban Spanish – 'Somos socialistas, pa'lante, pa'lante' (We are socialists, forward, forward!) – are not translated, yet the German characters and the German viewers understand these and other lines in a general way through contextual cues. This filmic technique conveys the foreign quality of the visit while underscoring the message that socialists throughout the world share a common idiom. Alfredo's musical rendition demonstrates this as well. Drawing his entire audience in with his roaming, warm gaze, the Cuban uses the 'we' that usually denotes citizens of his own homeland to create a 'we' composed of himself and his GDR addressees – in the diegetic and in the cinema houses.

The German characters also contribute to this transnational, interpersonal communication. As Alfredo taps and croons, Ulli strums this new melody, transposing the Cuban drum into a more familiar means of expression. In that viewers have been previously introduced to Ulli's guitar during the love ballad to Eva, this rendition of political fervour resonates with romantic fervour as well. On the bridge, the international revolutionaries sing a common song of solidarity that raises the spirits of the GDR partisans. The camera emphasizes the enthusiasm with which this German militia accepts their Cuban compatriot. Throughout the scene, Alfredo is centred in the frames, surrounded by smiling GDR militia. Close-up to medium-shot and counter-shot sequences that alternate between Alfredo and various GDR guards emphasize their mutual respect and communicative affection. The one-on-one discussion between Ulli and Alfredo also emphasizes the benefits of international socialist solidarity and exemplifies that in socialism, personal and political goals map seamlessly on to each other; the heartfelt interaction between the two moves easily between personal and political topics.

In these ways, the film parallels the global circumstances of the GDR and Cuba in order to shore up the actions of the GDR government. Cuba also models the unification of individual and social desires in this new Heimat. As the above scene suggests, the film transports this message in part by presenting Cuban sensibilities as more politically advanced than the sensibilities of GDR citizens. In contrast to the GDR, in Cuba there are no tensions between individual and social desires. From one perspective, this depiction expresses a typical trope in which characters of the dominant group are psychologically complex, while the peripheral group, often characters of colour, are psychologically undifferentiated. The Cuban characters in *Und deine Liebe auch* are psychologically straightforward, but rather than representing backward personality types or 'noble savages' of times past, their personal and political attitudes suggest a trajectory for the citizenry of the GDR. The aligned Heimat of Cuba helps to reconfigure German Heimat of the present and the future.

Cuba models the alignment of romantic and socialist aims particularly strikingly. In Alfredo's Southern Heimat, male socialists need not choose between personal and political, nor between pleasure and duty. Women participate fully in the revolution, while retaining their femininity even in uniform, as evidenced by the female soldiers that Alfredo greets as equals. Female socialists remain traditionally attractive and faithful spouses, as evidenced by Alfredo's feminine wife. The audience sees her showing Ulli around the island on her own in Alfredo's absence; her scarf remains chastely tied over her hair and under her chin.

The love triangle in the GDR contrasts with Alfredo's relationship in Cuba. While Ulli tells Alfredo that Eva is his girlfriend, under the difficult circumstances of a fledging socialism, Ulli can be married only to the revolution. His choice to guard the GDR border means in practice leaving Eva to Klaus. The theme song expresses this tension, linking romantic and patriotic love. Ulli first performs the ballad for Eva; in other scenes, a sound-over accompanies long shots of a pensive Ulli on the Warsaw/Oberbaum Bridge. In contrast to the actions of Alfredo's wife, Eva expresses her political immaturity through her sexual desires. Interior monologues articulate vacillation. Eva's attraction for Ulli is vaguely motivated by a scar on his chin, while her interest in Klaus – who, she muses, has no scar on his chin – is motivated by his Don Juan–style advances. At first, Eva prefers being objectified to entering a relationship with a hero who is marked by struggle. As her political consciousness grows through experiential knowledge of the political events of the early 1960s, she moves towards a steadfast desire for Ulli. In contrast, the self-proclaimed loner and perpetually underdeveloped socialist personality Klaus ends up in social limbo despite self-centred attempts to connect through his relationship with Eva.

This triangular relationship that expresses the generalized tensions between individual and social needs shapes the characters along traditional heterosexual, national, and masculinist lines. For Eva, the sexually desirable embodiment of socialism is Ulli, not Alfredo. While Cuba is the ideal of socialist Heimat in many ways, this ideal is not normatively masculine. The faithful, married Alfredo is only nominally attractive by normative standards and his mannerisms are comic, not sensual. Other Cuban males are also presented in non-sexualized ways. Only the GDR hero embodies socialist masculinity par excellence. Similarly, the film condones the expression of German socialist libido in terms of traditional gender inequality and sexual difference. An upbeat denouement legitimates Ulli's choice to leave his mousy, socialist colleague for the young, sexually attractive Eva, with her questionable political merits. Indeed, his libidinal realignment fulfils a call of duty; Eva is converted in part through her relationship with him.

Cuba thus models successful relationships between individuals and between individuals and society, and brings affective and sensual pleasures into socialism. International solidarity with this brother nation also refigures production and consumption within the socialist paradigm. Such reconfiguration was critical; consumption competitively measured national success.[23] Particularly after forbidding its citizens *Grenzgänger* lifestyles, the GDR increasingly attempted to provide a superior standard of living through manufacture, supply, and equitable distribution. It also sought definitional shifts; in *Und deine Liebe auch*, for instance, production and consumption are reconfigured away from Western/FRG affiliations and towards socialist/Cuban affiliations. Partnership with Cuba is superior because the nature of consumer goods and the meaning of consumption shift according to the economic system of which they are a part. Goods from the West are ephemeral and encourage decadent tastes that entice underdeveloped personalities into unsatisfactory and endless cycles of desire. Goods from the socialist bloc facilitate interpersonal and international exchange, and enable a sustainable cycle of production and distribution for necessary commodities.

Unsurprisingly, the capitalist and socialist modes of consumption and production are juxtaposed in Klaus and Ulli. Klaus earns his money thinking only of himself rather than of how his actions affect his fellow citizens. This attitude is exemplified in his habit of playing the lottery, a game of chance in which the payout is not based on the work put in. His spending is equally frivolous. In contrast, Ulli uses his marketable skills as an electrician to benefit the GDR and his spending reflects socialist values. Klaus fetishizes the ephemeral, vicarious pleasure of capitalist consumption. His use of the 1959 Peter Stuyvesant marketing slogan, 'The Scent of the Great, Wide World' (*Der Duft der großen Weiten Welt*), to characterize his own desire demonstrates that Klaus has internalized the values of capitalism.

Klaus's vague appeals to cosmopolitan freedoms remain insubstantial. In contrast, in socialism, goods facilitate communication. Thus on the Oberbaum Bridge, Ulli and Alfredo share cigarettes and cigars as a sign of their friendship. Modern, amateur photographic images evidence the GDR's technological wealth and, in the right hands, further interpersonal relationships. Upon finding photos of Eva that Klaus has left behind, Ulli takes a portrait over semi-nudes, a choice that emphasizes Ulli's interest in Eva's person and Klaus's consumerist objectification of his 'bed bunny' (*Betthäschen*). Eva's portrait cites the photo of Alfredo's wife that Alfredo has shared with Ulli. The images both connote communicative romantic relationships and facilitate interpersonal exchange between the two socialist men.

In the realm of international politics, goods are building blocks to a sustainable socialist future of brotherhood. Scenes of light-bulb factory production and general assembly meetings narrated by Ulli's voice-over emphasize international connections on all levels of manufacture and trade. In this model, the more technologically advanced nations, such as the GDR, share expertise and industrial products with their less developed brother nations, such as Cuba. The extended Heimat of Cuba enriches the GDR with not only the musical instruments and LPs that Ulli shares with his enthusiastic GDR colleagues but also with the powerful 'light of the revolution' that Ulli drinks in (*das Licht der Revolution tanken*) while being chauffeured through Havana streets.

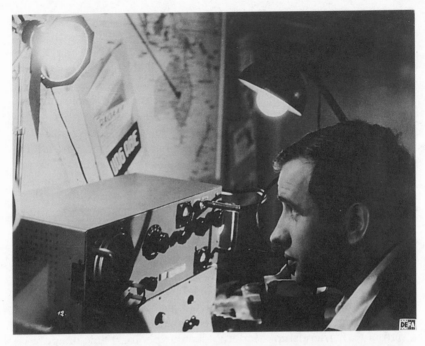

2.1 Armin Mueller-Stahl as the GDR patriot Ulli in *Und deine Liebe auch*.
Photo (17552) by Heinz Wenzel. Used with the kind permission of the BA-FA
for Heinz Wenzel.

In *Und deine Liebe auch*, opportunities for pleasurable communicative consumption based on international socialist exchange mediate the closing of the border to the West. Cuba concretizes the theory of expanded socialist Heimat. Socialist consciousness and international solidarity participate in the most literal sense here, as international socialism enables international travel for good socialist citizens. In contrast to Klaus, whose escape attempt leads to more strict confinement behind the Wall, Ulli enjoys all the benefits of intercultural exchange, as well as touristic pleasures legitimated by his convictions. In an intriguing interweaving of politics, product, and production, this diegetic rendition of the travel freedoms allowed to loyal GDR citizens was also rehearsed by those of the GDR film crew who were granted permission to shoot on-site in Cuba. *Und deine Liebe auch* is but one example; *Preludio 11* involved even more intercultural exchange.

2.2 Armin Mueller-Stahl as the Cuban patriot Quintana in *Preludio 11*. Photo (13131) by Waltraut Pathenheimer. Used with kind permission of Waltraut Pathenheimer and the BA-FA.

Preludio 11: Celluloid Solidarity as National Defence

Preludio 11 (1963) is one of three early 1960s co-productions between the Cuban national film studios ICAIC and the film studios of the Soviet alliance, the other two being Czechoslovakian Vladimir Cech's *Para quién baila La Habana* (*For Whom Havana Dances*, 1963) and Georgian Soviet Mikhail Kalatozov's *Soy Cuba* (*I am Cuba*, 1964). These cultural projects demonstrated international political solidarity, a term emphasizing collaboration not altruism. The visiting film crews trained Cuban workers, as many experienced film personnel had emigrated from Cuba with the departure of Batista, and their input and presence had the perhaps unintentional effect of calming nascent tensions within ICAIC.[24] These collaborations also expressed the widespread interest in revolutionary Cuba that brought many Western artists and intellectuals, such as Hans Magnus Enzensberger, to Cuba throughout the 1960s. In these early years, the new government invited foreign participation. For example, Maetzig, Cech, Kalatozov, and others participated in a high-profile round table on art and politics that coincided with both *Preludio 11*'s filming and the crisis in 1962 called 'Caribbean' by the Soviets, 'October' by Cuba, and 'Missile' by the Allies.[25] Visitors saw in Castro's famous statement 'nothing outside the revolution' an openness lacking in GDR and Soviet cultural policies. Cuba's sceptical relationship towards the socialist realism underwritten by the Soviet Union and its support of modernism were seen as particularly welcome evidence of pluralism.[26]

Although the GDR sought Cuba as a political ally, Cuba's uncertain relationship to the Soviet Union in the early 1960s complicated this aim. Perhaps it is surprising that *Preludio 11* was made at all. While documentation is lacking, interviews that I undertook with persons involved with the project offer some insights. Kurt Maetzig recalls that he and Wolfgang Schreyer suggested the topic to their superiors at DEFA out of their own enthusiasm about the events in Cuba. The late Cuban actor Miguel Benavides, who played the counter-revolutionary invader Peña, and the late Marco Madrigal, a technician on the film, understood the project as an act of solidarity that strengthened the GDR-Cuban relationship at a chaotic political moment. His criticisms of its execution notwithstanding, Benavides considers Maetzig's initiative at a moment in which GDR foreign policy towards Cuba remained unsettled an important sign of popular GDR interest in the success of the Cuban revolution.[27]

Both German and Cuban participants recall that the project aimed to raise awareness about Cuba abroad. Nevertheless, GDR concerns heavily influenced the narrative. As with the other co-productions, *Preludio 11* was a cultural project of political solidarity produced largely on the terms of the visiting partner. The GDR supplied the funds, materials, and most of the personnel and, by both German and Cuban accounts, dominated its production. Maetzig's recollections suggest what documentation and other interviews bear out, namely that while Cuban input was considered, the more experienced GDR production crew generally saw their compatriots more as apprentices than co-workers.

From the German side, DEFA supported the production enthusiastically and granted relative artistic freedom over the subject matter. It was Maetzig and Schreyer who decided on the theme of invasion on their preparatory visit just after the Bay of Pigs invasion in April 1961. This highly charged event that was on every Cuban's mind was manageable for Maetzig and Schreyer despite knowing little about the island. The invasion also lent itself to action-melodrama, a genre that was similarly manageable and more appropriate than documentary because ICAIC was already planning a documentary on said Playa Girón.[28] Whether DEFA would have supported a thornier topic such as the Cuban revolution itself remains speculative. What becomes clear upon closer inspection of the film is that the invasion theme engages with contemporary GDR concerns about domestic Heimat by mapping them onto the extended Heimat of Cuba.

Preludio 11 narrates an incursion undertaken by Cuban exiles with heterogeneous and irreconcilable aims and a romance between two Cubans from different class and racial backgrounds.[29] The white army officer Ramón Quintana (Armin Mueller-Stahl) has rejected his privilege in order to support the revolution. The mulatta Daniela (Aurora Depestre) has left her baby with her mother to devote herself to the cause as well, participating in the literary campaign during periods in which she is not needed as a soldier. Her former husband Miguel left Cuba for economic reasons and has secretly returned with the invaders led and financed by the United States. When the group becomes desperate in the face of popular resistance and infighting, Miguel meets with Daniela to ask for help. She rejects his request and him, but allows his escape. Feeling that she has erred, she recounts the incident to her commanding officer Palomino (Günther Simon), who is secretly collaborating with the invaders. Ordering her to bait the invaders, Palomino sends her to them in a jeep. In a move aimed to decrease troop strength at a key bridge, he then informs Quintana that she has deserted to join them and her husband. Meanwhile, the revolutionary prisoner of the invaders, Peña, has been raising consciousness within the group. He sabotages their attempt to destroy the bridge just as the next wave of invaders parachute in, which allows Cuban peasants to repel this backup force with burning branches. Quintana rushes to Daniela, uncertain of her political and romantic convictions. He arrives just as she has escaped the now commandeered jeep and Miguel's bullets. By field radio, Quintana hears that Palomino has committed suicide. The invaders are rounded up and Daniela definitively spurns her husband.

The camera zooms out in an aerial panorama as Quintana and Daniela walk towards each other across the road.

Preludio 11's articulation of Cuban struggles expresses domestic concerns, and in this way, its transnational solidarity shored up GDR sovereignty. Official discourse depicted the GDR's closed border as protecting citizens from the West, with armed invasion being one form of threat. Emigration had severely threatened national survival. Yet, in the heat of the Cold War, NATO's rollback policy (which aimed to contract Soviet influence to pre–Second World War borders) could be understood as a real menace, not just as a shell game. The parallel to Preludio 11 is clear; a fledgling socialist nation experiences invasion by expatriates under direction of the United States, common enemy of Cuba and the GDR. This North-South analogy promoted the GDR's East-West stance relative to the Federal Republic and the United States. Preludio 11's focus on the invaders also expresses popular interest in those who had made their way to the FRG. A closer look at the project will demonstrate this.

Media coverage highlighted the correspondence between Cuba and the GDR by paralleling Northern filming and Southern fighting, and emphasizing Preludio 11's verisimilitude. Kurt Maetzig's broadly disseminated statement, '[We] understand it as a thing of honour precisely now to fight on the "film front" as best we can, in order to help our Cuban friends in our way,' certainly expressed his sense of Cuban solidarity.[30] Its media resonance suggests that this declaration furthered an official agenda. In contrast, German scepticism was not reported. Cubans recall such tensions today; for instance, Benavides deemed actor Gerry Wolff the only truly solidarian member of the German crew. That filming inadvertently coincided with the crisis of October 1962 facilitated the equation of German film-making with the Cuban struggle. The analogy participated in a revolutionary romantic and implied that both the GDR and Cuban projects were equally supported by their respective populace. Consider this Filmspiegel (Film Mirror) journal essay: 'In these hours, filmic backdrop and reality blur at the Hotel "National." While movie scenes are being shot in the park, on the other side of the hotel, the machine guns are brought into position and Cuban militia and military units have taken their posts ... So in these hours it is not surprising that the real Cuban militia soldier turns at attention to the false German captain in order to make a report to him.'[31]

Other descriptions of the filming state that props included rifles borrowed from Cuban soldiers and a boat from an attempted invasion. In part they simply play up the adventure genre of the action movie, but their emphasis on verisimilitude, solidarian film-makers, and the alliance between the film and national self-defence also encouraged vicarious identification with the Cubans and analogy between the national situations on the island and at home.

The film also articulates a German perspective through its focus on the expatriates. Battle-worn, besieged, and recent witnesses of the court trials of the Bay of Pigs invaders, Cuban audiences cared more about their own experiences of national defence and nation building than about counter-revolutionaries.[32] And German audiences? The official term for the Berlin Wall – *Schutzmauer* (protective wall) – insinuated defence against external invaders. Yet, in contrast to the Cubans, GDR audiences had no experience with invasion. Newly separated from their loved ones and interpolated to reconceptualize their own national allegiances, they fixated on GDR emigrants. *Preludio 11*'s depiction of the Cuban emigrants as morally and politically deficient threats to the new German nation was a none-too-subtle critique of those Germans who had left. The Cuban emigrants' dissatisfaction with capitalism and their desires to return home speak to Western inadequacy. This specific narrative perspective casts GDR Heimat as worthy of defence and development by those who have remained and as enduringly attractive for those who have fled.[33]

The representation of the Cuban patriots privileges GDR interests as well. The counter-revolutionaries and a few Cuban soldiers are the well-developed characters. Civilians and partisans are undifferentiated and function as local colour; they seem a unified category. This diegesis belies the Cuban situation in which most able-bodied adults were militia with combat training. The GDR's very own media reported that Cuban citizens regularly participated in armed national defence against U.S.-led invasions.[34] An interesting twist on this narrative rule is the exception: the aforementioned scene in which Cuban peasants with burning faggots battle the second wave of invaders in a swamp. While this might be read as a typically neocolonialist vision that collapses the global South and nature, the scene has a forebear in Tomás Gutiérrez Alea's *El Mégano* (1955), in which charcoal burners who work in the swamp are depicted as nascent revolutionaries. Whether or not this particular resonance was deliberate, *Preludio 11* depicts Cuba and by extension the GDR as grassroots movements while emphasizing the importance of an organized military and state apparatus for national defence by distinguishing soldier from citizen. The USSR does not overtly figure in the film, yet the external threats to the small nation suggest the benefits of bloc aid. While the influence of the Soviets was increasingly debated in Cuba, it had been divisive for years in the GDR.

German actors play nearly all of the major Cuban characters. DEFA hoped that familiar stars would draw GDR audiences. The German production team found such casting pragmatic. Language was not of primary import, as the film would be dubbed in both languages, the crew had interpreters, and Maetzig had learned some Spanish. Experienced German actors were somewhat more available, but more importantly, Maetzig believed that it would be easier to work with Germans. He was one of many members of the crew and cast who were concerned that cultural differences would overwhelm this already logistically challenging project. While on one hand pragmatic, such perceptions suggest that supremacist attitudes inflected solidarity.[35] The *Filmspiegel* narrative of a Cuban soldier reporting to a German superior implies a similar viewpoint.

Casting and narrative mapped Cuba's broadly accepted national defence agenda onto the GDR's less broadly accepted national defence agenda. *Preludio 11* offers a spectacle of GDR citizens as combat militia involved in civic security. It worked to rewrite the contemporary GDR situation in which many of the average citizens were not proactively involved in the radical political changes. Seeing identificatory stars like Armin Mueller-Stahl as a GDR citizen and border guard in *Und deine Liebe auch* and as a Cuban soldier involved in national defence in *Preludio 11* invited audiences to parallel the situations of the GDR and Cuba and to become more actively involved in building the GDR. Such typecasting across films buttressed domestic Heimat while making extended socialist Heimat familiar.

In playing Cuban characters, these GDR actors 'drag' nationality in ways analogous to white Germans' 'ethnic drag' performances, to call upon Katrin Sieg's term. Sieg argues that the racialization of a given white German actor playing a foreigner of colour influences how viewers perceive that character. Similarly, not only do *Preludio 11*'s generic and aesthetic strategies invite identification with the Cuban protagonists, but also the extra-diegetic identities of Armin Mueller-Stahl, Günther Simon, and Gerry Wolff. Moreover, the reputed socialist convictions of these actors invite the inscription of Northern socialism as superior. With the exception of the black character Peña, played by black Cuban actor Miguel Benavides, principled socialist consciousness is embodied in whiteness. In these ways, *Preludio 11* incorporates a normative subtext in which Northern politics and whiteness lead and Southern people of colour follow. Moreover, the subjectivation strategy emphasizes social structures over individual character development[36] and also advances the film's Germano-centrism. Although the narrative is overtly about Cuba, it favours GDR concerns.

The gendering of national drag is highlighted by the exception: the fledgling Cuban actress Aurora Depestre plays the leading Cuban female role. This casting and its marketing capitalized on stereotypes of the hypersexualized mulatta. Newspapers attributed a fiery nature to Depestre herself; about Depestre's visit during the filming, a journalist noted that Potsdam's snow wasn't cold for her 'because one has fire when one is from Cuba.'[37] The white Germanness of Daniela's romantic interest Quintana and that Quintana is played by Mueller-Stahl encourage multifaceted identificatory pleasures. This constellation resonates with colonialist narratives in which the relationship between North and South is articulated as the relationship between a benevolent masculine colonizer and a feminine colonized.[38] It also invokes long-standing tropes of woman as nation and Southern nation as feminized. Demonstrating a typical Northern Marxist emphasis on class, the film allows traditional racial, gender, and even colonial discourses to further its national agenda.

Preludio 11 not only enhances socialist Heimat by embodying it in Daniela as object of German desire, but also in its depiction of this female Cuban revolutionary. Daniela's – and by imaginative extension Depestre's – actions figure as more than a straightforward remapping of her desire for the character Carlos onto the German actor Mueller-Stahl (and through character identification, onto the GDR audience themselves). Insofar as Daniela embodies Cuba, her libidinal shift from her emigrant, counter-revolutionary husband played by the Cuban Roberto Blanco to her revolutionary lover played by the German Mueller-Stahl functions as a GDR fantasy of Cuban desire for GDR Heimat. Insofar as her counter-revolutionary husband represents GDR deserters, Daniela's decision also shores up GDR desirability. Finally, because her affective transfer turns GDR viewers back upon the domestic sphere in these ways, it invites them along a third signifying chain that moves from Depestre and Daniela to tropical Cuban Heimat as extended GDR socialist Heimat that resonates with German homeland proper. Narrative yearnings and subjectivities weave the fabric of soli-

darity that yielded transnational island fantasies of Cuba and shored
up GDR domestic support for the GDR against the FRG.

Audience Reception and the Short Film *Carlos*

Und deine Liebe auch and *Preludio 11* were unpopular in the GDR and
attendance fell quickly. Moviegoers expressed their particular dissatisfaction with the former's representation of the German situation.[39]
Some GDR and much FRG press deemed the latter's representation of
Cuba stereotypical.[40] DEFA cast *Preludio 11* as both solidarity and adventure film, screening it in conjunction with *Tod den Invasoren* (*Death to the
Invaders*) and *Kuba, ein Reisetagebuch* (*Cuba, a Travel Diary*).[41] The first
documentary decries U.S. policy towards Cuba, a policy that shored up
GDR politics, without addressing Cuba's revolution and internal politics, which were more politically divisive.[42] Its perspective highlights
the docudrama qualities of *Preludio 11* that Maetzig strove for in much
of his work. In contrast, *Kuba, ein Reisetagebuch* presents a socialist
brotherland with exotic qualities, qualities that Progress film distribu-
tors emphasized in their publicity materials: 'The beauty of the tropical
island, hot playing of guitars and tam tams, and above all, spellbinding
women.'[43] DEFA blamed *Preludio 11*'s unpopularity on insufficient publicity,[44] yet adequate billing was a tall order. The disjunction between
the putative and de facto verisimilitude of this true-to-life, larger-than-
life, solidarity, adventure film[45] may have left audiences dissatisfied.

In Cuba, *Preludio 11* was not well received despite Spanish dubbing.
The film was criticized for those characteristics meant to appeal to
GDR audiences: tropical exotic, revolutionary romantic, and focus on
the mercenaries. Cubans in the film crew recalled that their German
co-workers were ill prepared for the project. Audiences found their
situation inaccurately represented, and the European actors left them
alienated. Such criticisms hearkened back to the time of U.S. film production on the island.[46] Most Cubans were critical of the Soviet and
Czech co-productions for similar reasons. For instance, the Soviet production depicted Lenin rather than Marti as germinal for the Cuban
nationalist movement of the 1950s. These attitudes undoubtably influenced assessments of their aesthetic quality as well. While *Preludio 11*
bears overt marks of technical difficulties, *Soy Cuba* is a cinematograph-
ic tour de force that continues to receive critical acclaim. Nevertheless,
Cubans seldom praised it, indeed Uruguayan film-maker at ICAIC,
Ugo Ulive, spoke for many when he referred deprecatingly to *Soy Cuba*

as a 'delirium for the camera.'[47] Such experiences inspired Cuban film-makers to create works that better reflected Cuba's historical, social, and aesthetic values.[48]

While these films were largely produced in Cuba at ICAIC, international cooperation took many forms and facilitated production in the GDR as well. For instance, the Hochschule für Film und Fernsehen 'Konrad Wolf' (HFF) in Potsdam hosted many students from the global South. The short film *Carlos* (1966) by Cuban HFF student Humberto Lopez presents an attempted invasion of Cuba that offers insights into differences between GDR and Cuba perspectives. *Carlos* opens with loud documentary footage of a U.S. attack. A voice-over specifies the date – 17 April 1961 – without marking it as the Bay of Pigs invasion, and states that many Cubans were injured in the fighting. The scene after the title frames begins with a near point-of-view shot into a quiet, clean hospital room from close behind the head of a man lying in bed. A young German nurse checks his wounds. The two wait for his scheduled surgery, with the camera alternating between the two figures and everyday objects in the room. She calmly adjusts the position of the window as a plane passes loudly, aurally linking this moment in the GDR with the loud passing of the warplanes in Cuba. The language barrier prevents much communication between the characters, yet the young woman who knows so little of the Cuban situation nevertheless regards the injured young man with concern, wonderment, and romantic interest. The patient practices her name, Bärbel; she does not repeat his name, Carlos. As Carlos is wheeled into the elevator, the camera shifts to a point-of-view shot from his exact perspective. Bärbel speaks with another nurse, confirming that the young patient is from Cuba and that his wounds are very serious. The next scene shows the young woman in the afternoon on a quiet city street in an overhead long shot whose initial perspective seems to derive from the hospital window. She calmly meets her boyfriend and the two scamper down the avenue to catch the streetcar; a plane screams loudly overhead, and the screen quickly turns to black.

This short thematizes solidarity between Cuba and the GDR while at the same time emphasizing its limits and the differences between the situations. Cuba is a nation of heroism and struggle, while the GDR is a haven where life is safe, organized, and uneventful. Although both Cuban and GDR youth play active roles in their respective societies, Cubans such as Carlos have larger concerns, defending their nation with their very lives, while GDR youths have time for carefree flirtation in a well-ordered, quotidian routine. The film privileges the former lifestyle through the attitudes of the nurses. In particular, Bärbel's awe for and sexual interest in Carlos is represented more forcefully than her interest in her German boyfriend. The camera work underscores this circulation of desire in close-ups of the faces of the nurses as they gaze at Carlos. These close-ups contrast with the distant shots of Bärbel and her anonymous partner.

The filming also increasingly aligns the spectators with Carlos's perspective. While the first point-of-view shot that situates viewers in the hospital positions them behind Carlos's head, in the final such shot, the viewer takes on the very position of the injured soldier on the moving gurney heading to the operating room and surrounded by nurses. Simultaneously, the filming distances the audience from the GDR characters. For instance, viewers see Bärbel adjusting the window from an angle very near to Carlos's perspective. Having seen the documentary footage, they connect the sounds of the passing planes with the Cuban events, much as the character that was injured in them logically would. This double shared perspective further links German audiences and the Cuban character Carlos. At this moment, viewers are alienated from the well-intentioned but naive Bärbel, who does not shy from the window as the plane passes. In the denouement, the distant shot of the street suggests a parallel with Carlos's separation from the carefree lives of the GDR couple because it seems to be taking place at the same time that he is undergoing surgery and also seems to be filmed (in part) from his sickroom. In these ways, the film emphasizes Carlos's importance in a world of extended socialist Heimat.

Carlos presents a case for solidarity by opening a Cuban national and a comparative transnational perspective to GDR viewers. In contrast, *Und deine Liebe auch* and *Preludio 11* seek to engender solidarity for both Cuba and the GDR by paralleling the two nations. While in the DEFA features international solidarity and Heimat organize sexuality, power, and politics around masculine GDR heroes and mark Cuba as feminine, in the HFF student short the GDR is embodied by feminine caregivers who desire a masculine representative of Cuba. Such contrastive takes are not the sole purview of works by Cubans, however. The novel *Rumba auf einen Herbst* (finished in 1963) by the woman-centric writer Irmtraud Morgner is a German exemplar that unsettles Northern stereotypes and engages Cuba as a hope for ameliorating, rather than stabilizing, the real-existing, young GDR.

Rumba auf einen Herbst: Partial Visions of Crisis and Creation

In *Rumba* the figure of Cuba refracts the contemporary GDR in multi-faceted ways. The Caribbean nation is a negative model in its position as a satellite of the Soviet Union, while 'partial visions' of revolutionary Cuba suggest alternatives for German domestic Heimat.[49] These latter representations speak primarily in relation to the first generation born in the GDR, youth disillusioned with what seemed an unchanging sociopolitical structure. Tensions between the demands of the GDR present and its foundational mythology are importantly allegorized in a son-father generational clash; the conflict is mediated through the extra-national island of Cuba.

Recent scholarship is recognizing this text (that was not published until 1992) as pivotal in Morgner's oeuvre. In 1965, the author referred to it as her first novel;[50] after its censure it was not until the 1980s that she referred to it again in this way, calling *Rumba* the first novel that she felt compelled to write due to the international political situation.[51] The complex, fantastic narrative is similar in form and style to her later work, rather than her earlier socialist realist novels *Das Signal steht auf Fahrt* (1959) and *Ein Haus am Rand der Stadt* (1962), and the form enables and furthers the content. *Rumba* is divided into four primary chapters, each of which concerns itself primarily with a pair of GDR characters. As events in this East Germany of the 1962 October crisis unfold, it becomes clear that all of their lives are intertwined. Framing these chapters are shorter ones set in the heavens that centre on goddess Persephone and her extramarital affair. Persephone is concerned with the survival of the earthly inhabitants out of a benevolence whose wellspring is her sexual desire and love. The potential for human destructiveness and the constructive power of love relationships is brought together through Persephone's larger-than-life feminine perspective.

The 'adventure' of *Rumba*'s dissemination highlights the significance of cultural production for GDR national politics and identity.[52] Submitted for publication in 1963, resubmitted in 1965, and definitively rejected in early 1966, the novel was one of the unexpected casualties of the eleventh plenum of the Central Committee of the *Sozialistische Einheitspartei* (SED), the December 1965 meeting that resulted in increased strictures on artistic expression. The manuscript then disappeared in the ministry of culture. Purportedly left with only an incomplete and poorly legible carbon copy, Morgner inserted extensive portions of *Rumba* into the voluminous and well-known *Leben und Abenteuer der Trobadora Beatriz nach Zeugnissen ihrer Spielfrau Laura* (*The Life and Adventures of Trobadora Beatrice as Chronicled by Her Minstrel Laura*), one of three novels in the Salman trilogy. *Trobadora* is even more modernistically fantastic and fragmentary than *Rumba*, and its messages are also critical of the GDR leadership and social structures; the timing of the manuscript submission during a period of political and aesthetic thaw in the early 1970s helped enable its printing and dissemination.[53] Although Simone Barck's and Geoffrey Westgate's detailed archival work on *Rumba* does not reveal extensive, overt considerations of international politics on the part of censoring editors, it is feasible that its critical commentary on the Missile Crisis, Cuba, and the Soviet Union influenced its suppression in the 1960s.

Rumba's publication history impacted *Trobadora*'s reception in the FRG and the United States. Critics often deem censored texts aesthetically and politically superior to those that received official favour. This tendency persists although, as with *Rumba*, volatile circumstances often heavily influenced the paths of artistic works. Such scholarly judgments can hold unexamined premises: governmental censorship evidences monolithic authoritarian structures, and favoured work calls for categorical rejection. The GDR itself remained a work in progress, with attendant struggles around ideology and practice, including structures of control. Many artists were interested in reform and expressed this in their artistic production.[54] In Morgner's case, the censoring of *Rumba* weakened her support for the system, but not her allegiance to what she held as her German nation.

The reception of such critical works outside of the GDR often speaks first and foremost about the interests of Western scholars. In the FRG and the United States, Morgner's oeuvre has been canonized according to a Western feminist lens that grants little attention to its sociopolitical context and the particularities of its gender critique that is always already deeply and explicitly connected to these concerns. *Rumba* exemplifies this. Consider its oblique, fragmentary, polyphonic style that *Trobadora* made famous. The style embodies and articulates the sensuality, subjectivity, emotion, and irrationality that the narrative itself argues is necessary for successful interpersonal relationships and socialist societies. By FRG and U.S. standards such stylistics and messages are feminist. And, such interpretation risks underestimating both how this narrative form critiques the GDR system expressed as socialist realist genre and how this oblique style enables the transport of politically problematic messages.[55]

Furthermore, few GDR citizens – including Morgner – identified as feminists, even when they struggled for sex and gender equality.[56] Western scholarship has had the tendency to discount such popular disavowal because it parallels governmental disparagement of feminism as a Western product.[57] Transnational feminist and gender scholarship encourages taking seriously those who find Northern perspectives limiting.[58] This approach has more often been employed in North-South relations; more widespread application in relation to Eastern texts would better local and comparative understandings.

While *Rumba* can be usefully explored from a traditional Western feminist perspective, more to the point is the way in which the novel reorganizes sex, gender, and power into an alternative national paradigm. The focus on Persephone inverts canonical hero narratives in which larger-than-life characters are male; indeed, Persephone's mortal lover is called only '*mein Freund*' (my boyfriend) for most of the text.[59] Persephone is the first-person narrator in the framing chapters and can be read as the third-person narrator of the events on earth. This reliable authority figure that prefigures Trobadora Beatriz advocates for increasing the presence and influence of feminine characteristics, decreasing masculine characteristics, and thoroughly integrating gender multiplicity in order to better the geopolitical situation. Its analysis highlights the limits of Western reception that reads Eastern notions as backward.[60] This early 1960s text performs a gendered humanist critique of national and international politics that remain a challenge today. Representations of Cuba transport and embody such alternative visions.

The Caribbean nation marks both emergency and opportunity in *Rumba*. As the focal point of the October crisis, Cuba portends a Cold War apocalypse. It comments on the problematics of the GDR's geopolitical positioning, masculinist rationalisms, and sexuality that does not involve personal transformation. Cuba also opens partial visions of a grassroots, socialist-style utopia that extends and transforms GDR Heimat. Refracted transnationally, these dialectical visions mediate generational boundaries and aim to inspire the second generation to transform the existing GDR into a socialist nation according to their own vision.

The Cuba crisis opens the novel. In the heavens, Persephone worriedly apprises her sleepy boyfriend about the reappearance of a second sun. This strange yet increasingly frequent occurrence threatens human survival. Connoting atomic testing and a world of nuclear winter, these two suns also represent the two superpowers that dangerously vie for global control; der Freund remarks that the suns have existed since 1945.[61] In the subsequent chapter set on earth, this binary expands to a plethora of meanings. Such profusion characterizes Morgner's style, in which recurring images blend and separate, refiguring interpretations. In the earthly chapters, the suns oscillate around linked articulations of the Soviet sphere of influence: the island of Cuba and the walled GDR. The volatility of these geopolitical constellations is exacerbated by the unprincipled psyches and actions of the characters.

Consider the engineer Lutz Pakulat and the architect Evelyne B. (Ev). Self-centred and driven by reason, Lutz lacks emotion and empathy. These traits mean that he apprehends only particular aspects of situations, which encourages him to confidently opine on many topics. In contrast, Ev's impulsiveness, sensuality, and emotive abilities drive her actions. These characteristics make it difficult for her to garner respect in her profession, yet her work is valuable precisely because it overcomes problems that rational thinking cannot surmount. Lutz and Ev's differences draw them to each other; unknowingly they seek what they lack. The narrative reveals Ev's motivations. Although content in her being on a personal level, she is debilitated by its inadequate validation in a society based in science. She is therefore attracted to Lutz's confidence and public success and most enamoured when he explains scientific problems because he seems so completely one with these abstract thoughts. Ev's intense attraction to reason and her ambivalence towards her abject creativity comments on how dominant value systems form the psyches of resistant as well as willing subjects.[62]

The sexual energy between Lutz and Ev evokes Morgner's 'Produktivkraft Sexualität' (productive force of sexuality), which combines socialist values of productivity with the creative power of sexuality.[63] Their interaction is powerful and exciting in comparison to the superficial relationships between the other guests. Yet their relationship falls far short of Morgner's liberatory model. They do not connect deeply, achieve lasting satisfaction, or shift in consciousness through their physical union. Instead, the denouement suggests parallels between the power dynamics of their relationship and contemporary geopolitics. The last scene consists in an alienated description of the sleeping Lutz told in the third person, yet suggestive of the close-up perspective of Ev, who lies next to and partially trapped under him on the bed:[64]

Pale, short undergrowth grew from the cotton firn field up to a high plateau that was multiply furrowed. In the foreground it ended in on overgrown ledge, under whose overhang an eye boll became vaguely visible. In the background a nose mountain arose at the feet of the brows, big-pored, oil-gleaming, ascending steeply until the summit … Ev saw how the right nostril tensed, stretched and relaxed again. The fat lids that were occupied with pale, bent lashes twitched once in a while. Ev observed the uniform movement under the skin covering of the neck that was stuck with solitary redly-shining quill-like stubble, and the bumping in the centre of this movement … The body lay stiff as before. He had pressed Ev against the wall. He seemed to swell up in sleep. If he continued to sleep in this manner, the moment in which he would inevitably crush her seemed foreseeable.[65]

This description of Lutz resonates with his description of the *doomsday-machine*, which in turn recalls the reconnaissance photos of the Soviet rockets stationed on Cuba that were broadcast internationally during the crisis:

'A large, but definitely manageable construction,' said Lutz P. to the hotel guests …Through the breath flecks [on the glass façade] they looked into the October sky. And they thought vaguely to discern what was repro-duced there in a strange reflection over the lake and what had been ver-ified by Lutz P. with a definition: a torso, bulky, island-like, but full of movement, in its entirety as well as in parts of the surface, dead and ani-mated material in symbiosis, mostly steel and humans, it seemed, the hol-low spaces were filled with concrete, at the places where barrel-like objects protruded from the torso, it [he] was, as far as one could tell, spread with leaden plates, the barrel-like objects wore dragonhead-like swellings at their ends and moved themselves stiffly, and when one looked careful-ly, one also recognized the cover that had covered the monster until just now, which was known under the technical name: doomsday-machine. 'I have been there five times already,' said a young man. 'The last time eight weeks ago. I have a girlfriend in Baracoa.' He took a photo out of his pants pocket and showed it around.[66]

Seen through Ev's eyes, the stiff male body of the egocentric engi-neer has a torso of deadening weight that, shifting and inert, traps and threatens her. Seen through the eyes of the watching vacationers, the doomsday-machine is a torso with phallic protuberances, dead and alive, moving and still, that threatens them. Indistinct movements of the bodies are disconcerting, whether under the '*Decke*' (cover) of skin on

Lutz's neck or newly emerged from under the Decke of the monstrous doomsday-machine. Both objects are alien and somewhat indistinct to the viewers. The neologism '*Augenkogel*' to describe the lidded eyeball and eye socket, accentuates the narrative alienation effect. Commonly understood as primary in interpersonal communication, the eye here becomes a site of estrangement through its mobile, absent presence under the layer of skin and under this new linguistic term that suggests a monstrous union of eye and socket. Lutz's face as a landscape suggests the terrain of the doomsday-machine. The text links the dangers of Ev and Lutz's relationship and those of the doomsday-machine.

These passages touch on three of *Rumba*'s primary themes. First, the ontology of becoming is privileged over being. The stasis that characterizes Ev's relationship with Lutz makes it ultimately unsatisfying and confining. The monstrous machine in the sky moves, but it does not vary; later in the text, precise repetition of the above description underscores the stasis of the threatening entity. The Cuba of the crisis is itself bound into such unwelcome strictures. It is a 'spot of dust the size of a sun, which cannot swim. That always sticks to the same place, determined by the same coordinates.'[67] This reflection of the sun mirrored in the sea is unable to determine its own national or international course. It is bound to the position determined by the Soviet Union. Indeed, insofar as the sun, the sea, and the spot represent the GDR's positionality, both nations are trapped within the constellation designated by bloc forces.

This fixed mode of being is linked to the masculinist logic that the text critiques. Lutz embodies it and shows its limits in practice. Consider his exposition of the doomsday-machine, a description significantly located at the opening of a chapter, as is the above quote as well. This scientific definition is both unsolicited and inadequate. '"A large, but definitely manageable construction ... One could perhaps describe the dimensions as enormous," said Lutz P., "as enormous or tremendous, as you will. But an engineer does not judge a machine by its dimensions, but rather by its technical specifications."' A young female guest calms her fears with the authority of scientific logic by repeating this superficial, yet soothing definition: '"An enormous construction" said the miss, "but thank God one does not judge a machine by its dimensions, but rather by its technical specifications, isn't that true?"'[68] Similarly, Ev recalls that her fear of the night sky subsided when Lutz defined its content. GDR readers who had lived through the harrowing October 1962 would presumably have found Lutz's approach lacking; to underscore its inadequacy, an old male professor supplies information about the probable results of nuclear war. Although the topic is relevant, the character himself is another source of misinformation based in scientific knowledge. He laments the death of all fauna, while prognosticating human survival. As it is evident that humans cannot survive outside their ecosystem, his model generated entirely by rational thought turns out to be irrelevant because it is too circumscribed. Similarly, the professor enumerates in precise scientific terms the negative impacts of controlled atomic experiments on human health without showing any concern about these results. In such ways the text suggests the dangers of the situation and that stolid, masculinist, scientific logic cannot apprehend circumstances adequately. *Rumba* does not, however, dismiss science as a method, despite critiquing its real-existing form. Rather, a discussion between the free-thinking physicist Kai, the critical journalist Uwe, and the anti-fascist hero Kantus in an underground blues club suggests that a scientific knowledge that incorporates the irrational, the emotive, and the creative can contribute to a real-existing utopian future.[69]

Finally, these examples problematize underdevelopment in political, social, and interpersonal relationships. Reason, emotion, science, and irrationality do not come together in principled ways, and Lutz and Ev's union does not generate Produktivkraft Sexualität. The setting of their affair – a lakeside resort in the GDR countryside – foreshadows this failure. The location well away from their productive lives implies alienation from labour and society. Despite the obvious relevance of the events in Cuba for their immediate futures, all of the GDR vacationers demonstrate limited interest; they soon return to their trivial parlour games and head off to sleep. Such apathy in citizens exacerbates crises. Similarly, the ultimately meaningless sexual encounter between Ev and Lutz begins as the discussion of the doomsday-machine has subsided and Lutz asks Ev to dance. Ev's perspective shows the relationship as escapist, occurring as it does in an island-like setting distanced from daily cares and in immediate contrast to the concerns in the night sky and the German present and recent past:

> She opened the eyes and squinted into the sky. It was deep as an overturned well, narrow and uncannily deep, and the shaft was bricked up with colourful foliage. On top. Naturally the brickwork was not brought down to the bottom, it extended perhaps one hundred beech years down or one hundred and fifty. The bottom was blue; the longer that Evelyne

B. looked down, the bluer the bottom became and the farther it distanced itself. It/She seemed to fall. Evelyne B. threw lucky pennies in the well and counted. But the echo failed to come. The bottom fell and fell, and Evelyne B. fell with it.

She laid the left hand on his upper arm, he took the right, she felt his breath on her forehead and the yellow tones of the trumpet, dark blue iris, big pupils, rhythm ... Evelyne B. lay stretched out on a blanket, to get tan. The sun was not worth very much, it was worn out, emaciated from the ecstasies of the summer. But it still managed it; it acted as though it stood at the zenith. Here, where it never stood at the zenith. Where it always looked down at the country a little askance and a little incidentally. The little country. The little, orderly country. Upon which an enormous, over-turned well with a blue bottom was placed. Evelyne B. stared down in the narrow, uncannily deep shaft and threw lucky pennies and waited and waited, but no echo came, only blue came. Dark blue, and she fell and fell and rushed towards the bottom.[70]

In this passage, the blue of the sky and Lutz's eyes becomes an increasingly direct commentary on GDR border politics, yet the unprincipled Ev escapes into it while the couple also skirts the problems of the suns and their energy. In contrast to the night sky of obvious threat, this is a blue sky of ambivalent hope. Consider the wall with its brickwork extending about 100 or 150 'beech [tree] years' (*Buchenjahre*). Although the colourful autumn foliage seems inviting, the name of the Buchenwald concentration camp echoes in the neologism *Buchenjahre*, connecting this wall with internment and authoritarian structures. The endless, dark blue bottom stretching into the heavens suggests bi-directionality and a world turned upside down; perhaps the Wall and Ev's relationship with Lutz are simply based on misguided romantic hopes. Are these utopian trajectories merely disorienting vortices in which no wishes made on pennies come true, no traction can be found, and no future is reached?

The last paragraph triangulates the GDR and Cuba through the sun. Here again the sun connotes the Soviet Union, this time as a powerful force that neglects its orderly satellite that has been walled in since summer. The description of its slanted shining on the GDR recalls by contrast its shining on the more equatorial Caribbean. Might both island nations be under unwelcome stricture? At the same time, the paragraph suggests that the specific positionings of the nations influence the energy of the sun. Might Cuba employ this energy for revolutionary changes? Might the orderly GDR avoid the same, because of or despite the enormous barrier surrounding it? In this narrative strand, the Cuba of the doomsday-machine, the respectable little GDR, and Lutz and Ev's relationship are locked into externally mandated global coordinates and troubled by half-disguised local movements. The partial mapping of each of these constellations with each other critiques the domestic situation in the GDR.

Elsewhere in the novel, Cuba means differently. From the mythic perspective set largely in the heavens, the island embodies a paradisiacal site accessed through creative sexuality that Persephone relishes as life-affirming (*Rumba*, 317). It is an inspiration for alternative living that incorporates sensuality, sexuality, wholeness of body and mind, and wholeness of human and nature. This potentially exotic utopia conforms to escapist desires born of over-industrialization. Yet the novel also gestures towards undercutting this othering by repeatedly citing Baracoa. It makes explicit that this is the site of Christopher Columbus's first penetration; the GDR vacationer visits his trophy girlfriend in this town; and it is also where the euphoric Persephone landed. Such repeated foreign intrusion recalls colonial legacies and invites consideration of ways in which they might be advertently or inadvertently reinscribed.

From the more denotative perspective set on earth, Cuba models a socialist-style alternative. This extra-national grassroots, emotional, sensual nation suggests a road map for the becoming of the GDR and mediates its generational conflict. This conflict garnered particular significance in the Democratic Republic although it was widespread in both Germanies. The state focused on the tension between those who had experienced the Second World War and its immediate aftermath and those born into an established socialist society. Official narratives heroized the first generation as the Germans who had successfully defeated fascism under Soviet leadership and cast national development in anti-fascist terms.[71] Officials argued that de-emphasizing anti-fascist tradition would undermine social and state cohesion, even though this foundational mythology was already greeted half-heartedly by the second generation. *Rumba* critically articulates the domestic and international significance of this generational conflict by refracting father-son relationships through an extended Caribbean Heimat.

In narrative strands set on earth, then, familial generational conflict tropes struggle around GDR identity and are mediated by the extra-national entity Cuba. The conflict occurs between Old Pakulat, a war hero and heroic construction worker of post-war reconstruction, and his son Benno Pakulat, a university student and jazz musician. The anti-fascist Old Pakulat's experiential knowledge of the Second World War strongly influences his understanding of and actions in the contemporary GDR. Benno does not value the lessons that Pakulat imparts through monologues on socialist anti-fascism and his war experiences, but instead seeks personal fulfilment in his own manner. The altercation reaches its climax when Pakulat attends a concert at which Benno, as band leader, 'twists' a traditional communist-worker march into jazz, a politically dubious genre. To Pakulat this reinterpretation insults the GDR and his own history and values. When his son does not return home, Pakulat breaks open and reads Benno's diary while searching for him throughout the city, engendering a dialogue of sorts.

Here in particular, *Rumba* expresses these themes and their potential solutions through its textual form. By means of a multi-perspectival narration that includes Benno's diary passages, Pakulat's interior monologues, Pakulat's present experiences, and flashbacks to Pakulat's past experience, both sides of the conflict emerge with similar intensity. Moreover, the shifts between these perspectives emphasize that rational thought does not drive the intercommunication that finally enables the anti-fascist father to accept his son. Instead, Pakulat's understanding is engendered by the interaction between his experiential knowledge, the relation of his past to his present experiences, and his love.

The influence of these multiple discourses on Pakulat is epitomized in flashback, which telescopes past, present, and emotion. In contrast to narratives typically associated with anti-fascist heroes, these passages are poignant, sensual descriptions of daily life. They emphasize the extensive influence of Pakulat's wartime experience on his GDR existence. Flashbacks occur when Pakulat is weak. Sudden and complete shifts in his perception emphasize the anguish in any moment. For instance, while looking for Benno, Pakulat's experience in front of a firing squad suddenly remakes the present, and the former partisan 'sees' a man near him explode. Flashbacks that reveal the widower's sustained love for his wife Anna evidence his sensitivity and modest humanity. His interior monologues describing her peaceful sleep during bombing raids underscore his tenderness, even while the zinc bathtub and blankets in which she sought protection recall wartime hardships and coffins. Her protective motorcycle goggles suggest adventure in another, happier life that Pakulat seems to have forgotten. In these passages, the dogmatic, righteous attitude of this older character becomes tolerable and even comprehensible.

Pakulat's partisan history is linked to Benno's present interest in the Cuban armed revolution and new society in other ways as well. The historical moments are brought into dialogue through their contiguous placement in the text. This association validates Benno's transnational impulse as part of a trajectory of struggle, as well as validating the Cuban project by linking it to the internationalist German effort. Moreover, Pakulat had enthusiastically converted to the anti-fascist struggle in Germany; now his son walks near his footsteps through Cuba. As music importantly expressed Pakulat's communist sentiments, Benno brings his jazz horn into the service of this new revolution; the band name, 'Bearded Stompers,' cites Cuban fighters. For Benno, 'twisting' traditional communist-worker songs validates the GDR socialist past while claiming it for his generation. The text suggests that youth can become impassioned about their society by making it their own. Synchronic revolution abroad invites rearticulation of the German revolution as diachronic. The marches of the first GDR generation inspire more forcefully in conjunction with the rumba of Cuban contemporaries. African rhythms of protest gain new meaning within the socialism of the Cuban revolution and as a call for grassroots socialism in the GDR.[72]

The text links Pakulat and Benno across struggle while at the same time demystifying war. Although readers are privy to the wartime experience of the father, his son has no conception of its brutality. Pakulat's reluctance to share the experiential knowledge that is so intimately linked to his political attitudes has inadvertently contributed to the glorification of state violence that *Rumba* critiques. Masculine role play thwarts communication; Pakulat rejects his flashbacks as unseemly signs of weakness. Waiting for Benno to return home, the anti-fascist hero leaves his removable glass eye burning uncomfortably in his right eye socket. He bears the pain for the sake of appearing whole in front of his son. This choice also maintains the pretence of a binocular, dialectically objective vision. Yet doctrine marks his body; through his left eye the old warrior sights only along a GDR Marxist-Leninist trajectory.

Such communication barriers and predetermined structures in his own country encourage Benno to engage with the developing possibilities of the nascent revolution in the South. Cuba wins over the GDR youth for the larger socialist project and attenuates the German generational conflict. Benno values sensuality, emotion, and adventure, in which youth have important roles to play. Pakulat cannot accept the domestic sociocultural ideals that Benno has developed for himself, as they seem to evidence disrespect for the GDR society that the first generation built with so much effort. However, Pakulat can and does learn to respect those that involve the new Cuban project. Through this new interpretation of revolution abroad, the father accepts the attitude of his son that socialism at home must be dynamic.

As a metonymy, this familial narrative critiques the GDR more broadly. Pakulat's mention of Fidel Castro – 'a statesman with such a temperament' – is of particular interest. Despite Pakulat's scepticism, the statement itself invites readers to compare such leadership to lacklustre GDR heads of state and against the Soviet leader Stalin who had died in 1953 and who was publicly denounced in 1956. Read from this perspective, Pakulat's acceptance of Benno's shift in political allegiance implies support for a shift in GDR and Soviet governance without direct articulation of this thorny domestic issue.

Overtly, the text remains focused on more modest and grassroots domestic change. Benno's internationalist sentiments do not inspire flight from his political circumstances; rather, the Cuban model inspires this representative of the younger generation to engage in the GDR project. After Pakulat has come to understand and respect Benno's political and social attitudes, he finds a note from his son stating that he has left to find work in Schwedt. This industrial city, centrally planned and enthusiastically built, symbolized a bright future in the GDR in the 1960s. The possibilities that it offered for personal advancement, including better housing, pay, and professional advancement, meant that this socio-economic engineering project promised to attenuate tensions between individual and social needs. This sudden and conveniently happy denouement to the novel may be a politically suitable ending tacked onto an otherwise ambiguous text. The cultural production of the GDR was no exception to this widespread tendency of self-censorship, and archival evidence does not elucidate this question. Yet the status of the final scenes does not change Cuba's function as a mediator and catalyst throughout *Rumba*. Moreover, it is thanks to its revolution that the younger generation, embodied here by Benno, is granted and takes up the challenge of extending domestic Heimat within the GDR on some of its own terms.

Conclusion

In the early 1960s, the GDR was struggling to position itself within the international discourses of bloc politics. To do so, its thinkers turned in part to traditions such as Heimat that had historically undergirded national sentiment. GDR Heimat reclaimed domestic space as a socialist space of belonging that extended well beyond newly constraining boundaries. Thus, far from focusing inward, this German cultural agenda also looked outward to shore up support for its national project. Films such as *Und deine Liebe auch* and *Preludio 11* and the novel *Rumba auf einen Herbst* demonstrate this phenomenon. They variously employ the extended socialist Heimat of Cuba to engage domestic border politics and work towards increased domestic social cohesion. While they are texts of solidarity with socialist brother nations, a primary objective is to engage contemporary issues most salient within the GDR. The film *Carlos* highlights this as, in contrast to the GDR texts, it seeks to bring the German viewer to a more Cuba-centred perspective while simultaneously emphasizing distinctions between the nations.

As the 1960s progressed, the Cuban agenda increasingly centred beyond national boundaries, in part as a means of survival in the face of geopolitical pressures. The GDR selectively thematized this shift; perhaps just as selectively, the West Berlin anti-authoritarians embraced what they saw as a Cuban model of island revolution that they hoped would enable escape from the nation-state as normative polity.

Chapter Three

Translating Revolution:
Cuba and the 1960s Federal Republic

In the GDR, the government encouraged popular and cultural interest in Cuba. At the same time, GDR texts that feature Cuba show that the interest of GDR citizens in the island exceeded their civic duty. In the Federal Republic, the government discouraged similar attentions. This U.S. political, military, and economic partner generally adhered to the U.S. program of active economic and cultural neglect. FRG citizens who were interested in Cuba were often politically engaged and organized. They aimed to educate themselves about and support what they perceived as Cuba's new agenda. Their specific engagement with the politics of the island was generally correlated to their particular interests in official politics and political activism at home. Such solidarity often expressed itself in the dissemination of Cuban political and cultural texts in Germany and in attempts to develop relationships with Cubans. The music and sun-drenched land with a language far more accessible than Chinese, Vietnamese, or Russian had particular charms. Yet, for those who were serious about their politics, Cuba was a unique beacon, a model to be emulated.

This chapter focuses on an exemplar of such engagement, the reception and translation of Cuban-style struggle to the metropole of Berlin by the West Berlin anti-authoritarians around Rudi Dutschke. Dutschke is perhaps the most well-known FRG student leader. The West Berlin anti-authoritarians were those close to Dutschke who were involved in the radical activist group *Subversiver Aktion* (Subversive Action) and/ or the meeting in Pichelsdorf, as well as those who self-identified and worked closely with these groups. As is characteristic of grassroots organizations, participation shifted. Subversiver Aktion later formed the basis of the *Sozialistischer Deutscher Studentenbund* (Socialist German Student Union – SDS).[1]

Scholarship of the 1960s traditionally considers Dutschke and the anti-authoritarians within a German or a German-U.S. framework.[2] Their agendas and activism are interpreted as catalysts that matured into reformist change within the Federal Republic, notably the new social movements and the Green Party.[3] This is only part of the narrative, one that does not account for the significance of Southern theories and practices for Northern thinkers and activists. Recent transnational perspectives in scholarship go a long way towards making Northern activists such as the anti-authoritarians comprehensible.[4] In this chapter I make three related arguments: Dutschke and the anti-authoritarians had significant interest in the global South, especially revolutionary Cuba; their vague plan for revolutionizing West Berlin relied on this Southern example; and their interest and agenda were based in the adoption of particular Southern understandings of nationalism that opposed what for many were tainted Northern models.

Defining Nationalism

Following the Second World War, FRG nationalism was being redefined. The concept of the zero hour (*Stunde Null*) functioned as a tabula rasa for the Federal Republic, and the new nation was to be thoroughly bound into Western alliances to assure that it would remain within its post-war borders.[5] FRG national identity was to be based on economic strength and parliamentary, constitutional, socio-governmental structures, not emotive, racialized mythologies that had contributed to the success of Nazi Germany. Many on the left in the FRG rejected even this Enlightenment-style 'constitutional patriotism' and focused on articulating forms of post-national or supranational identification.[6]

These vexed relationships among left-leaning Germans and patriotism may contribute to the relative silence surrounding Dutschke's interest in nationalism. Ulrich Chaussy's well-respected biography, for example, downplays it.[7] Historian Wolfgang Kraushaar has attempted such a project,[8] but interestingly, his more recent work tends to assess the student leader within a German framework.[9] I assert that in this case and related cases, scholars misinterpret the meaning of nationalism. Consider Nick Thomas's note in relation to the group around Dutschke: 'It is necessary to acknowledge the Left's contradictory opposition to nationalism while supporting a war of national liberation [Vietnam].'[10] While it may lie beyond the scope of Thomas's worthwhile project to engage this seeming paradox, these positions are not contradictory. What is required in order to make sense of the situation is to better understand the meaning of nationalism in this context. Analysis of Dutschke's work yields a particular conception that suggests a basis for rethinking the anti-authoritarian agenda. Similar reassessment may help us to better understand other left-leaning thinkers and activists as well.

The anti-authoritarians sought to define an identity for themselves based on notions of nationalism professed by third-world liberation movements in the global South. By nationalism, I mean both a shared sentiment of caring about an imagined community and the desire to act in the cause of this national community. Yet, an important distinction must be made here. Anti-authoritarian Germans rejected what (borrowing from Marx) Michael Hardt, and Antonio Negri have called 'bourgeois' nationalism associated with the global North in favour of 'subaltern' nationalism associated with the global South. The bourgeois nationalism devised in eighteenth- and nineteenth-century Europe is imagined as homogeneous and enabled by the subjugation and elision of the racialized other. In such cases 'the construction of national identity guarantees a continually reinforced legitimation, and the right and power of a sacrosanct and irrepressible unity.'[11] In contrast, subaltern nationalism is formed defensively against unwelcome dominant forces and is based in communities that exist in the imagination rather than as actual polities. Subaltern nationalism is double-edged, for in as far as it succeeds, it risks becoming oppressive itself. Nevertheless, the distinction between bourgeois and subaltern nationalism is significant: 'whereas the concept of nation promotes stasis and restoration in the hands of the dominant, it is a weapon for change and revolution in the hands of the subordinated.'[12]

The anti-authoritarians legitimated their radical project by identifying it with what can be best understood as the subaltern nationalisms of decolonizing Southern polities and against bourgeois Northern nationalisms. By relatively uncritically embracing such emerging nationalisms, they were able to claim a positive notion of German identity in a manner that, for them, opposed the homogeneous, oppressive conceptions of Nazi Germany, the FRG, and even the GDR. These anti-authoritarians' notion of subaltern nationalism that was fomented in the highly charged and politically contested space of West Berlin was deeply influenced by third-world liberation movements and expressed their internationalist agenda.

Third Worldism and 'Left Fascism'

Although the anti-authoritarians were among the first in the FRG to consider the discontented people in the South as ideological partners, they were not alone in their interest in these groups. In his groundbreaking work on third-world critique in 1960s literature of the Federal Republic, Rüdiger Sareika cites the importance of international development aid programs, media exposure, advertising, and international tourism in creating broad awareness. The expansion of television, coupled with public funding for broadcasting, yielded a wide distribution of substantive programming on international themes. Advertising marketed with exotic motifs and travel fantasies, although jet travel remained prohibitively expensive for many.[13] In this environment, left-leaning thinkers began to criticize North-South relations. Some drew parallels between what they saw as wartime imperialist and post-war neocolonialist tendencies. Even policies such as those involving development aid were deemed to be primarily concerned with supporting corporations based in more industrialized nations.[14]

By the early 1960s, predecessors of the anti-authoritarians, such as Subversiver Aktion, were deeply involved in such neocolonial critiques.[15] The contributions of these radical activist groups have been largely overlooked in cultural and literary scholarship on Germany and third-world liberation movements in favour of early works by those who became more accepted and popular public intellectuals. An example of this phenomenon is the scholarly focus on the literary journal *Kursbuch*, founded in 1965 by Hans Magnus Enzensberger, which is often credited as having initiated interest in Southern themes.[16] Rather than being seen as foundational, *Kursbuch* should be understood as part of a heterogeneous web of critical discourses about such issues. In another example, although *Kursbuch* gave writers of third-world movements an important forum through which their work could reach a German-language public, publications such as *konkret*, the leftist journal with communist tendencies popular among students, for which Enzensberger wrote before founding *Kursbuch*, have an earlier tradition of this practice.

The nuances of influence and reception are significant, because historiographies shape the way that the South is understood to have influenced the North depending on which South-North connections they foreground.[17] The oft-cited, public dispute between the German intellectuals Enzensberger and Peter Weiss on what they term first-world/third-world solidarity illustrates this phenomenon. The debate exemplifies dominant positions among left-leaning thinkers of the FRG in the early and mid-1960s.[18] Read against the grain, however, it also suggests the limits of these dominant opinions, limits that functioned productively for the anti-authoritarians.

In these early and mid-1960s texts, Enzensberger asserts that first-world/third-world solidarity is impossible. Meant as a corrective to overzealous and unreflective attitudes, this position risked promoting quiescence and diminishing accountability. Moreover, his stance that third-world revolution improves life solely for third-world citizenry destabilized particularly efforts of first-world actors to mobilize across national boundaries or to even think seriously about global interdependence as resistance to the status quo. Weiss's Northern solidarity, in turn, can be read as expedient in that its ultimate goal was to atone for German fascism through aid to the South.[19] Weiss's notion skirted issues that were divisive in the FRG, even when such questions were crucial for Southern revolutionaries and thus for defining solidarity. Notably, Weiss does not define 'oppositional violence' or consider under what circumstances such direct violence might legitimately be used against what some left-leaning thinkers saw as 'structural violence' in the form of state-sanctioned governmental and social organization.

To focus on the global perspectives of groups such as Subversiver Aktion or the anti-authoritarians is to articulate a different reception of the South in the North. Both Enzensberger and Weiss largely agreed that revolutionary change in the FRG was impossible, a position that suggested acquiescence to what they agreed were global systems of inequity. In their paradigms, well-established nation-states remain in positions of authority, knowledge, and power. Symbolically at least, the anti-authoritarians avoided such intellectual stalemates through their intense identification with third-world liberation theory and practice.

For the anti-authoritarians, the rebellious South acted as a role model for global change and suggested a domestic blueprint – the South was a forerunner, not a supplicant. Third-world revolutionary theories offered promising alternatives to existing FRG nationalism that was tainted by history and reinscribed existing power structures. Stated in Hardt and Negri's terms, for the anti-authoritarians, subaltern nationalism offered an alternative to bourgeois nationalism. Their desires for domestic national change increased their interest in countries such as 1960s Algeria, Cuba, and Vietnam. Their own critical attitudes towards the United States were reinforced by their analysis of how U.S. policies impacted such nations.[20] In these ways, moreover, the anti-authoritarians' alliance with the South was about critique of National Socialism rather than about belying it, as many have argued.[21]

The anti-authoritarians also saw these proto-socialist, emerging nations as alternatives to the increasingly discredited socialist GDR. Dutschke's 'Vom Antisemitismus zum Antikommunismus' (From Anti-Semitism to Anti-communism) expresses this position: 'Precisely the engagement with international questions was the result of our contradictory situation: None of us loved the Wall, only a few considered the GDR and the SED to be truly socialistic, but almost all hated the hypocritical [FRG] Adenauer-"Republic" … Nevertheless, we saw in our own reality no possibilities for a useful political praxis.'[22]

Dutschke's essay exemplifies this international engagement by articulating the position of emerging Southern nations such as Cuba. For instance, it criticizes U.S. practices of the United States as neocolonial and disparages the policy of peaceful coexistence as beneficial only for the U.S. bloc and the Soviet bloc countries. In particular, the essay faults the USSR for bettering its own economic position by neglecting Latin American revolutions.[23]

The piece also demonstrates solidarity through identification. In Dutschke's text, the global geopolitical conflict is often shaped by physical geography, but always defined by ideology. Anti-authoritarians mapped what they read as the neocolonialist relationships between the United States and third-world countries onto the U.S.-FRG relationship. For example, the position of the FRG as a U.S. trading partner under the Marshall Plan was criticized as having brought the FRG under the political and cultural sway of the United States.[24] This identification across lines of privilege may seem surprising and it has often been read as self-serving. Organized along ideology, it downplayed difference. Yet, this identification is worth taking seriously, in part because Southern actors such as the Cuban government and intelligentsia supported it. If the intensity and logic of this felt and theorized solidarity is understood, then an unpublished document by Dutschke that Kraushaar revealed in 2005 suddenly becomes comprehensible as further evidence for this identification of solidarity. In it, Dutschke aligns the anti-authoritarians with the revolutionaries in Latin America and places the ruling classes across the globe on the other side of the division.[25]

This identification with third-world liberation also further explains why the anti-authoritarians downplayed the influence of the GDR on their own thinking although these trans-Wall connections were not insignificant. Dutschke and Rabehl had been schooled in the GDR, where the international scope of capitalist influence was studied and articulated as global exploitation.[26] The group also had access to translated printed materials from the Soviet bloc that were not printed in the FRG until the mid-1960s when market demand rose. For example, Che Guevara's influential 1960 text *La Guerra de Guerrillas* (*Guerrilla Warfare*) was available to West Berlin anti-authoritarians in 1962 through the GDR's translation, *Der Partisanenkrieg*.[27] The GDR also supported some of the FRG left financially and logistically. For instance, Kraushaar has shown that it funded the newspaper *konkret*,[28] while journalist Bettina Röhl, daughter of the *konkret* editor Klaus Rainer Röhl and *konkret* columnist Ulrike Meinhof, shows that this support ended in 1964, when the paper repeatedly strayed from the SED's agenda. Röhl's work highlights that financing did not mean complete control.[29] In another example, debates between the GDR youth group *Freie Deutsche Jugend* (Free German Youth) and the FRG youth group *Die Falken* (The Hawks) suggest both that the GDR subsidized Die Falken and that the group was nevertheless quite autonomous in determining its political agenda.[30] Scholars variously attribute the historiographic elision of trans-Wall affiliations to the strategy of peaceful coexistence and its aftermath.[31] It would be unsurprising that the Soviets supported the anti-authoritarians – in that case, the anti-authoritarians' scepticism towards such ties would have accorded with their conviction that both superpowers instrumentalized the South, as well as with their preference for more radical socialist projects.

Dutschke's interest in the Southern hemisphere involved radically changing the situation both at home and abroad. He considered the third-world movements important for West Berlin activists for three reasons. First, theories from authors such as Frantz Fanon and Guevara analysed contemporary international politics in ways that Marx's texts, written earlier, could not.[32] Second, transnational solidarity opened the possibility of cooperation between GDR and FRG youth, thereby bringing Germans closer together on terms that Dutschke supported. German unification under a socialist organizational system was an aim shared by the SDS and the SED.[33] Third, the student leader saw the West Berlin demonstrations against political constellations in countries such as Iran and Congo as the first politically and socially conscious grassroots initiatives in the city. He concluded that these demonstrations were as significant for domestic politics as they were for colonial critique.[34]

The anti-authoritarians' reception of third-world liberation theory and praxis furthered a shift in their alliances from Western European to Southern role models. Much work has been done on the relationships between the more established European left and the student movement. Intellectuals such as Weiss and Enzensberger influenced student reception of the global South. The Frankfurt School and the circle of thinkers around it, as well as intellectuals in the United States and France such as Herbert Marcuse and Jean-Paul Sartre, were well received. Yet, the younger generation had not lived through the Second World War, was more impatient for social change, and believed that the necessary conditions for it were proximate. The students became frustrated by models that seemed to neglect practice for theory.[35] More established left-leaning thinkers famously spoke against the use of political violence to promote the conditions necessary for a radical social shift. For instance, Marcuse came under attack by student audience members when he was seen as an apologist for categorical non-violence.[36]

Professorial ally Jürgen Habermas's famous use of the term 'left fascism' to criticize student enthusiasm for overt political violence is telling here. The phrase highlights that the older generation judged these young Germans according to a bourgeois nationalist paradigm. The well-established state was construed in the Weberian sense as the sole legitimate wielder of force and as the guarantor of national unity and stability under already-existing conditions. On these terms, oppositional violence would amount to sedition. Moreover, the spectre haunting Habermas's charge was German fascism, and it was a haunting spectre indeed.[37] While the parties involved disagreed about the potential suitability of overt violence, they all agreed that a voluntaristic attack against a democratic German state was unacceptable because it revisited National Socialist patterns.

Recognition of this context further clarifies that alignment with Southern national revolution opened a perspective from which activists could entertain ideas about the legitimacy of political violence without inevitably conjuring the fascist past. According to third-world liberation models, 'subaltern nationalism' and its struggles can be justified means of constituting independent new nations. Figures such as Fanon and Guevara argued for violence as popular force – in their models, the existing state was not the only legitimate administrator.[38] The anti-authoritarians' sustained concern, even fascination, with violence in the opposition was more than a vague, romantic notion. Grounded in theories of subaltern nationalisms current across the globe, their interest expressed and furthered their attempts to reconstitute Berlin and, finally, German identity through these third-world liberation models of nation building, amid and despite the historical baggage of National Socialism.

Guevara's 'focus theory' and his international directives were particularly inspirational for the West Berlin anti-authoritarians. Focus
theory hypothesizes that an advance guard acts like the focal point of a
magnifying glass, igniting the general populace to revolutionary action.
Ingo Juchler has shown some of the ways in which Dutschke's practices
and theories respond to Guevara's demands for an internationalization of focus theory.[39] Kraushaar has recently come to similar conclusions.[40] By at least 1967, Dutschke described student group actions in
Guevarian terms. Consider his analysis of a clandestine anti–Vietnam
War protest involving postering in West Berlin: 'How and under what
conditions can the subjective factor write itself into the historical process as an objective factor? Guevara's answer for Latin America was that
the revolutionaries are not always to wait for the objective conditions
for the revolution, but rather that by means of the Focus, they can create
the revolution through subjective activity. This question also stood in
the final analysis behind the poster campaign, still stands today behind
every campaign.'[41]

Dutschke's portrayal of an SDS street demonstration also closely
echoes Guevara's ideas about praxis creating consciousness.[42] Sometimes read even by sympathizers as fetishizing violence,[43] Guevarism
nevertheless spoke forcefully to this group of youth who felt impotent
against the status quo.

As the anti-authoritarians sought to translate focus theory into West
Berlin, they looked to thinkers like Guevara. His texts of the early
1960s suggested that violent protest was inappropriate in the European context. In *Guerillakrieg: Eine Methode*, these Germans read: 'In
places where a government has attained power through more or less
democratic means, with or without voting fraud, and where at least
the appearance of constitutional law is upheld, no guerrilla movement develops, because the possibilities of legal struggle are still not
eliminated.'[44]

Such statements implied to them that activists in the Federal Republic should work with established political structures such as the Social
Democratic Party and labour unions to create political change.

The local and the global situations seemed to the anti-authoritarians to have changed radically by 1967. In the FRG, the so-called grand
coalition between the mainstream conservative and mainstream progressive parties left little room for dissent through government chan-
nels. Clashes between police and activists were also increasing without
much apparent impact on governmental policy. During this time, Cuba

was leading in organizing government and party officials and rebels from Latin America, Africa, and Asia. Western thinkers were coming to believe that in Latin America 'Cuba [had] emerged as a third, independent communist centre, more actively committed to armed revolutionary struggle in the Third World than either the Soviets or the Chinese.'[45] The January 1966 Tricontinental Conference in Havana ended with its participants calling for a radical, non-aligned platform to counter the superpowers' doctrine of peaceful coexistence and for an alliance between Southern socialists and the proletariat in the Northern metropoles.[46]

Guevara's focus theory formed the official basis of the resultant Havana-based Organization of Solidarity with the People of Asia, Africa, and Latin America (OSPAAL). Although many of the established communist parties of the participating nations disagreed with this strategy, arguing that initiatives for change should be party-led, Cuba pressed its agenda. Guevara's well-known letter to the executive body of OSPAAL, with its call to create 'two, three, many Vietnams,' was published in April 1967 in Cuba and its theoretical counterpart, Régis Debray's *Revolución en la Revolución?* (*Revolution in the Revolution? Armed Struggle and Political Struggle in Latin America*) was published that same year in Cuba as well. Cuba reaffirmed focus theory by convening the first Organization of Latin American Solidarity (OLAS) conference, held in early August 1967 in Havana, controlling the guest list, and pushing its official internationalist agenda of non-alignment. Criticizing the Soviet Union and bloc politics, Fidel Castro called for grassroots internationalist revolution and transnational solidarity.[47]

The anti-authoritarians were deeply inspired by such events and sought guidance from their Southern role models. The results of the OLAS conference were considered directly relevant to the European struggle. In the small West Berlin paper in which many anti-authoritarians published, *Oberbaum Blatt*, author G. reports on OLAS: 'A strategy of the urban guerrilla for some countries was not treated by the conference, but it was also not fully ruled out. The development of such a strategy seems to be the task of the revolutionaries of the countries whose populations mostly live in the cities.'[48]

This account reads like a response to a question formulated prior to the meeting, the question of violent political action in the urban North. It reports that OLAS participants tacitly supported such struggle – its phrasing implies conference debate on the topic. The conclusion that the article draws may or may not have actually been discussed; it responds primarily to questions in West Berlin when it suggests that the Southern delegates had vested the decision-making authority in interested Northern radicals. The report adds that the participants had unanimously chosen focus theory as their method and that 'the best contribution to the continental revolution, the best expression of solidarity is the liberation of one's own nation. "Imperialism must be beaten at every and any place" (Che).'[49] The OLAS conference focused on Latin America, and G.'s article also primarily treats this region. Yet, the report also emphasizes what the anti-authoritarians read as Guevara's new message of ubiquitous struggle shaped by indigenous revolutionaries, including those living in Northern metropoles.

Guevara's letter to OSPAAL also seemed to the anti-authoritarians to have opened a new space for their involvement. Dutschke considered the letter so groundbreaking that within days he and fellow West Berlin student leader Chilean Gaston Salvatore had finished translating it as 'Schaffen Wir Zwei, Drei, Viele Vietnam!' (Let us create two, three, many Vietnams!)[50] In 1967, they published an excerpt in the *Oberbaum Blatt* and shortly afterwards printed the entire letter. The segment in the *Oberbaum Blatt* emphasizes Guevara's call for physical solidarity with Vietnam against the United States.[51] In the complete text, Guevara's words seem to predict some type of revolution in the European metropoles: 'The situation of the world shows a great multiplicity of tasks. Even the nations of old Europe are still waiting for the task of liberation. Although they are developed enough to be able to feel all of the contradictions of capitalism, they are too weak still to follow imperial goals or to pursue this course. In the next years the contradictions there will take on an explosive character. Their problems, however, and because of this in the final analysis also their solution, are different from those of our dependent and economically backward nations.'[52]

In 1967, particularly after the killing of the first-time student protestor Benno Ohnesorg, the situation in West Berlin seemed explosive to the anti-authoritarians. Guevara's 1962 missive had expressly forbidden overt political violence within real-existing democracies. Some now saw the end of the 'appearance of constitutional law.' The government that in the eyes of many had led primarily through tacit, ill-informed, public consent seemed to now be exposing its similarity to colonial powers abroad by ruling with cudgels and pistols at the heads of protesters. Guevara's 1967 communiqué focused on the role of advance guards as liberators seemed perfectly translatable into the European context and the task of activists in the North.

Taking Guevara's predictions literally, some argued that West Berlin, as the first revolutionized metropolis, would function as another Vietnam in so far as it would be the next focal site of the spreading anti-imperial revolution. In this way, the West Berlin struggle would serve both national and international liberation. In Dutschke's words it would be a 'mounting political struggle against "our" existing order, which distinguishes itself precisely through the open and undercover complicity with the USA, to concretely support the Vietnamese liberation struggle through our own emancipation process.'[53] The intended revolution itself was paralleled not with the prolonged and bloody battle in Vietnam, but with the assumedly populist and quickly successful revolution in Cuba. The specificity of this parallel was critical. Relating to an idealized Cuban revolution rather than to the struggles in Vietnam meant that the anti-authoritarians could appropriate theories of third-world liberation without appropriating its bloodshed in practice.

Translating Cuba to West Berlin

Two texts that scholars have deemed uncharacteristic of Dutschke's oeuvre show the centrality of subaltern nationalism by styling West Berlin as a revolutionary island modelled on third-world theory (Guevara's and Castro's) and praxis (Cuba). One is an essay based on the Pichelsdorf meeting, which sources as diverse as Dutschke's wife Gretchen Dutschke and colleague Rabehl describe as a gathering meant to work on plans for taking over West Berlin.[54] A core group of anti-authoritarians around Dutschke met on 24 and 25 June 1967, shortly after the shooting of Ohnesorg and directly after the publication of Dutschke and Salvatore's translation of Guevara's Vietnam letter. The essay, *Zum Verhältnis von Organisation und Emanzipationsbewegung – Zum Besuch Herbert Marcuses* (*On the Relationship of Organization and the Emancipation Movement – On the Visit of Herbert Marcuse*), published by Dutschke under a pseudonym on 12 July 1967 in the *Oberbaum Blatt*, summarizes the results of this meeting and was influential among the anti-authoritarians.[55] The October 1967 interview with Enzensberger, *Ein Gespräch über die Zukunft* (*A Conversation about the Future*), published in *Kursbuch* in 1968 focuses on similar issues and reached a larger audience.[56]

Few scholars have attended to these texts, perhaps because they seem to implicate Dutschke in a Soviet-led or a rightist agenda. In his study of Dutschke's relationship to the question of unification, Kraushaar emphasizes the internationalist ends of Dutschke's national interests. Consider his analysis of the strident call of the student leader to 'Crush NATO' that Kraushaar reads as expressing Dutschke's goal of a neutral course for Germany between the United States and Soviet blocs: 'To crush NATO or – in a milder variation – to want to leave it, means, in terms of the politics of the Alliance, to strike a neutral course, and this means, in turn, to win back the lost national sovereignty. It fits this perspective that Dutschke spoke of the "American army of occupation" in his speech at the Vietnam conference. Probably he thinks complementarily of a Soviet army of occupation and the departure of the GDR from the Warsaw pact. However, to say this openly in 1968 in West Berlin would have been not only more unrealistic than the explicated demand would have been but also unwise from tactical perspectives.'[57]

Kraushaar's analysis engages Dutschke's interest in German nationalism in relation to the power struggles of the Cold War in the North. Rather than exploring the precise meaning of the nation and nationalism for the young German, Kraushaar focuses on demonstrating that his later life was spent working for national liberation through unification as a necessary step towards international socialism. Kraushaar mentions that Dutschke considered the U.S. military an occupying force, that he saw structural similarities between the anti-authoritarians' efforts against NATO and third-world liberation struggles against colonialism, and that he was fascinated by third-world issues. Kraushaar, however, does not link these concerns.

Yet, such ideas were deeply interconnected and were legitimated by notions of subaltern nationalism. Southern paradigms informed what Dutschke saw as national liberation for Germany, sparked by the liberation of West Berlin. Neither a covert attempt to open the way for Soviet occupation of West Berlin, nor a crypto-fascist agenda, Dutschke's national vision sought its inspiration across what was for him the first world–third world divide.

Precisely the Dutschke texts that have proven so discomfiting for scholars of leftists in the FRG illuminate Dutschke's conception of German national liberation through the metropolitan focus of West Berlin. In these two texts in particular, the city is positioned in the South – the West Berlin revolution is to liberate it from the '"false" East-West perspective.'[58] Castro and Guevara called for a similar goal of tricontinental independence from the Western and the Eastern blocs.[59] West Berlin is described as distinct from the FRG; indeed, it is understood as in a neocolonial relationship with West Germany, and by extension, the

United States. Dutschke writes, 'As a consequence of its dependence on the FRG, West Berlin is especially "endangered"; indeed 75 per cent of the commodities produced go to West Germany.'[60] For Dutschke, the more oppressive the colonial situation was, the higher the probability of a successful subaltern independence movement in West Berlin.

Within this paradigm, Cuba and West Berlin were similarly positioned. Each 'island' was sheltered by the policy of peaceful coexistence. Many understood Cold War tensions to have protected Cuba's move for sovereignty.[61] Dutschke explicitly argued that such tensions would also stop the larger powers from taking over a small independent West Berlin.[62] Each polity sought to lead an international coalition of non-aligned states – Cuba in Latin America, and West Berlin in Europe. For the anti-authoritarians, Cuba set the example of non-aligned, grassroots socialism, and West Berlin was to be model in the first world. The focus would transform the Northern metropole into an independent urban island, which would provoke the GDR into support not only of Latin American revolution, but of domestic reform,[63] and might enable German unification.[64] Following the example of Cuba in Latin America, West Berlin was to be a revolutionary model in Europe. This parallel was enabled by the claiming of subaltern nationalism in the North.

The twenty-second delegate conference of the SDS in Frankfurt in early September 1967 was an important testing ground for this claim. In their suggestions for structuring the organization (*Organisationsreferat*) Dutschke and Hans-Jürgen Krahl translated Guevara's organizational model for use by the group. '"The propaganda of shots" (Che) in the "third world" must be completed through a "propaganda of deeds" in the metropoles, which makes the urbanization of rural guerrilla activity historically possible.' With the universities as 'safety zones,' student focus groups were to instigate change and the rest of the populace would be enlightened into socialist consciousness.[65] The anti-authoritarians aligned the roles of student agitator and guerrilla fighter. In his *Zum Verhältnis von Organisation und Emanzipationsbewegung*, Dutschke uses populist rhetoric when addressing his audience: 'I don't know how to address you, all forms of address have been occupied by our masters in East and West, unless you accept the term and the title of revolutionaries.'[66] Dutschke's request draws in his audience and binds them linguistically with the weapon-carrying attendees of the tricontinental and the planned OLAS conference.

Indeed, some of those in West Berlin did not need Dutschke to identify themselves with the Latin American fighters. A series of letters to

Dutschke from the Berlin communist Konrad Born seemingly playfully cast street demonstrations as 'street battles,' used some of the terminology of *Guerillakrieg: Eine Methode*, and called Dutschke a German Guevara. According to notes from their meetings, members of the Projektgruppe 3. Welt/Metropol, of which Dutschke was a part, considered themselves qualified to judge Southern guerrilla activities in order to assess the appropriateness of focus theory and the effectiveness of Guevara's Bolivian project.[67]

The high-profile 1968 Vietnam Congress in West Berlin was a significant articulation of subaltern nationalism. The conference aimed to define solidarity with Vietnam. Could and should the anti-authoritarians' theoretical model be used to foment a West Berlin revolution and what would this revolution look like in practice? The podium backdrop reveals that Southern directives guided these questions. The second line from the enormous banner, 'Für den Sieg der Vietnamesischen Revolution – Die Pflicht jedes Revolutionäres ist es die Revolution zu machen' (For the victory of the Vietnamese revolution – The duty of every revolutionary is to make the revolution), was translated directly from the backdrop of the 31 July to 10 August 1967 OLAS conference in Havana, and both included images of Guevara.[68]

The uses of this phrase and image reveal both the internationalization and the idealization of the Cuban agenda. The words are Castro's, and Guevara explicitly attributes them to him.[69] Yet, this statement is overwhelmingly ascribed to Guevara in Latin America, within activist movements, and in critical literature. This attribution suggests that the mobile, idealistic, and romanticized fighter Che more readily embodied an international revolution than the governmental leader Castro. At the OLAS conference, the Cubans had already internationalized the appeal beyond Cuba and the non-aligned nations by omitting the specificity of the Latin American context. The Vietnam Congress organizers welcomed the internationalization of the directive. Their embrace of Che as icon suggests their idealization of the Guevarian 'New Man.'[70] Their acceptance of a figure that represents self-subordination to a group may seem surprising. The Frankfurt School–trained anti-authoritarians were highly sceptical of such discourses in German contexts; the very name anti-authoritarian articulates the value that they placed on individuality. This reception of Guevara speaks to the intensity of their desires for alternative models of identification.

There is also some evidence that during the large conference, smaller meetings between radical European leaders took place. Until recently, the most direct evidence of this conference-within-a-conference stemmed from Rabehl.[71] These leaders predicted that if the student revolution gained real momentum, NATO under the command of the United States would attempt a putsch. Accordingly, they sought to prepare counter-measures to halt what they saw as imperialist actions and to unseat U.S. dominance in Europe. This understanding placed the Vietnam Conference in West Berlin into direct articulation with the OLAS conference, one of whose stated aims was to free Latin America of the U.S. imperialist yoke. It would be a different project to analyse the contested discourses involved in the retelling of these alleged events. Rabehl's assertion that some Vietnam Conference organizers narrated European strife in terms of North-South oppression and resistance supports my contention that the anti-authoritarians imagined their German nationalism in terms of subalternity.[72] Chaussy's assessment that the anti-authoritarians vacillated over the use of overt violence remains salient.

Conclusion

For the anti-authoritarians, the Cuba of the 1960s was an inspirational model for change in the North. The Berlin and October crises mutually informed; West Berlin was in a position as strategically important as Cuba's, and long-time residents and 'Berliners by choice' felt the political weightiness of their position in the newly walled-in city. The anti-authoritarians imagined leveraging Berlin in the North as the revolutionary government had leveraged Cuba in the South. Their solidarian identification enabled these Germans to feel that they were struggling for progressive global change in a manner that worked against what they saw as the neocolonial legacy of the National Socialist past. Moreover, Cuban nationalism offered them an alternative to German nationalism.

This underrecognized case of the importance of the global South for the North suggests that the relationship is traditionally underestimated. The significance of this North-South alliance can be understood in terms of its material expansiveness; its ideational weight in terms of cultural capital and imagined community is of even more significance. In the mid- to late 1960s, Cuba functioned for the anti-authoritarians and others on the left as an inspirational role model with an alternative trajectory seemingly at odds with both superpowers.

The next chapter, focusing on the 1970s, explores how this role shifted in relation to changes in Cuba and the Germanies and by the increased experiential knowledge that Germans gained through increased exposure to the island. Many left-leaning Germans reproved decisions of the Cuban government that took it further under the wing of the Soviet Union; notably its ambivalent support for the violent suppression of the Prague Spring, its ten-million-ton sugar harvest program and the aftermath, and its acceptance of rigid cultural guidelines that ushered in the 'grey five years' (*quinquenio gris*) of repression beginning in 1971 and de facto extending well beyond 1976. Meanwhile, the Germanies were experiencing struggles of their own that gnawed away at hopes for national and global change. The resultant German Cubas work through and gesture beyond these concerns.

Chapter Four

Siting Trials: Cuba as Cipher for German Governance around the 1970s

As the FRG and the GDR factionalized internally from the late 1960s, intellectuals explored these tensions through Cuban themes. Events in Cuba that involved individual, collective, and national sovereignty, and governmental form and authority, were of particular interest to Germans confronted with these questions at home. Political violence as expressed in decolonizing efforts in the South and social unrest in the North was an important concern. Yet, Northerners increasingly problematized liberation theories that seemed to them to bear little resemblance to on-the-ground practices. In the FRG, third-world solidarity groups were prime exceptions to a general turn towards putatively domestic issues. These grassroots organizations tended to focus on the new independence movements, such as in Chile and Nicaragua, struggles whose contours were inspiringly embryonic. More militant associations in particular identified with prolonged 'hot' struggles, such as in Vietnam. Post-1959 Cuba held a distinct place in this constellation, for relative to these fledgling movements, it was a firmly established nation. Increased travel to and information about the island exposed its arduous development. Stable official relationships with the GDR and the Soviet bloc meant both that the island nation was more accessible to GDR citizens and that it was less subversive from the perspective of German left-leaning circles. Yet, its positioning as a fresh socialist-style nation lent itself to styling as a testing ground for salient concerns. Many 'Cuban' texts of the period are shaped by concrete experiences with German politicized violence and the specific exigencies of the geopolitics of peaceful coexistence. By and large, the earlier texts interrogate the nexus of national political structures and individual rights, territorial boundaries, and the effects of transboundary influences by individuals, interest groups, and extra-national entities. Although still socially critical in the broadest sense, later texts demonstrate increased disillusionment, increasingly stylized representations, and few alternatives to the situations narrated.

This chapter focuses on two exemplary texts by well-known public intellectuals and writers, Hans Magnus Enzensberger's *Das Verhör von Habana* (*The Havana Inquiry*, 1970) and Volker Braun's *Guevara oder der Sonnenstaat* (*Guevara or Eldorado*, written in the mid-1970s), to demonstrate how they wrestle with divisive questions of political violence that were suppressed in the Germanies. Framing these works in relation to other contemporary 'Cuban' works, the analysis highlights how each theatre piece interrogates voluntaristic radicalism while attending to the emancipatory and destructive potentials of overt and structural violence in the FRG and the GDR, respectively.

Enzensberger's documentary-style play based on the 1962 protocols of the public trials of the Bay of Pigs invaders addressed mainstream society and its discontented. First, the narrative questions the authority of the state. If organizations are systems of structural violence, is it legitimate to engage them with overt political violence, as third-world revolutionaries had done? In an FRG in which such violence was being shut down, this text opened space for a public debate on its legitimacy. Second, the theatre piece engages with the articulations of violence and jurisprudence through the example of the Cuban court system. According to *Das Verhör*'s logic, direct struggle may be warranted to achieve just societies outside Cuba because, in the Cuban case, it engendered functional and equitable legal structures. A double refraction enables these considerations. Through Cuba the FRG can be seen more clearly; through the judicial system overt violence can be considered more clearly. Third, the work engages questions of national sovereignty and borders. The example of the Bay of Pigs invaders overtly criticizes U.S. influence in Cuban, and by extension FRG, politics. Finally, the text speaks for the contemporary borders of the Germanies, addressing the topical issue of claims that German expellee organizations were making on land east of the post-war German borders. *Das Verhör*'s representation of the Bay of Pigs invaders suggests that contestation of the eastern border was about economic gain rather than ethical, patriotic, or affective considerations.

While Enzensberger's theatre piece explores overt violence by analysing social structures, Braun's exposes structural violence through critiques of overt violence. This avant-garde GDR work treats tensions between citizen, state, and change through a recounting of Guevara's departure from Cuba and the Bolivian struggle. In a nation in which criticism of the government was tightly controlled, Braun's text opened a space for a public debate on the legitimacy of existing political structures. For underlying its overt theme of Che's direct engagement, Braun's text questions the conservative elitism in the party and state structures, prescriptive engagement with the global South, and the USSR's sway over the GDR. As does *Das Verhör*, *Guevara oder der Sonnenstaat* speaks for more democracy and more socialism in its Germany, and implies that foreign influence impedes them. Interrogating individual, collective, and national sovereignty, it judges organizational structures according to individual actualization. The singular revolutionary must have a place in real-existing nations, and state socialism must not preclude global revolution. Otherwise, what course of action is an activist to pursue? Read allegorically, the query becomes whether the critical intellectual should abandon the GDR, as so many were. Without suggesting that staying a reformist course is appropriate, *Guevara*'s proto-neocolonial critique suggests that leaving one's own real-existing socialist nation is not the ideal means of creating global change.

Whereas, both *Das Verhör* and *Guevara* critically embrace Cuba's problematic yet vibrant potential, in texts of the later 1970s, the Southern experiment becomes dreams deferred. In GDR works, Cuba increasingly represents the exotic rather than the revolutionary. Political transformation gives way to pragmatic alternatives; change is reimagined through consumerism. For instance, Fritz Rudolf Fries's travel narrative, 'Kubanische Kalenderblätter' (Cuban Calendar Pages, 1976), and Frank Beyer's film, *Bockshorn* (*Ram's Horn*, 1983), employ Cuba to represent vicarious pleasure-driven consumption.[1] In the FRG, Enzensberger's text *Der Untergang der Titanic* (*The Sinking of the Titanic*, 1978) is emblematic of a generalized shift from support for change through direct politics to support for change through artistic expression. That revolution has largely given way to reform is evidenced aesthetically as well. Moving away from unifying, overt messages such as those of *Das Verhör*, this epic poem offers a global critique to a newly sceptical audience through multiple associations that speak obliquely to individual readers. In all of these texts, refraction through Cuba furthers insights into domestic situations.

Radicalization I: Agit-Prop for Global Change – *Das Verhör von Habana*

In the late 1960s and the early 1970s, contests between the FRG govern-

Regie: **FRANK BEYER**

Bockshorn (1984)

4.1 Mick and Sauly enjoying tropical decadence in *Bockshorn*. Photo (30855) by Klaus Goldmann. Used with the kind permission of Klaus Goldmann and the BA-FA.

ment and protesters were turning increasingly violent. This period was rife with well-publicized, divisive events. In 1967 the student Benno Ohnesorg was killed by a West Berlin policeman (who incidentally may have been a GDR agent) during a street demonstration against the visit of the Iranian Shah. In 1968, Rudi Dutschke was shot by a West German citizen after a mainstream media campaign against the agitators, which was tacitly supported by the city government. Mass protests and street fighting followed such incidents. More radical activists garnered significant public support as well. Andreas Baader and Gudrun Ensslin were tried for arson of a department store; the arson meant to draw attention to the firebombing of Vietnam. Jailed in 1968, they were freed in 1969 and went underground when it appeared that they would be sentenced. In 1970, Baader was captured and convicted again, only to escape with the help of Ensslin and others in what became known as the birth of the RAF (*Rote Armee Fraktion*, Red Army Faction, Baader-Mein-hof Group). An enormous state force entered into a violent cat-and-mouse game with this and allied groups. When many RAF members were captured in 1972, their long, involved trials, their imprisonment in a specially constructed high-security institution, various attempts to force their release, and their deaths – shrouded in what was for many an unconvincing narrative of suicide – all continued to further already widespread deliberations about the proper roles of states and citizens.

Hans Magnus Enzensberger was at the forefront of these debates so central to public concern. Many have noted his long-standing tendency to shift his expressed viewpoints slightly ahead of and slightly more radically than the critical mass of the intellectual milieu.[2] Recently, for instance, he has taken the increasingly common move to the right of his generation a step further in his essays against the Middle East and in favour of military activities there. Whether such moves that keep him on the crest of new trends are signs of a genius ability to assess the present, expedient ways to maintain his culture capital, or should be understood differently, they are an Enzensberger trademark. Similarly, yet on the other side of the political spectrum, in the earlier, post–Second World War decades, his writings and translations of thinkers of the global South were particularly influential among left-leaning FRG citizens. Enzensberger himself was radicalized by the West Berlin student movement and, despite his expansive knowledge base, there is little evidence that the philo-U.S. intellectual was influenced by GDR reception of Latin America, such as Anna Seghers's oeuvre, including *Das Licht auf dem Galgen* (1961).[3] The 1968 *Kursbuch* issues on the student movements across the globe offer in-depth commentaries and include Enzensberger's own interview with West Berlin student leaders, in which, as I have shown, his interlocutors hypothesize reshaping the city on the model of revolutionary Cuba. He was also variously involved in direct political action. For instance, Enzensberger intervened on behalf of activists with an open letter to the Ministry of Justice, was involved from early on in the debate around the emergency laws, and supported legal services for those who were arrested based on their political stripe. His acceptance speech for a Nuremberg cultural award in 1967 occasioned a stir when he declared that his prize money would go for such legal aid.[4]

Enzensberger's texts on Cuba were published as these events were gaining momentum and engage with these events through particular aspects of the Southern nation. Reinhold Grimm focuses on *Freis-prüche. Revolutionäre vor Gericht* (Acquittals: Revolutionaries on Trial,

1970) as evidence of Enzensberger's approval of Cuba's Marxist revolution.[5] This anthology of court statements features Castro's well-known defence of the 26 July Movement's attack against the Batista government. For Sara Lennox, Enzensberger's gloss of 'History will absolve me' (*La historia me absolverá*) shows that the German thinker interpreted Castro's socialism as a grassroots rather than a top-down movement.[6] In this way, Enzensberger's understanding articulated the understanding of many in the German left who appreciated what they saw as Cuba's validation of individual praxis and concretization of a dialectic between theory and praxis. But more than this, *historia* argues for the right of citizens to rebel against what they deem to be illegitimate governments. And Frank Dietschreit and Barbara Heinze-Dietschreit have compellingly argued that *Freisprüche* was meant to advise the FRG opposition, part of which was radicalizing towards armed violence on a national and international scale.[7] This collection by activists accused of going beyond the law garnered little critical attention in the Federal Republic, however. Many public intellectuals hesitated to extol texts that granted a platform to oppositional politics and thereby challenged government and media. In another non-fiction, thematically related example, Enzensberger's October 1969 *Kursbuch* essay on the Cuban Communist Party (CCP) also speaks to the Cuban and German situations. It describes in careful detail how the CCP followed Castro rather than a defined political platform. The text argues that the CCP benefits Cuba by improving economic well-being and political participation for the working classes, yet it criticizes its hierarchical structure and rule.[8] This more sober assessment of the Cuban situation resonates with the FRG left's criticism of both Germanies as authoritarian.

Several of Enzensberger's 'Cuban' texts are librettos for musical co-creations developed with the well-known German composer Hans Werner Henze. These and Henze's own Cuba-related oeuvre would be more insightfully analysed in co-authorship with a musicologist; I will highlight the musical-theatre piece *El Cimarrón*, which is of most direct relevance for my argument. Notable is that in 1972–3, Enzensberger and Henze again collaborated on a made-for-TV opera based on Miguel Barnet's *Canción de Rachel* (*Rachel's Song*, 1970) entitled *La Cubana oder ein Leben für die Kunst* (The Cuban Woman or a Life for Art, 1972–3). Cuba variously inspired Henze. For instance, he collaborated with Gaston Salvatore, who had translated Guevara's letter with Dutschke. The composer also dedicated his oratorio 'Das Floß der Medusa'

(The Raft of Medusa, 1968) to Guevara, which led to its premiere being thwarted when the SDS hung a red flag and Che poster in the hall as a reminder, prompting the RIAS choir to boycott.[9] In a move meant to draw public attention, Henze also accepted a lectureship in Havana in 1969–70 and premiered his Sixth Symphony there.[10]

Performed in Berlin at nearly the same time as *Das Verhör*, *El Cimarrón* forms an as-yet overlooked generic and thematic complement to *Das Verhör*'s sober, documentary-style fictionalization of revolutionary Cuba and the elliptic, allusive epic poem *Der Untergang der Titanic* in which the contemporary island signifies variously between concrete specificity and sweeping metonymy. *El Cimarrón*'s script historicizes the struggles of 1960s Cuba using a local source, Cuban writer, sociologist, and convinced revolutionary Miguel Barnet's *Biografía de un cimarrón* (*The Autobiography of a Runaway Slave*, 1966), which Enzensberger had translated and published in *Kursbuch* in 1969. Barnet's ethnography relates the long life of Esteban Montejo, a Cuban of part African descent who had struggled as a slave, a fugitive in the wilderness, and in the war for independence from Spain. *El Cimarrón* articulates a revolutionary subject for whom violence is a necessary but distasteful activity. The narrator Enzensberger's commentary on *El Cimarrón* specifies the relevance of Montejo for an FRG audience surrounded by political struggle that was becoming increasingly violent: 'The Cimarrón is not the "New Man": he carries the birthmarks of the old society, his thinking shows the deformations, limitations, mythologies of that society ... He understands the necessity of a war of the people, but he sees it soberly, free of romantic hysteria. In his eyes I don't find any of the ominous gleam of one who sacrifices himself to the cause in order to forget his own life. The Cimarrón protects his own skin and fights for his brother in one breath ... Is he still living? I see you shrugging your shoulders and I know that you don't believe me. But I say: Yes, he lives.'[11]

This assessment of Montejo negotiates the FRG reception of Che Guevara and the consequences thereof. On one hand, it sketches a counterpoint to a romanticized vision of Guevarian-style heroism. Montejo is not the hero imprinted into martyrdom through the words 'Che lebt' (Che lives) on the cover of Dutschke and Salvatore's translation of his Vietnam speech; nor can this Montejo be dismissed as a voluntarist zealot who chose death as antidote to personal existential crisis.[12] The Cuban native Montejo recovered by Barnet and Enzensberger as a proto-revolutionary subject is written poetically into history in ways that offer an alternative to the individualistic adventurism and excesses of the FRG.

While *El Cimarrón* warns against voluntarist excesses, *Das Verhör von Habana* interrogates state legitimacy by thematizing the juridical system, somewhat in the tradition of *Freisprüche*. However, unlike *Freisprüche*, *Das Verhör* depicts the court proceedings and thereby invites closer consideration of the larger structures of power. Indeed, perhaps surprisingly given the public debates between Enzensberger and Peter Weiss, *Das Verhör* resembles Weiss's well-known text *Die Ermittlung* (*The Investigation*).

Published in 1965 in the FRG and shortly afterwards in the GDR, Weiss's documentary play based on the protocols of the Frankfurt war crimes trials speaks about the Federal Republic through consideration of National Socialism. Selective, verbatim reproduction of courtroom testimony demonstrates the continuity of National Socialist social structures post the Second World War. It casts fascism as the apotheosis of capitalism by depicting a camp life ruled by pure market logic. As Arlene Teraoka has shown, Weiss's project aims to resist fascism in its post–Second World War form: North-South world imperialism. Enzensberger's afterword to *Das Verhör* makes a similar link: a corporate lawyer who had been involved in U.S.-Soviet spy exchanges and in the Nuremberg Trials also brokered the famous exchange whereby the Bay of Pigs invaders were traded for baby food and U.S. medicines.[13]

First performed in 1970 in the FRG and in 1972 in the GDR, Enzensberger's text builds upon Weiss's in its representation of the judicial system. In each, the testimony of the accused exposes the injustice of their actions. Weiss's documentary highlights similarities between the logics of the camps and the courtroom, showing that the existing FRG judiciary is marred by its continuity with the past system. Rather than focusing on the flaws in the FRG system, *Das Verhör* employs the Cuban court as a model for emulation; the contemporary court system of the Cubans embodies a fragile possibility of grassroots, radical justice.

Das Verhör consists of selections from protocols of the public hearings of the U.S.-financed invaders, which took place shortly after their capture in 1961. The choice of this particular topic at the end of the 1960s reinforced public recollection of early, popular actions of the new government. Castro's arguably generous and certainly media savvy treatment of the Bay of Pigs invaders had encouraged an international groundswell of support for the tiny nation.[14] Such events had convinced many Northern sympathizers that the new Cuban government had the support of the Cuban people. *Das Verhör* also de-emphasizes the violent aspects of the Cuban revolution precisely by depicting a struggle of words in a courtroom and a narrative of universal justice rather than, for instance, the Cuban's armed defence during one of the many attempts made to invade their country.

Its allegory is not hidden. Paratexts of the play in its book form, as well as its playbill, make clear that *Das Verhör* speaks about the Federal Republic.[15] Here, the specific represents a universal that illuminates another specificity. As if anticipating the postcolonial counter, the notion advanced is that it is precisely the specificity of Cuba that makes it translatable. Only in Cuba is a class-conscious, popular will embodied in state institutions. Only in a Cuban court in which the accused are the ruling class does this class articulate the system of oppression endemic to capitalist nations. According to the essayist Enzensberger, 'the prisoners are interchangeable.' These accused, whose true character has been revealed for the first time in history, are part of an international class, any of whom should take the stand. This assessment resonates with the description of the FRG in which the leaders are, in the Marxist phrasing used by Dutschke a few years earlier, 'character masks' and 'interchangeable.'[16] In contrast to Cuba, however, in the FRG, as in most of the world, few citizens share this understanding because their society has not achieved radicalization. Thus, the Cuban situation models the exposure of structural violence in a manner not possible elsewhere.

Particularly interesting is *Das Verhör*'s message that censorship does not serve the cause of justice, but rather that free expression exposes truth. It is precisely in the course of their own defence that the prisoners recognize the structures they support as discriminatory and their own aims as self-serving. Such a message resonated in the FRG, whose government was increasingly controlling public speech and in which much mainstream media was corporate. It also spoke to the Cuban situation by implying that this freedom must be cemented in a democratic system in which participants have an equal voice. This proviso, in an otherwise optimistic depiction of the revolution, takes place over the figure of Castro when, in the last scene, the charismatic speaker powerfully compels the invaders to his perspective. Klaus Berghahn recognizes parallels between the assessment of Castro's authority in Enzensberger's essay on the CCP and its depiction in *Das Verhör*. For Berghahn, the concentration of power in the heroic leader functions as a warning against socio-political hierarchy, his progressive messages notwithstanding.[17] Although governmental power and ethics are unified in the fictional Cuba, *Das Verhör* underscores that this fusion must be ensured through continued democratic practice.

Although the text exhorts that many in the FRG could stand accused, one group would have suggested itself to audiences of the time: German expellees from Czechoslovakia and Poland, lands that lay east of the Oder-Neisse line. Many of these people ended up in the GDR, whose policy was to largely ignore their specific, often arch-conservative histories and assimilate them as completely and as quickly as possible.[18] In the FRG, on the other hand, some organized into a formidable political force that the government felt necessary to appease, yet whose strident and often unrepentant voice was particularly detrimental to foreign policy.[19] These groups called for the reunification of Germany and the right of return even to areas outside of the 1937 German borders, as well as recognition of their post–Second World War expulsion from Eastern and Central Europe as unjust.[20] This debate was prominent in the late 1960s and early 1970s. Particularly between 1965 and 1968, the time of the Grand Coalition between the Christian Democrats (CDU) and the Social Democrats (SPD), many in the expellee associations believed even the latter to have become increasingly open to their perspectives. When (at the 1968 Nuremberg party meeting) SPD Chancellor Willy Brandt stated unambiguously that the Oder-Neisse line was to be respected, the associations felt surprised and betrayed; hot debate and political jockeying continued into the early 1970s (and since 1989 has gained momentum again).[21] The parallel to the Cuban situation described in *Das Verhör* is obvious. As the expellees on the witness stand emphasize pride of place, the questions of the interrogators gradually expose their patriotism as imperialistic nationalism. Their ostensive love of the land is revealed to be love of the fruits that this former property brought.[22] Some invaders are opportunists who follow first one political leadership then the other, as long as it maximizes their profit.[23] Through its Cuban narrative, *Das Verhör* supports sovereignty of the GDR and Eastern European countries, as well as that of the FRG. It depicts the demands of those who would return to that which they call their homeland as hypocrisies camouflaging imperialistic greed.

These earlier 'Cuban' texts by Enzensberger address concerns about state power, citizen resistance, and global change through narratives about violence. From the perspective of some Northern intellectuals, to articulate such parallels between the situations in Cuba and the Federal Republic was to strengthen the possibility of a transnational solidarity of violence. Yet bloc and state politics intervened. Cuba's more complete entrance into the Council for Mutual Economic Assistance (Comecon) in 1972 and its attendant emphasis on state-directed governance rather than the global dissemination of revolution cooled infatuation between most independently minded Northern intellectuals and the Cuban government. In 1968, a significant number in the Federal Republic justified Castro's ambivalent support for the Russians' military action against the popular uprising in Prague as necessary for continued protection from the Soviet Union. The purging of political splinter groups was similarly rationalized. However, few could understand or support governmental crackdowns on Cuban intellectuals and artists, such as the trial and imprisonment of the Cuban poet Heberto Padilla. Cuba increasingly seemed to embody not the successful use of overt violence in the service of social change but the failure of overt violence as an enabler of democratic realities. Against what was seen as a failed experiment, the political statements of the RAF, with their emphasis on collective will for violent national and global political change, sounded hollow. In the FRG, the idealistic focus on violence for social change split into several perspectives. Some refocused on the newer solidarity struggles of fledgling nations abroad as the appropriate global locus. Others, such as Hans Magnus Enzensberger, shifted away from support of violence altogether. *Der Untergang der Titanic* is an example of this move. Before considering the shift that it represents, let us look more closely at Volker Braun's mid-1970s play in which similar themes of bloodshed, social change, and sovereignty articulate somewhat distinct messages.

Radicalization II: The Upright Gait of Global Change – *Guevara oder der Sonnenstaat*

'This is the time of the [political] machine no more.'[24] Spoken by the violent revolutionary Che Guevara, this retort may have been too explosive for popular consumption in the GDR, yet it exemplifies the domestic message of the text. Recall that as acceptance of radical direct action in the FRG waned, Enzensberger's text strategically employed Cuban courts abroad to criticize structural violence at home more effectively. In the GDR, it was overt violence that seemed distant, and Braun's text employs this circumstance strategically. On an abstract level, *Guevara oder der Sonnenstaat* philosophizes about the relationship between the individual and society through the overt example of Cuba and the allegorical example of the GDR. More concretely, the piece on one hand demonstrates the limitations of alternatives to governmental structures as embodied in Guevara. On the other hand, it exposes the violence of ruling structures precisely through its articulation of Guevara's overt violence in his Bolivian project.

The play was written in 1975, shortly after a shift in the political course of the GDR. First Secretary Walter Ulbricht, with the support of most of the Socialist Unity Party, had sought a nationally oriented agenda. This GDR aimed for German unification and to further its own interests, even ahead of Russia's. By the 1960s, however, the USSR decided that the GDR's future lay with the socialist community, not in the large, putatively neutral Germany that the Russians themselves had suggested in the 'Stalin note' of the 1950s. By the 1970s, USSR President Breschnew reiterated his enthusiasm for the presence of Soviet troops in the GDR, and by 1971 the Soviet Union was instrumental in replacing the aging Ulbricht with Erich Honecker, a change meant to further closer international ties. This relationship offered the GDR benefits as well as restrictions. In the short term at least, the alliance facilitated the GDR Central Committee's aim of offering more consumer goods in a Germany that had largely focused on industrial production. Soviet aid in conjunction with loans from both the Soviets and the FRG enabled such appeasement of a populace weary of hard work for seemingly little material benefit. This time of material liberalization also saw putative cultural liberalization, yet domestic security and surveillance increased.[25] In part, artists had simply learned to adapt. Grand social analysis gave way to 'subjective' stories that cleverly united the social and the personal. Subtle motifs were easier for the censors to ignore, whether naively or in support of a spirit of resistance. Many readers developed sophisticated reading and viewing skills, certainly others took away primarily the dominant messages. Braun's play speaks into this time of social negotiation in the GDR.

The global South played a significant role in this spirit of hope and hypocrisy. Indeed, the historian Ulrich Mählert contends that the optimism of the 1970s depended on the independence movements in Africa, Asia, and Latin America – especially Cuba, Chile, Vietnam, and Portugal: 'The Left was also gaining ground in Western Europe. Both on this and on that side of the Iron Curtain, the heroes of the freedom fights – especially Ernesto Che Guevara – served as identificatory figures. The revolutionary romantic of a socialism under the palms allowed the contradictions in one's own daily life in the GDR to move temporarily into the background. Setbacks such as the U.S.-supported military putsch in Chile in 1973 provided within – as well as outside – the "Camp of

World Peace" for a common cause from which even the critical Left at least for a time could not withdraw.'[26]

Mählert's text reveals a limiting Northern perspective on the Germanies, yet it does rightly emphasize the impact of Latin America on the public imagination of the GDR. These independence movements figured importantly in popular identity. For some, third-world socialists were the litmus test for the GDR's theory and justification of its practice, and many heroized Che. For these reasons, Braun's work that tests socialism on a Latin American example functions as a particularly effective appraisal of the Democratic Republic.

Guevara oder der Sonnenstaat plays on the specific meanings that Latin America, Cuba, and Guevara held in the GDR. Even more than of Enzensberger's documentary piece, scholars have argued that *Guevara* instrumentalizes the global South for domestic national purposes.[27] *Guevara's* representation of the closed-door debate between Castro and Guevara exemplifies this alleged misappropriation that, I suggest, was seen as significant at the time because it intervenes so directly in Cuban debates. The content of Castro and Guevara's discussion remains a state secret. The official Cuban narrative holds that the two state leaders did not part ways, but that the *Commandante* supported Che to the bitter end.[28] In contrast, Northern leftists scrutinize what they see as incompatibilities between the exigencies of Castro's nation building and Guevara's revolutionary ideals. The Cuban assessment furthers Cuba's actual political goals; the Northern reading metonymizes this historical moment as the tension between state and individual socialist theory and practice. The fascination of German critical intellectuals with the putative split between Castro and Guevara points primarily to their own struggle with reform versus revolution. Braun's text articulates this split and also works to reconcile it. The play closes with an ambivalent image of a quixotic Che riding the 'steed' Castro through the windmilling arms of Cuban and Guevara's own children. Both reformist and revolutionary forces are necessary, if not sufficient, to meet the challenges that the future holds. The text obliquely supports Cuban self-representation and, as will be shown below, it raised the ire of Cuban officials.

Philosophical questions are at the core of *Guevara oder der Sonnenstaat* and Braun's other works. *Guevara* explores long-standing debates around individual/society through a contemporary example: the nexus of revolutionary ideals and state socialism.[29] It continues Braun's investigation of anarchism's political potential and the limits of state power that he first investigated in *T.* (Trotsky, 1968) and *Lenins Tod* (Lenin's Death, 1970).[30] As the names of these earlier plays suggest, the GDR-trained philosopher (whose first disillusionment came with the Prague Spring in 1968 and who protested the expatriation of singer-songwriter Wolf Biermann in 1976) increasingly engaged politically thorny themes.[31] Never rejecting the GDR nor rejected by it, this critical, state-supported artist endorsed the movement for a third way between state socialism and capitalism after 1989. His works from the mid-1960s onward attest to his efforts as a political gadfly in the cultural realm. At least three other censored plays of the 1970s deal with the theme of power and revolution: *Grosser Friede* (Big Peace, 1976), *Simplex Deutsch* (Simplex German, 1978–9), and *Die unvollendete Geschichte* (The Unfinished Story, 1975). Each highlights the taboo disjunctions between theoretical Marxism and real-existing socialism. Dieter Sevin explains how these disjunctions are expressed through *Die unvollendete Geschichte*'s generational narrative, for instance: 'Braun's prose work portrays the conflict between the generations as a clash between the high, idealistic expectations of the young – ideals that were impressed upon them by the older generation – and the shortcomings, failures, bureaucratic inadequacies, and arbitrary manipulation of human lives by the established order. While the older generation shows much more tolerance for the misuse of state power, the younger generation is unwilling to compromise. It does not share the older generation's memories of worse conditions, nor does it want to measure the present by the past. Rather, it compares the existing reality with the ideals instilled in them.'[32]

Guevara negotiates these overarching concerns of idealistic individualism and staid objective conditions through a story of third-world revolution. The questions here become: What can one achieve and what does one risk with revolution? What should revolution look like? When are which actions justified? Are practices of revolution and reform mutually exclusive? Through fictions of Cuba and Bolivia, German audiences confront these theoretical questions that speak to their domestic circumstances. Guevara embodies the heroism that seems necessary for a truly socialist stance, while Castro represents the putatively objective realities of a real-existing socialist state. This Latin American example of the abstract, dialectical tension recalls the generational model of *Die unvollendete Geschichte* while engaging them with a unique specificity.

Guevara opens with Che's death at the hands of the Bolivian military and its scenes move backward in narrative time to his resignation from the Cuban leadership. Much has been made of this temporal organization that falls out of the socialist realist tradition of a 1970s Cuba and GDR. Braun did not have close contact to Cuba, and it is unlikely that he was consciously reacting to Cuban literary norms. What is the import of this structure in the GDR setting? In the afterword of the GDR hard-copy edition, the publisher Hans Marquardt quotes Volker Braun from the playbill of the planned GDR premier. According to Braun's statement, the reverse temporality helps the audience understand the necessity of Guevara's trajectory, while at the same time deromanticizing Guevara's project.[33] This paratextual framing overtly evacuates the activist potential of the play.

Marquardt's didactic gloss suggests that the temporal structure actually promoted acceptance among functionaries sceptical of Braun's work in general and of the Guevara material in particular.[34] Marquardt's and Braun's statements certainly aimed to diffuse contemporary political criticism; an unproblematically heroic Che would have been rejected out of hand. 'Revolutionismus' – a synthesis of revolution and tourism – is a term that Braun uses today to describe the Bolivian project. The vicissitudes of memory notwithstanding, *Guevara*'s temporal structure was more than a nod to the censor. By channelling the dramatic suspense, the form indeed invites critical analysis of all of the events as they unfold backward from the first scene onward. The text does not withhold dramatic tension altogether, rather it dispenses only with a dramatic build-up to Guevara's death. Subsequently, it employs a 'why-done-it' style reminiscent of the mystery genre, building narrative tension and drawing the audience in as the narrative progresses into the past. The final and penultimate scenes become the most significant. Moreover, the reverse structure that invites analysis of the events leading to the death simultaneously encourages analytic reading more generally and promotes mapping of the overtly Latin American narrative onto other situations, such as those in the GDR. In these ways, the structure furthers affirmative and subversive political messages.

Political functionaries understood Braun's text about Cuba as a narrative that was very much about the GDR.[35] Volker Braun corroborates what Matthias Braun's research in files from the secret police and the culture ministry has shown. Nevertheless, just before the premiere, it was the Cuban embassy that stopped the production, objecting to several elements: the fictional representation of Castro, who was their acting head of state; the negative representation of Guevara; and the difference of opinion between Castro and Guevara. Finally, they objected to the representation of a romantic liaison between Che and

Tamara Bunke. Tamara's mother, Nadja Bunke, was the catalyst for this diplomatic intervention.[36] Always driven to protect the heroic image of her daughter, she first apprised the Cuban embassy in the GDR of the potentially problematic work. Yet although Nadja Bunke had clout, issues larger than Tamara's legacy were at play. In overemphasizing Nadja's influence, Nadja's detractors underrate GDR domestic and foreign policy. Volker Braun recalls about a later discussion with a Central Committee member primarily responsible for cultural questions, Kurt Hager, that GDR officials were happy to comply on the unassailable grounds of good foreign relations.[37]

The Cuban connection both hindered and furthered *Guevara*'s influence in Germany. The topic garnered interest, but the play remained problematic into the 1980s. Indeed, what Hans Marquardt neglects to note in his 1983 afterword, the very afterword in which he quotes Braun from the 1977 playbill, is that the play did not premiere in 1977. Rather, it first opened in a theatre in Mannheim in 1978 and did not reach the GDR stage until 1984. The 1984 illustrated hardback was expensive; few copies also meant little distribution. GDR scholarly commentary on *Guevara* remained concerned with presenting the piece benignly, a situation that attests to its explosive potential even in the 1980s. Thus, for instance, the Marquardt afterword emphasizes the influence of Che for the West student movement, thereby shifting the relevance of the topic outside of the Soviet bloc. In a 1981 critical essay on Braun's work, Germanist Frank Hörnigk took pains to emphasize that, unlike Braun's earlier pieces, *Guevara* is not of pedagogical value in the contemporary GDR.[38] Certainly scholars such as Hörnigk believed precisely the contrary.

Three motifs important to the GDR debate are national and community sovereignty, the place of the individual revolutionary in state-driven reform, and popular versus party leadership. Attention to *Guevara*'s title offers a way into the first. Scholars tend to understand the terms 'Guevara' and 'Sonnenstaat' as two labels for the same social utopia that according to the narrative is difficult, perhaps even impossible, to achieve.[39] I propose 'or' as a dialectical fulcrum between Guevara and Sonnenstaat. Read in this way, the text questions the Soviet Union's influence on the GDR.

'Der Sonnenstaat' references Giovan Domenico (Thomas) Campanella's *Der Sonnenstaat*. In 1955, the GDR Akademie press published a German translation of this utopian narrative of the 1600s that included translations of the introduction and the commentary from the Soviet

Akademie press edition. A philosopher trained in Marxist-Leninism, Braun had most probably been exposed to this work. The introduction's author, W.P. Wolgin, explicitly casts Campanella's imagined society as communist but finds fault with its hierarchical character: 'If one considers that the democracy of the People's Assemblies in "Sonnenstaat" does not appear as objective driving force, [but rather] that the highest ruling organ basically completes itself, then one can characterize the political structure of "Sonnenstaat" as a strange oligarchy of the intelligentsia under a formal democracy.' Wolgin argues that in contrast to this fictive world the contemporary 'technological socialist' systems are democracies led by the proletariat.[40]

If in the diegesis Castro's nation is understood as a real-existing Eldorado in dialectical opposition to Guevara's as-yet-unrealized vision, then, understood quite programmatically through Wolgin's Soviet interpretation of Campanella, the play criticizes the Soviet system itself. For in this fictional Caribbean Sonnenstaat guided by the Soviet system, state socialist structures are oligarchies of the intelligentsia – precisely what the Soviets disapproved of in Campanella's Sonnenstaat. Moreover, in Castro's Eldorado foreign rulers have forced the citizens to return to a money-based economy whose abolishment in Campanella's state decreases inequity and alienation. Finally, this foreign leadership forces adherence to state capitalist logics that, in turn, make global equity impossible.

The closed-door debate between Castro and Guevara prior to the departure of the armed revolutionary from the island makes this oligarchy and its global consequences clear:

GUEVARA: ... The Revolution must / If it now shall last, question all the structures / in order to be brotherly.

FRIEND: Must. Now. All. / Those are too many words for one / simple thing. Is not the Must enough for you / The new human being must feed / And let's not ask about the cutlery ...

GUEVARA: ... Open the doors, Vietnam lies there. / Bleeding the dirt under the feet, there / [Feet] [w]ith which we go our proud course / of affluence in the so-called peace / East and West, [Vietnam], however, is alone. Delivered naked to the murderous Yankees / Close to our cowardice, almost left behind / And indifference, with which we chatter / of solidarity. The absurdity / Binds my throat closed. There will / be no socialism, if we ourselves don't

FRIEND: change / And be brotherly instead of holding fast to everything /

What we own this property / that we save for ourselves that separates
the peoples / This life for ourselves and inequality / And alien and
meaningless trade between us / As between capitalists we accomplices /
The oppression and trade in friendship / Blackmailing also the Friend in
equilibrium / The blocs blocks around our necks / And Vietnam bleeds
to death and we look into the / Arena as the blood flows this game / That
drives us to the limit. I hear, I hear.

GUEVARA: Cuba, hope of the world.
FRIEND: Keep silence, Comrade.
GUEVARA: Everything is true, can't you hear it, Friend / What you are saying?
FRIEND: You can't talk that way.
GUEVARA: I cannot, aha, I cannot. / Then the struggle is also impossible here.
FRIEND: We / will come into the devil's kitchen through your speeches / The
hell of war in front of our eyes.[41]

In this hierarchical Sonnenstaat, Castro and Guevara, not the people, make the decisions. As Castro's ambivalent speeches evidence, he
believes his actions constrained by the transnational yoke of peaceful
coexistence. The Cuban leader bends to ostensive practicalities such
as monetary systems to supply his 'new [socialist] men' with necessities. For Braun's Guevara, this compromise spells failure. Consciousness cannot be altered in a system based on capitalist values.[42] Guevara
asks: 'Do you want to have a financial system or a / New human being.
Namely, as / important as the production is the consciousness / That
it produces. Socialism / you cannot build with the decaying weapons
/ That capitalism leaves behind.'[43] This debate recalls Cuba's domestic
attempt at a moneyless society and links its failure to global pressures
driven by bloc politics, not by communist ideals.

As part of the terms of publication, Braun replaced the name Castro
in this scene with 'friend,' yet the denotation does more than describe
him and the relationship between the two main protagonists. It underscores the relationship between Cuba and the Soviet Union, and by
extension between the GDR and the Soviet Union, by referencing the
term used in the Soviet bloc to refer particularly to the Russians and
also to fellow socialist states. The text articulates the benefits and costs
of such ties. Aligned nations profit in the form of material goods from
the milk, shoes, and chalk of the fictional Cuba to the consumer goods
available thanks to the GDR's strengthened relationship with Russia.
These countries also avoid war on their soil. In exchange, they quell
dissent – such as Guevara's and Padilla's in Cuba and Braun's in the

GDR. They also replace radical global solidarity with an instrumentalizing solidarity based on material gain. The statesman of the small socialist nation feels the blocs around his neck. As Guevara reconvinces his friend of his former standpoint, the leader exclaims: 'Keeping still hatred breaks from my neck / Against the force that holds us on wires / In the old time, and I don't know myself anymore.'[44] The use of the present tense (holds) aligns the colonial and neocolonial power structures of the past with the strings of the superpower puppetmaster of the present. As satellite states, Cuba and by extension the GDR benefit from the unequal relations between the North and the South at the expense of more underdeveloped nations and to the extent that their providers wish.

The intermezzos interspersed among the primary scenes further articulate the postcolonial sensitivities of the piece. Two tragicomic figures, Bumholdt and Bedray, engage in farcical interactions while lauding the wonders of the ancients and the Cuban revolution. Unlike in the gravediggers' scene of *Hamlet* or Beckett's *Waiting for Godot*, which the interludes recall, events here turn brutish and violent, culminating in Bumholdt cannibalizing Bedray. These depictions of the explorer Alexander von Humboldt (Bumboldt is an archaeologist digging for the utopia of the Incas) and the French philosopher Régis Debray (Bedray is an explorer looking for the utopia of authentic guerrilla fighters) might at first seem surprising. The aristocratic traveler Humboldt was acclaimed in official GDR discourses for his work as a naturalist, as well as his anti-slavery views. Régis Debray was a staunch supporter of the Cuban revolution who taught on the island, travelled to Che's forces in Bolivia, wrote in support of the Cuban project, and worked politically in France.[45] His *Révolution dans la révolution* (published in 1967 in France and Cuba) complemented Guevara's focus theory, which opposed the Leninist principle that party precedes practice.[46] For Debray, Cuban praxis trumped state socialist doctrine.[47] We might expect a more positive representation of Debray in this politically thorny text. Although the presence of the revolutionary tourist did inadvertently hamper Guevara's project in Bolivia, his writings furthered the cause of unseating superpower orthodoxy. The negative depiction might reflect pragmatic concerns regarding censorship, as the radical Western Marxist was in some ways as problematic for the GDR as Guevara was. On a more abstract level, the depictions of both the aristocratic explorer, whose work prepared the way for further colonization, and the radical philosopher highlight the problems that inhere in their prescriptive utopian visions of the other. Whether their search is in the materialist past or the idealist future, their attitude leaves no space for the real-existing communities that they ostensibly seek. These two foils of the 'revolutionist' Guevara suggest that North-South solidarity must involve communicative exchange and respect for sovereignty across persons and polities.

The final interaction between Guevara and Castro, then, outlines the paradox of heroic idealism versus reformist pragmatism and criticizes regulation by the superpowers, while the intermezzos critique other foreign influence. In the penultimate scene, the meeting between Guevara and Mario Monje Molina contrasts the voluntarism of immediate revolution and the opportunism of party-led compromise. Guevara meets this secretary general of the Bolivian communist party at his jungle camp, where Monje asks him to hand over leadership of the guerrilla operation, an act that would end Guevara's armed struggle. Monje pleads for a strategy of dialogue with those in power for the sake of the people:

MONJE: ... and your case / Is not as new, as your death will be. / And old we
    would look, so foolishly led / And without leadership all with two leaders
    / And demoralized the power, confused / of the people. That is not only
    your death, Guevara
    grabs him
    you liquidate all of us, the Party / as it now lives, in that you knock us out
    / With your emergence and we watch / Like cowards and can't help our-
    selves / because you are no more to be helped.
    lets him go.
    But
    Your heroism is not the dunged hothouse / Of revolutions, and your death
    / Will lead us as little as your life.
GUEVARA *laughs*: Build the guerrilla force, and the rest comes on its own. /
    And only the guerrilla can lead it / And after the victory also he, that risked
    everything / He should get everything and not you / Who hesitate in the
    cities, sluggish, public officials / and zealously wait for orders.
    grabs him:
    How I will like it to be in power / And if it is only to pull the flunkies of
    every / clan into the light and with their snouts / push them in their piggy
    mess.
    lets him go
    Comrade
    This is the time of the Machine [Apparats] no more.

MONJE: How should I understand that.
GUEVARA: As you can.[48]

In its overt depiction of the Communist Party of Bolivia, this scene covertly addresses the governance structures of the GDR. Indeed, Guevara's description of party members as public servants (*Beamte*) aligns much more closely to the GDR situation, in which party members were actually government officials, than to the Bolivian situation, in which the military under René Barrientos had taken over in 1964 and the party was in the opposition. Intertextual connections further strengthen the allegory. The relationship between Braun's Guevara and Hölderin's Empedocles has been studied in some detail.[49] The resonance between the line from *Guevara*, 'This is the time of the Machine [Apparats] no more,' and that from Hölderin's *Empedocles*, 'This is the time of the kings no more,' casts the party as a monarchy, a far cry from a party that serves the citizens. These indictments of existing structures speak for radical change. Yet, the text demands, how can such necessary change take place under the current conditions (in Bolivia and in the GDR) when the average citizen is uneducated, dependent, and dully satisfied with his or her lot? The political disinterest of the GDR citizenry was one of Braun's largest concerns.[50] Can Guevara's martyrdom bring the masses to consciousness, as Monje so anxiously denies?

Many critics find that *Guevara oder der Sonnenstaat* presents Guevara negatively.[51] Yet, the character is powerfully ambivalent. He revels in power and authority. Unwilling or unable to engage intersubjectively, he aims to replace the existing power structure with one in which he is in charge. The self-styled, brash hero does not have the popular support of the farmers or his troops. Guevara's metaphor decrying public officials even contains a parodic double entendre. His pejorative term 'snout' or 'trunk' (Rüssel) is not species specific, yet the German word 'mess' (Schweinerei) contains the word 'swine' (Schwein), which connotes the historical Che's nickname that referenced his hygiene habits. However, the play nevertheless suggests that Guevara's actions have important influence. It is not only that the party representative is concerned that Guevara's continued activity – even his death – will alter the reformist movement. Guevara also points out to Castro that leaders of the increasingly authoritarian French and Russian revolutions quickly killed non-conformist radicals to decrease the influence of these revolutionaries.

Intertextual analysis grants somewhat more insight on the status of radical, visionary individualism as seen through the ambivalence of Guevara. In Hölderin, Empedocles's self-immolation in a volcano calls his people to consciousness. In a draft version of Braun's text, Guevara explicitly compares himself to Empedocles; his individual death can catalyse global social change. This burnt offering might cause the suffering, bloody world to erupt – or implode.[52] Moreover, the brutality of objective circumstances justifies Guevara's death in that these conditions preclude revolutionary influence in life. The connection to Empedocles in the published version is suggestive, not direct; the staged version opens with Guevara's burnt corpse falling through a hole in the ceiling. This change in the written text may have been a concession, although Braun himself recalls that it was merely stylistic; Guevara's individualistic and anarchic qualities were a high-profile problem in the GDR.[53]

In the final analysis, the work is less concerned with judging the individual than with the dialectic of the 'or.' Guevara's attempts at revolutionary life and revolutionary death highlight the flaws of the world. Under different conditions, his actions would have different effects and in this way would gain their practical justification. An immature world precludes an 'upright gait' (aufrechter Gang). This is why neither Guevara nor Castro is castigated for actions that are less than legitimate and less than adequate. Braun's Guevara offers an extreme antidote to learned helplessness and to the pyramids of power that further this mass disengagement.[54] Castro's attempt to save Cuban citizens at the price of citizens in non-aligned nations is similarly caring and brutal. Guevara's and Castro's work of improving the lives of others takes place – fatally – on their own terms; and others are not able to demand.

The ineffectiveness of both political strategies is the most important commentary on the GDR. The text is precisely not a call for disenchanted GDR artists to follow their revolutionary aims in a space beyond the confines of their nation, as SED officials feared. Guevara is no more effective or satisfied abroad than he would have been at home. However, that there is no place for his kind in real-existing socialism decries the decay of that volcano that once portended global change.

Enzensberger's earlier texts on Cuba and Braun's Guevara treat the relationships between and possibilities of overt and structural violence. Das Verhör represents an early Cuban justice system to highlight flaws in the FRG judiciary. Cuba's example demonstrates that overt violence in the form of grassroots resistance can birth ethical social structures that further equality. This text thus begs the question of the place of overt violence in the FRG, while *El Cimarrón*'s protagonist functions as a role model in his principled resolve towards armed struggle. In a nation in which such political violence was not actively under public scrutiny, Braun's text presents an ambivalent take on overt violence to perform a multifaceted interrogation of structural violence in the form of the national and international governance structures of real-existing socialism. Instead of praising the possibilities of a governmental system formed in the crucible of overt violence, Braun's piece resoundingly attacks the entire governmental structure in its violent quiescence. Perhaps more stoutly swathed in revolutionary romantic than its counterpart birthed under state socialism, Enzensberger's work makes a stronger case for overt violence in fomenting change. In addition to interrogating power in these ways, the texts contain quasi-postcolonial perspectives that shore up claims to national sovereignty. These latter messages articulated neatly with the increasing stabilization of global power constellations in Europe in the late 1960s and the 1970s, particularly the solidification of the FRG border through Chancellor Brandt's politics of border normalization.

Reformism I: Where Have All the Rifles Gone? Popularizing Cuba in the GDR

While *Guevara oder der Sonnenstaat* takes Cuban ideals seriously, it also expresses the increasing disillusionment of German intellectuals. One of the last exuberant portrayals of Cuba's real-existing socialist project is of Havana's urban space as free of racism and classism in Braun's poem *La Rampa, Habana* (1976). Yet, its famous line, 'The future is a mulatta,'[55] employs logic more prevalent in GDR texts of the later 1970s and the 1980s. From this time, programmatic works that thematize Cuba frequently and overtly exotify and sexualize it. This tendency away from socialist realism is, more importantly, part of a shift towards depicting the non-socialist world, one that bears not the marks of production but of consumption and desire. In this context, Cuba was functionalized to represent the exotic outside of the socialist experience in narratives meant for mass consumption, such as Fritz Rudolf Fries's literary travel narrative, 'Kubanische Kalendarblätter' and the DEFA film *Bockshorn*.

A favoured GDR intellectual, Fritz Rudolf Fries was deeply involved in Latin American and GDR cultural relations through his publications and translations. 'Kubanische Kalendarblätter' is part of a collection about his travels between 1959 and 1979. Written in 1976, 'Kalendar-

blätter' recalls an officially sanctioned trip taken in 1963 with his mentor, Werner Krauß.[56] This text about Cuba is as interested in sensual
consumption as an accompanying tale about a quintessentially capitalist site, Paris. In 'Kalendarblätter' this focus on the exotic is facilitated by its setting five years after the governmental change in Cuba,
a time period when its gains were evident but Cuba's relationship to
the Soviet Union was not normalized. The 1970s frame the tale in a
politically appropriate manner: the narrator's friend, who just returned
from a visit to the island, mentions that little is left of Fries's Cuba: 'If
one leaves the palms and a drink named mojito out of the game. Everything else is seven league boots, year plans, Cuban economic miracle.'[57]
'Paris, doppelt belichtet' (Paris, Twice Exposed) provides a similarly
politically appropriate introduction that enables subsequent revels in
the exotic pleasures of the Western metropolis. The narrator recalls the
socialist heritage of the Enlightenment and its revolution and criticizes
the return to capitalist excess. In both texts, the political sentiments of
the traveller are identical to these politically appropriate standpoints.
Such didactic framing around the narratives that move outside of these
norms both opens a space to articulate what could be politically problematic pleasures and reminds readers that good socialists may enjoy
the pleasures of travel.

The plots are driven by the exotic of the visited sites articulated
through desire, consumption, and sexuality. The narrative on Cuba
links the power and popular support of the revolution to the island's
history of magic. For instance, it depicts the well-known incident of
the dove alighting on the orating Castro's shoulder as a credibility test
instigated by the pagan Cubans of African heritage. According to the
text, the Cuban leader employs cultural syncretism strategically, allowing the bird to perch until the santería followers are converted. Such
device also drives a theatre performance. The director casts a tall man
to play a revolutionary who is not even in the script to 'present the
utopian mythology of the bearded one (in the minds of the audience)'
because the audience expects it. 'Can we, when it comes to Cuba, not
get by without magic and mythology?' muses the narrator.[58] The 'we'
here refers to more than the Cuban audience. Is this a textual self-
critique against the romanticization into which citizens of bureaucra-
tized Germanies can so easily fall? This potential reflexivity is at best a
rationalization, for under the guise of cultural difference, the text offers
titillation, particularly through the long-standing trope of black, feminine ur-sexuality.

As is often the case in left-oriented travelogues of the period, the principled standpoint of the male visitor renders exotic sexual pleasures at travel destinations politically permissible. Fries's narrator is distinct from the typical sex tourist in other ways as well; he is an unlikely combination of passive victim, ethnographer, and expert socialist. An upstanding, revolutionary Cuban broaches the topic of sex work: 'Morales, our guide, young and hip, came around, who knows why, to talk about prostitution that had once made Cuba the brothel of Latin America. The prostitutes, said Morales, disappeared with the last North American tourists.'[59] The interjected phrase 'who knows why' releases the narrator from responsibility for the topic. The text now moves the naive and defenceless narrator inexorably into the otherworldly, twilight zone of commodified sex. The narrator abashedly describes his night-time walk through the old city as the wanderings of a flâneur – a passively consumerist occupation made famous by Baudelaire and anathema to the socialist purpose. As if to avoid this negative connotation, the next sentence surprises with a stated purpose for his wanderings: testing Morales's theory that sex work does not exist in socialist Cuba. As if to demonstrate the depth of his innocence, the narrator bungles his first attempt at even talking to a 'dark-skinned [girl] in a luminous light blue dress.'[60] Again a Cuban male character initiates the narrator, this time by guiding him to a certain street filled with wandering men. Relative to the rest of the text, the sex work scene employs more metaphors and is more visually suggestive. It evokes the realm of the senses and depicts the course of events as inexorable and natural, while focusing on irrationality and instinct: 'Again and again one [of the waiting men] is swallowed by a house entryway ... The doors to the houses flush with the earth seem to have a magical attraction, abruptly I also allow myself to fall into their depths and find myself in a brothel run by negro women. An unlit hallway, therein along the walls the dark figures. The youngest had opened the door. Later she would ask me for money for her sick mother – like in a scene from the bad novel, *The Gringo.*'[61]

The waiting men are de-individualized, part of a flowing mass determined by their common drives – as the term 'the driven ones' emphasizes – hungrily swallowed by nearly incarnate, domestic openings contiguous with the earth – the masculine enveloped by the feminine. The narrator gives in to the force, yet keeps his analytical wits about him, as the phrase 'find myself' (*befinde mich*) and his recognition of being treated as a typical foreign customer suggests. Here is a stereotypical exotic fantasy in which the white, Northern visitor has his

desires serviced by the overwhelming, untamed natural forces of dehu-
manized, de-individualized black females.

This night-time commerce is counter-revolutionary; the Cuban man
who brings the narrator to the site has deserted from the army to seek
his pleasures. Far from considering his own participation disloyal,
however, the narrator immediately and openly relates the experience
to his GDR travel companion. The two seek the house by day, but find
no trace. The socialist mentor exonerates the narrator of any trans-
gression: 'You became a victim of black magic, said K. [his mentor] ...
Morales will not believe this story from you ...'[62] Interestingly, the narrator's analytic abilities do not engender scepticism about his actions;
rather, they support his understanding that his motives were to test the
Cuban revolution. Such aid is needed; natives like Morales are blind to
such weakness in their system. The text has already depicted the visitors as helpful experts. Earlier, a Cuban geologist asks the two writers
for advice on an agricultural project, suggesting that first world status
bequeaths knowledge in all areas. Such passages not only emphasize
the superiority of the GDR over their fellow socialist state, this positioning justifies pleasurably exoticized descriptions of Cuba such as the
one above, a decadent diegesis that would otherwise be inappropriate.

Exoticism, commodity, and sexuality drive the Parisian tale in a similar manner. The narrator revels in the sensual pleasures of a women's
clothing store: '... I dive in blouses and skirts, scarves and mufflers,
spread out at home, warmed by the flesh of women, swelled by femininity, they will be proofs of this trip.'[63] This scene denotes the bounty
of consumer capitalism in the fashion metropolis of the West. The
apparent purchasing power of the visitor creates a fantasy in which
socialist citizens have ample access to such products, at least if they
are citizens whose behaviour at home has resulted in freedom to travel
abroad. The scene also connotes access to non-normative sexual pleasures. The 'dive' of the narrator may suggest transvestism pleasures and
he revels at adorning multiple libidinal interests. In a second instance,
a Western journalist entices to infidelity towards socialist values. As
any good enemy, this embodiment of capitalism has power and voice.
Perched on the edge of his hotel room bed, icily wrapped in a fur coat,
she interviews him. Their innuendo-laden intellectual jousting heightens the sexual tension. In response to her question '[but] don't you love
France?' the narrator responds, '(I plunge myself into a proposal of
love, explain the little difference, God, she is really naive, talk my way
out.)' After this heated exchange, the pair dine together, and 'discover

in doing so mutual tastes, preferences.'[64] The revolutionary tourist and the readers savour vicarious pleasures.

Both Cuba and Paris, then, are about commerce and sex. Unlike in the socialist site, however, in the capitalist one, the narrative variously thwarts a climax. In the clothing store, although the sexual connotations heighten the enjoyment of consumer goods, they also disarm the potency of the latter; these commodities are surrogates for interpersonal relations. Moreover, two matronly shopkeepers with the Berlin accents of home remind the narrator to keep his wife's measurements in mind while handling the wares. This policing reminds that choice based on need is superior to accumulation based on desire. Marital fidelity here parallels political fidelity. In the hotel room scene, the extent of the exchange is more ambiguous. The parentheses around the narrator's description of his responses separate the reader from his responses towards his fictional interlocutor. Within this indirect speech, his declaration of love suggests more than one object, his excuses more than one indiscretion. Nevertheless, unlike in the Cuban tale, this narrative overtly relates fidelity.

In Fries's programmatically acceptable texts, the small difference remains, allegorized in differing sexual relations. In Paris, restraint prevails because consummation would represent contamination by capitalism. In Cuba, in contrast, the narrator consummates his relations. Carefully legitimated through rhetoric, this sexual act is a politically acceptable expression of international solidarity. Yet, more heavily than in most earlier GDR texts, this representation conjures a fantastic, pre-revolutionary, feminized stereotype. It draws on bourgeois tropes of the hypersexualized black woman and sexual commerce, while debunking the success of the revolution's intense campaigns against racism and sex work. Reading the tales side by side highlights the exoticization of Cuba as a means of marketing socialism, an exoticization, moreover, that is racialized and gendered according to neocolonial North-South logics.

This shift is even more pronounced in the 1983 DEFA film *Bockshorn* (*Ram's Horn*) in which Cuba depicts a debauched capitalist society – in this case a distant, yet ever-present quintessential actor: the United States (see fig. 4.1, page 110). Based on the novel by Christoph Meckel, written by Ulrich Plenzdorf, and directed by Frank Beyer, *Bockshorn* tells of two homeless orphan boys seeking happiness and safe haven in a contemporary, capitalist society. Their journey takes them through various scenes of poverty, corruption, and wealth, including decadent

beach and cruising scenes in tropical surroundings barely identifiable
as Cuba. The tale ends in the tragic death of the younger boy, Mick,
which leaves his best and only friend Sauly alone in the world.

There is space for neither a revolutionary Cuba nor a revolutionary
GDR in this project. Instead, the film uses Cuba to criticize capitalism
through mimesis rather than counterpoint. In doing so, it participates
in the trend of the times. By the 1980s, the positive representations of
socialism that had proven increasingly ineffective at capturing audience attention were disappearing in favour of depictions of Western
capitalism. In this case, the enemy appears as nightmare: Brooklyn
as jungle; opulent (Cuban) beaches as despoiled, decadent U.S. play-
grounds. Rather than socialist heroes building a new society, in the
West the downtrodden are the main protagonists, victims struggling
their way through an endless school of hard knocks. Their misfortunes
are meant to warn GDR youth by offering a counter-narrative to the
fantasies of Hollywood-style life portrayed in Western media to which
there was increasing access. The narrative seeks to develop a critical
gaze in the disillusioned fascinated with the land across the Wall. Yet in
the minds of young audiences, the filmic nightmare of Mick and Sauly's footloose adventures could function as real-life daydreams. Indeed,
DEFA staff themselves saw their offer of this vicarious freedom as a
way to draw young audiences to half empty cinemas.[65] The film tempts
with foreign lands, while pedagogically deconstructing these capitalist
castles in the sky.

The difference between *Bockshorn* and earlier films involving Cuba
is striking. On-site shooting would have enabled any manner of positive representation of the socialist brother state in addition to its actual
use as a decadent tropical backdrop. Recall that in *Und deine Liebe auch*
(1962), for instance, representations of revolutionary Cuba had been
written into the script after filming had already begun. This decision
was pragmatic – the crew was under pressure to complete the production on time, while the main actor, Mueller-Stahl, had been asked to
attend a film week in Havana.[66] Yet, Cuba was also integrated into the
narrative and featured as a socialist brother state in ways that went
beyond necessity. In *Für die Liebe noch zu mager?* (1973), revolutionary Cuba represents expansive socialist horizons even without on-site
shooting abroad. In the TV series *Das grüne Ungeheur* (which began in
1962), Cuba is both the revolutionary model and the needy socialist
brother nation. In *Bockshorn*, in contrast, not only is there no GDR vision
of revolution or reform, but international solidarity is evident only in

the praxis of cooperative filming efforts. Cuba is largely unrecognizable, interchangeable with any tropical backdrop. This brings up an interesting question, for select audience members should have recognized the uniquely Cuban palms, the signature 1950s U.S. automobiles, the seawall promenade so quintessentially Havana. Do these traces, all of which mark pre-revolutionary times as well, suggest a return of the island itself to a U.S. playground? Considering Cuba's role as a screen for GDR domestic hopes, such a subtext offers a dark vision of the future by DEFA producers who spent their professional lives furthering the German socialist project.

In both the FRG and the GDR, the representation of Cuba shifted from revolutionary model to challenge-ridden potential disaster. In each nation, these depictions flirted variously with violence; this topic drove interest in Cuba and criticism of it. In the FRG, artistic embrace of violence went somewhat further because of selective attention to the structural violence of socialist nations and to the presence of overt violence. In the GDR, more nuanced understandings of the aligned Cuban brother state engendered scepticism earlier. From the late 1970s, German texts not only move away from the representation of violence, but from a documentary aesthetic. As in the case of DEFA's *Bockshorn*, artistic work increasingly depicted Cuba in a more commercialized manner. In the FRG, Enzensberger's epic poem of 1978, *Der Untergang der Titanic*, engages both of these shifts. In it, the crux of the political and aesthetic problem is the notion of an idée fixe: utopias, social structures, ideological trajectories, semiotics, belief in seamless mimesis. Stasis leads to disaster. In the poem, the Cuba of the FRG left exemplifies fixed notions. The proposed solution of multiple readings both results from fear of violence at home and encourages flight from violence.

Reformism II: Educational Aesthetics? *Der Untergang der Titanic*

Untergang articulates disillusionment with world revolution through modernist, even post-modernist multiplicity in form and content, which in turn expresses the social climate of the late 1970s in the FRG. Most hopes for violence as progressive force had dissipated. Populist political struggle inspired by Southern models had not united the citizenry, toppled state power, or crystallized new organization. Instead, the majority had not legitimated it and the political violence that had inserted itself into mainstream society had polarized, radicalized, and paralysed the nation without clear progress. As Western intellectuals expressed their disillusionment, Cuba began to oppose them. Consider Fidel Castro's response to their protest against governmental censure of the dissident artist Heberto Padilla:

And thus, while capitalist Europe decays, and progressively so, and no one knows where it will eventually wind up in its descent, like a sinking ship ... And together with the ships, in this stormy sea of history, their intellectual rats will sink as well. When I say intellectual rats, let it be clear that we are not referring, not by any means, to all of the intellectuals. No. There as well they are a minority! I mean the sailors, the rats that want to convert their miserable role of a ship's crew sinking in the stormy seas of history into something of great importance. That's the way it is. It is a question of years, and perhaps not even very many! It is a question of time. Those decadent societies, made corrupt and rotten to the core by their own contradictions, will not last a long time. And while they sink to the bottom, we with work, with effort, and certainly many difficulties, we are steadily advancing.[67]

While the words of the political leader leave open the possibility for solidarity between Northern intellectuals and Southern nations, this vivid image makes clear that earlier hopes for robust cooperation were deeply damaged. Most intellectuals, including Enzensberger, were relegated to the ranks of the Northern ruling classes, their own political aspirations and inspirations notwithstanding.

Castro is certainly not the first to employ a sinking ship as a metaphor for civil collapse; more canonical examples abound and, notably, rock star Tamara Dansk would famously use it in 1989 to allegorize the GDR. Eight years passed between Castro's brusque and well-publicized rejection of Northern intellectuals and Enzensberger's publication of *Der Untergang der Titanic*. Yet it is not unconvincing to see *Untertang*, in its thematic similarity to Castro's words, as a response to this painful rejection. Enzensberger's work transforms Castro's graphic indictment into a poetic eulogy for a global ideal and legitimates the path taken by the accused in the process. *Untergang's* ship is global civilization, especially Cuba and Berlin, and the plentiful rats unable to save it are saving their own skins. Unlike Castro's sinking vessel, the *Untergang's* Titanic is a commonly fated, interconnected world of constrained actors and that simultaneously forecloses the possibility for fundamental improvement. Through subjectivity and multiplicity, the poem suggests reform rather than radical change.

Untergang variously highlights personal subjectivity. It performs its critique of ideological inertia through a reworking of Enzensberger's personal visit to Cuba, which engendered texts such as *Das Verhör* as well as his break with the Cuban government. Many have noted *Untergang*'s subjective epistemology and have suggested that it marks political disillusionment. Focusing on the scenes of the shipwreck, as do most scholarly works, Hinrich Seeba's analysis argues that in the world of the poem, dystopia is a natural force too powerful to fight; struggle for change has become personal struggle for survival. His scholarly essay from 1981 is at once an insightful analysis and a documentation of the intellectual climate. Through its assessment of Enzensberger, it points to the 1970s shift from public to personal and emphasizes the limits of this perspective.[68] *Untergang* participates in the retreat from official politics that new subjectivity often entailed; Enzensberger's documentary politics had become personal political poetics.[69]

The text also variously articulates individual subjectivity itself as multiple. Its reflexive form is a conduit into a rewriting and writing that (re)constitutes both the past and the present as personal. The loose plot is structured around the reported loss of a first version of the poem. Thus, two *Untergang* poems are involved in the narrative, one the figure within the epic, the other the epic itself. The former represents single-minded standpoints, the latter writes an ambivalent alternative to such fixity. According to the narrative voice that asserts authorship, the first was written during an earlier stay in Havana and vanished in transit when the writer returned to Berlin. In the diegesis it remains a phantasm, an expression of a lost ideal and a particular subjectivity in which and of which it was created. On the biographical level, it references a work by Enzensberger that criticized Cuba and that he ostensively did not publish. In a quote that evidences his characteristic attempt at critical solidarity through attention to audience, Enzensberger said: 'For reasons that are easy to see, I would have most liked to publish the book in Cuba, but this possibility was not open to me ... The book would only have been constructive in the Cuban context, but not in my own.'[70] The regret haunting this statement speaks to the understood limits of art to effect change, whether due to active censorship, media and political influence, or readership. The statement itself highlights that multiple subjectivities are also multiply intersubjective.

The remembrance of the first visit is personally specific and the tension between the past lived as ideal then and the past seen as dystopia now drives the narrative. The 1970s narrator recalls his then younger self in his struggles to write of the Cuban revolution there and the chaos elsewhere.

We had tried to get lost and to find something
on this tropical island, where the grass grew
over ancient Cadillac wrecks. The rum had gone,
the bananas had vanished, but we
were looking for something else –
hard to say what it really was –
but we could not find it
in this tiny New World
eagerly discussing sugar,
liberation, and a future abounding
In light bulbs, milk cows, brand-new machines.
There, where the young *mulattas*
cradling their automatic rifles
smiled at me at the street corners, at me
or at someone else, while I worked
and worked on *The Sinking of the Titanic*.
It was so hot at night, I couldn't sleep.
Young I was not – What does it mean, young,
I lived by the sea – but nearly ten years
younger than now, and pale with zeal.
[author's note: I have retranslated the nine preceding lines]
It must have happened in June, no,
it was April, shortly before Easter,
we took a walk down the Rampa,
it was past midnight, Maria Alexandrovna
looked at me, her eyes shining with rage,
Heberto Padilla smoked a cigar,
he had not yet gone to prison, but who
remembers him now, a lost man,
a lost friend, Padilla, and a deserter
from Germany shaking with shapeless laughter,
he too went to prison, but that was later,
and now he is here again, back home, boozing
and doing research in the interest of the nation,
and it is odd that I still remember him.
There is not too much that I have forgotten.
We talked and jabbered away in a medley

of Spanish, German and Russian
about the terrible sugar harvest
of the Ten Million Tons – nowadays
nobody mentions it anymore, of course,
Damn the sugar! I came here as a tourist!
the deserter howled, and then he quoted
Horkheimer – Horkheimer of all people,
in Havana! We spoke of Stalin, too,
and of Dante, I cannot imagine why,
cutting cane was not Dante's line.[71]

The extra-national influence is pronounced, the focus studiedly ego-centric. The classic canto form of the 1970s poem articulates with European more than Cuban or internationalist traditions and debates. The mention of Dante recalls Peter Weiss in that *Die Ermittlung* references the *Divine Comedy*. From the retrospective vantage point of this extant version of *Untergang*, Cuba is not the precarious panacea of *Das Verhör* radically shaped by island citizens. Instead, either Cuban artists and intellectuals play little role in the society, or their roles are not visible to the German eye. The character of Heberto Padilla introduced in these lines is uninspiring and evidences no interest in problems of art and politics, rather here his place 'Out of the Game' entails nothing more than puffing a cigar of an evening. Padilla's titular work (*Fuera del Juego*, 1968) came under intense scrutiny for its suggestion that critical artists had no place in the revolution; *Untergang*'s representation of the Cuban poet elides this debate, offering no rationale for Padilla's disaffected position prior to his imprisonment. While this silence may have had some practical considerations for Padilla himself, it narrates this moment of early solidarity as a time of Cuban inaction.

In contrast to the absent and impotent Cuban intellectuals, the visitor struggled to engage with the revolution by capturing it in writing. Yet, from the retrospective of the extant poem, circumscribed and disparate subjectivities engendered many troubles. For instance, the personal tunnel vision of the narrator was trained solely on his own acquaintances and the tropical heat of the urban revolution. The German metonymized his new Cuba as the young, female, creole militia standing at street corners with rifles rather than johns or babies on their arms. The desire of this redefined femininity roamed on their terms and the zealot yearned to be interpolated into more intense communication with the revolution. Was it his dedication to their smiles or to his work that raised the ire of the character's wife, Maria Alexandrovna? The sexualized exchange with Cuba in the form of these young women seemed to upset the bourgeois bonds between the German and the Russian.

According to the extant *Untergang*, not only did the Cuban revolution challenge Northern subjectivities, these turn out to have challenged the revolution. The melange of Northern characters saw Cuba personally; their 1960s concern with the sugar harvest was but trendy chit-chat. The knowledgeable individual reader may fill in the blanks and recognize that such talk did not ameliorate the disastrous effects of the campaign. Such a reader might consider that foreign subjectivities were at play here in another way as well by driving the fixed national policy that produced the harvest as inadequate. Ten million tons made sense within Soviet demands for trade-and-export orientation. *Untergang* itself does not provide such context directly. Rather it focuses on the personal and intimates its vicissitudes with such glimpses, while offering subjectivity as the only reality and, elsewhere in the text, the lesser malevolence.

The clearest embodiment of the limitations of the personal is the figure of the 'German deserter.' Günter Maschke was part of the Cuban landscape during Enzensberger's personal visit and used *Stalinismo tropical* to describe Cuba in *Kursbuch* and elsewhere.[72] The SDS youth had left the FRG to resist military service. A member of the FRG communist party, he helped organize extra-parliamentary opposition in Vienna until his arrest due to anti–Vietnam War protests. Deportation to the Federal Republic would have meant trial as a deserter and Maschke chose exile in Cuba instead. His stay from the beginning of 1968 to the end of 1969 concluded with his arrest and deportation by Cuban officials in response to his support of Heberto Padilla, support that expressed his increasing scepticism towards the Cuban system.[73] Back in the FRG, he served thirteen months for draft resistance and then settled in Frankfurt.[74] As a writer and lecturer, Maschke has become increasingly nationalistic, supportive of the German government, and critical of his former Caribbean refuge.

Castro's biting criticism of Western left intellectuals such as Enzensberger resonates here as the poem deflects Castro's charge onto this dogmatic, narcissistic visitor and his 'misshapen' expressions. Maschke's criticism of Cuba had already found a venue in Enzensberger's *Kursbuch* issues, and Enzensberger's essay on revolutionary tourism that followed Maschke's 1972 essay suggests scepticism towards it. *Untergang* furthers this critique in its portrayal of Maschke as self-proclaimed revolutionary tourist, a role that absolves him of attending to topical, material concerns on the island. The imported theories of the culture industry and the negative dialectic of capitalist mass culture obscure understandings of this Southern constellation whose problems and potentials arise from underdevelopment. The tension between North and South is represented here as an individual tale of misguided beliefs and inappropriate actions.

The narrative strategy does gesture towards one larger issue by means of an important distinction between individual circumstances that it does not make. It does not distinguish between Maschke's and Padilla's prison terms. This seems surprising. Maschke is not represented as a sympathetic character. Nor would popular opinion have rehabilitated him; although his Cuba essay was influential, Western leftists increasingly disparaged him as a political turncoat. In contrast, the character of the 'lost friend' is sympathetic despite his apathy. Many were supportive of Padilla's activities as a critical poet in Cuba. What does it mean that the poem does not differentiate between the circumstances of a Maschke, whose credentials were so questionable, and those of a Padilla, the idealistic colleague to whom Enzensberger dedicated *Das Verhör*? By presenting these characters so differently, yet paralleling their sentencing, the poem emphasizes that they both suffer under governmental control. The point and the problem is that neither the FRG nor the Cuban state tolerates resistance from its citizens, regardless of what form that state or the resistance takes.

Both systems of state control are destructive; does the poem distinguish between the results? Yes, and this difference also makes a point. Maschke's actions subsequent to his incarceration follow immediately upon its description. This placement suggests that his 'research in the interest of the nation'[75] and his excessive drinking result from his prison experience. It gestures towards the effects of industrialized systems of discipline on political belief structures in a real-existing democracy that was combating political dissent through tactics such as isolation cells. In contrast, the poem does not speculate on Cuban measures or on Padilla's public self-criticism after his imprisonment. Rather, only his artistic censorship is mentioned. By means of this distinction, the poem speaks more loudly against German state power and differentiates the two situations. According to *Untergang*'s description of its first version, written at the time of *Berliner Gemeinplätze*, *Das Verhör*, and *Freisprüche*, this early iteration also treats the tensions between citizen and state power. It questions critical and affirmative expression in a Manichean world of civil disobedience against structural violence. For all of the described difference between the standpoint of the 1960s version and the multiple perspectives of the 1970s work, both share concern over the limits of structural power, whether in a real-existing capitalist-democratic-nationalist state or a real-existing socialist-nationalist state.

This is one of the few nodes at which their perspectives meet. Generally speaking, the late 1960s world that engendered the first poem is radically different from the late 1970s world of the primary narrator. The 1970s situation that the narrative voice also describes calls the strategies of the earlier period into question. Not only does the underdeveloped nation lack even light bulbs (those symbols of socialist cooperation in *Und deine Liebe auch*), the 1960s tenets seem to have been dangerously misguided. The narrator distances himself from this idealistic historical moment in which activists, artists, and texts seemed to describe truth and in which exposure to such truth seemed to have had the potential to spark mass conversion. In the 1970s poem, signifiers are multiplied in a striking shift from Enzensberger's earlier work. This stylistic change marked scepticism of German and Cuban-Soviet socialist realism. Breaking with the Lukacsian formula for Brechtian didacticism, the symbolically rich and multiply layered epic invites readers to help create meanings. The poem counters rhetorics of abstract, univocal logic that were seen to stifle dissent. This allusive work offers readers a pedagogical playground without a singular trajectory.

Untergang's embrace of multiplicity over univocality means a rejection of global revolutionary change. Although Cuba itself continued to foment global radicalism, this new narrative strategy favours local reformism. Turning from the transnational, it turned towards a factionalized FRG. The reformist approach encouraged readers to participate in newly popular methods for engendering political change through critique of ideology. The questions the poem suggests – Has engaged literature entrenched radical groups without moving the masses? Can mass education unseat the culture industry? – also expressed Enzensberger's own questions at the time. While critics have noted his fascination with catastrophe and violence,[76] the public intellectual distanced himself from the concrete violence of groups such as the RAF early on.[77] Enzensberger's *Untergang* works through what it casts as a lost utopia to offer assessment tools for the contemporary crisis. In doing so, it bemoans Cuba's former status as utopia that has led to its 1970s categorization as a place just like everyplace else.

The differences in the division of power and political camps can be gleaned through *Untergang*'s description of the subjective realities for Northern sympathizers. The narrator writes:

> Nobody ever gave a thought to Doom then,
> not even in Berlin, which had outlived
> its end long ago. The island of Cuba
> did not reel beneath our feet. It seemed to us
> as if something were close at hand,
> something for us to invent. We did not know
> that the party had finished long ago,
> and that all that was left was a matter
> to be dealt with by the man from the World Bank
> and the comrade from State Security,
> exactly like back home and in any other place.[78]

As in Castro's metaphor, here Cuba seems a stable element of a hopeful and productive future distinct from the reeling Titanic. In the fictional world of the first poem, Cuba represents that which is opposed to the cruise vessel. The idealistic author of this early, now missing text sought with his writing to further the sinking of the ruling class, that object of critique familiar from *Das Verhör*. The visitors to Cuba fancy themselves on firm ground; they are participants in the struggle for the new future. This first *Untergang* participates in a hopeful experiment whose epicentre is Cuba.

In its rewriting of the text and context of its putative first draft, *Untergang* highlights the failure of the island utopias of Cuba and Berlin. As embodied fantasy, Cuba is the destructive quintessence of monolithic meaning. Understood by its progressive sympathizers as static, it wreaks destruction as it collides with material shifts. Much scholarship has wrestled with interpreting the poetic images of the Titanic and the iceberg. These multifaceted metaphors are also Cuba and the multifaceted metaphor of Cuba are they. Significant as well is that under the interpretive weight of these significations, Cuba itself cannot change according to its own needs and desires. This real-existing nation will come to symbolize the defeatist dystopianism that disillusioned visitors see in it. The poem suggests that reading in multiple ways offers an alternative to these perilous conundrums.

Despite its perspective that embraces difference, the 1970s narrative develops a particular notion of unity. While in earlier texts, Northern and Southern protagonists were pitted against each other (whether the

Northerners knew it or not), this narrative redraws the lines of global power. On the *Untergang*'s Titanic, Northern travellers retain their
oppressive position relative to those of the South even during crisis,
yet nevertheless their mutual circumstances are so closely linked that
all lose in the sinking. This 'one world' metaphor foreshadows Enzensberger's later work on environmental destruction.

This interdependence alters the valence of the descent. In this new
understanding, the catastrophe will not enable that revolutionary
rebirth that had been written for in the 1960s. Instead, the event is but
a radical shift into chaos. That dinner on board will continue rather
than end is not a misfortune but a mercy because there is no paradise
on the other side. Moreover, in the world of this *Untergang*, the bourgeois narrative voice depicts how monumental changes harm Southern inhabitants the most. This assessment is quite different from that of
Northern thinkers who favoured revolution as effective assistance for
the South. Unlike in texts such as *Das Verhör*, moreover, the state is not
a controlling force here. Instead, market-based structures engender the
demise of the Titanic: inequitable distribution of wealth, fetishistic over-
consumption, technophilia, and the hegemony of media discourses that
deify the hubristic project that is modern life. There is no clear enemy in
this constellation. This epic tale that invites subjective and multivalent
engagement through the perspective of a commonly fated, interconnected world also forecloses the possibility for its radical improvement.

Conclusion

German authors who were critical of their own nations and supported
solidarity with Cuba were confronted with a paradox. A turn away from
political violence also meant a turn away from the belief in the possibility of radical change in their own countries. Thus, the rejection of
violence was also expressed deep disillusionment with contemporary
realities and future developments. As a nation practicing political reor-
ganization on a large scale, Cuba embodied these hopes and expressed
this shift. After Northern malcontents had styled the Caribbean polity
an angel in fatigues, German disillusionment grew as Cuba developed
within the constraints of global power dynamics. Texts such as *Guevara* and *Untergang* interrogate the prescriptiveness of utopian visions.
Braun's work offers a continued search for a better world. Enzensberger's suggests retreat into individualism and individual survival.

Identification was also a driving force in the creative process of Braun and Enzensberger. In each case the writer fantasizes the artist into the role of revolutionary for whom his praxis becomes his art. In *Guevara*, Braun identifies with the revolutionary for whom there is no place in the brittle system, yet who pushes leaders towards a possible better future. In his notes to his block print illustrator, published in the hardback edition, Braun explicitly parallels Guevara's life as a revolutionary with the life of a revolutionary artist: 'I hope … you can / must live like Che, with the knife / of language cutting his case open to the bones of this century.'[79] Similarly, Enzensberger's introduction to *Das Verhör* connects violence to artistic struggle by paralleling language and the court trial to armed combat: 'As The Inquiry takes its course, in the swamps of the Zapata peninsula two hundred and fifty kilometers from the doors of the theater the armed struggle continues. The same truth is fought for here as there. The discursive dialogue in front of the microphone continues another type of encounter that at the same hour is carried out with the machine gun. The weapons of critique take to their conclusion what the critique of weapons has begun. Every word that falls here can be measured by a material experience. From it The Inquiry draws energy, it marks every sentence and every gesture.'[80] Not only does this quote emphasize the purported transfer of the armed struggle into the war of words, but it rhetorically collapses the court and the theatre proceedings. The phrase 'Das Verhör' (the inquiry) refers most obviously to the play, yet the use of the shortened version of the name allows the title to reference the court inquiry itself. Although the Germanies (where *Das Verhör von Habana* was performed) were much further from the site of battle than Cuba's Chaplin Theater in which hearings took place, the use of the term theatre recalls the FRG performance venues. The author becomes a virtual soldier at the beachhead. As I hope to demonstrate in the next chapter, such identification was critical among young audiences in the GDR and the FRG as well.

Chapter Five

Touring Revolution and Resistance:
Tamara Bunke and Che Guevara

In 1961, the German Democratic Republic closed its Western border. In 1962, the Federal Republic of Germany's first commercial aircraft carrying mass tourists landed on the tropical island of Mallorca.[1] GDR and FRG travel and tourism would remain as radically different as their ongoing projects of post-1945 nation building.

In 1967, the United Nations inaugurated the Year of International Travel under the slogan 'Tourism – Passport to Freedom.'[2] That same year, East German/Argentinean/Cuban Tamara Bunke and Argentinean/Cuban Ernesto 'Che' Guevara were killed in the Andes jungle by U.S. and Bolivian forces. They were part of an international group whose long-term, international travel was necessitated by their goal of fomenting populist revolution throughout Latin America. The fame of these two figures became as international as their project had been. In the GDR and the FRG, Tamara and Che were politically troublesome personages who simultaneously served as role models for many young people. German constructions of these extra-national heroes were influenced by and intervened in state, social, and citizen aspirations for German nation and national identity, particularly as these interpretations related to the gendered notions of international travel and tourism.

Che Guevara and Tamara Bunke in the GDR

It is well known that the GDR government worked to produce socialist citizens. This aim materialized diversely: in legislation, education programs, in canonical culture. So too the GDR wrought its heroes. By definition, the personal goals of these exemplars furthered social aims; they were anti-fascists, 'heroes of the construction of the new society'

(*Helden des Aufbaus*), 'heroes of work' (*Helden der Arbeit*). This notion of man-furthering-society contrasted with the man-versus-society schema more common in the West. Through these heroes, citizens were to come to identify with the state with which these role models were so closely aligned. It was particularly crucial that this theory function in practice among the youth, as the first generation raised under socialism was to prove the success of the socialist experiment. Moreover, labour short-ages made the nation dependent on these new workers. The 1963 Polit-buro Youth Communiqué voiced an attitude of pragmatism, hope, and concern that remained relatively constant,[3] although practices to fur-ther this aim shifted extensively. Slogans linked the next generation to the GDR project: 'trust and responsibility to the youth' and 'mould the face of tomorrow's society through the education and self-education of today's youth.'[4] Heroes were to further this connection. Yet, para-doxically, precisely because orthodox socialist heroes embodied the establishment, they were ineffectual in reaching the disaffected; youth critical of the GDR accepted both their nation and their nation's heroes half-heartedly.

In contrast to most GDR heroes, Che Guevara and Tamara Bunke were popular among young people. On into the 1980s, Guevara in particular embodied the GDR dispute around socialism in the global South. Even the programmatic *Jugendlexikon* attests to this debate. This pedagogi-cal reference for young people states seemingly paradoxically both that national liberation movements reject 'peaceful coexistence' and that the new nations of Asia, Africa, and Latin America support this very policy.[5] Official and popular attitudes towards third-world struggle spoke to less apparent tensions as well. The contemporary international heroes Che and Tania at once personified and challenged multiple orthodox GDR socialist views; they spoke to non-conformist desires of youth for themselves and their nation. GDR officials exploited this rebellious mystique to draw youth into their socialist project while simultaneously seeking to shape these heroes in ways that furthered the GDR's agenda.

GDR depictions of Che Guevara are part of the fabric of interna-tional relations between the Democratic Republic, Cuba, and the Soviet Union. Guevara's outspoken critique of what he saw as the Soviet Union's reformist communism, his support of China's Maoist revolu-tionary communism, and his aim of inciting revolution in the South were all anathema to the Soviets and by extension to the GDR. Gue-vara's revolutionary theory and praxis had the potential to unsettle the international peaceful coexistence supported by the Soviet bloc, as well as to encourage populist dissent. As I have shown in my discussion of the West Berlin anti-authoritarians, the Western bloc considered Guevara threatening for similar reasons.

Despite these concerns, the GDR eventually found it necessary to construct a programmatic version of Guevara that could supplant narratives from the West that were entering their youth culture by the late 1960s.[6] Although this decision responded to international interest in Che, officials were particularly concerned with their direct competitor ˎacross the Wall. GDR silence on a topic that was popular in the FRG could also quickly be labelled censorship. Moreover, without domestic interpretations, interest in Guevara encouraged identification with the bourgeois FRG youth movement and even with the U.S. youth movement.

The Strawberry Statement (*Blutige Erdbeeren*), a U.S. production that was popular in the FRG and that achieved cult status in the GDR, exemplifies this phenomenon of identification.[7] In this feature film about a 1960s student uprising, images of Guevara were aligned with what GDR critics saw as *Revoluzzertum* (pseudo-revolutionary activity) and sexual conquest, associations inappropriate for a GDR socialist hero. Moreover, the film links Guevara to Mao, whose call for immediate, populist revolution was unacceptable for GDR officials. Feuilletons approved of the film nevertheless because it treated popular protest against the U.S. system and because it could be read as demonstrating that the student movement failed because of its lack of a more structured socialism. Yet, *Blutige Erdbeeren* increasingly inspired youth protest, with 1980s GDR teenagers re-enacting its representations of civil disobedience during public gatherings such as dances and film screenings.[8] This tension between official and popular reception brings home the difficulties involved in allowing the West sole proprietorship over cultural icons such as Che.

The relationships between Cuba and the Soviet Union also influenced GDR reception of Guevara. As sketched previously, by the early 1970s, beset with political and economic struggles, Cuba turned to Soviet-style organization and ties with the USSR were strengthened. These changes impacted the GDR's reception of Cuba and Guevara. In 1969 and 1975, Cuba and the Soviet Union made important attempts to find a mutually acceptable reading of Guevara. So, for instance, the lecturer in scientific communism (*Dozent für wissenschaftlichen Kommunismus*) at the Institute for Marxist Leninism of the Central Committee of the SED (*Institut für Marxismus Leninismus ZK der SED*), Kurt Müller, quotes an official

Soviet overview of the Latin American situation and Guevara in his report urging a GDR edition of *The Bolivian Diary*: 'the blood of thousands of Latin Americans [flowed] ... It is the blood of communists and fighters of different viewpoints, symbolized today by the name of that great Argentinean, Cuban and Latin American – Ernesto Che Guevara.[9] In the first half of the 1970s, with such cultural pressures, increased political and economic interest in Cuba, and Guevara's partial rehabilitation in the Soviet sphere, a well-tempered GDR representation of Guevara was brought into its cultural life.

The Democratic Republic often limited public knowledge of important but politically ambivalent personages by disseminating texts about them, rather than their original writings. Che is a good example. Recall that until this point solely Guevara's *Der Partisanenkrieg* had been published in the GDR. In early 1973, the official youth organization Freie Deutsche Jugend (FDJ) first ran a series on Guevara in *Forum: Zeitung der Studenten und der jungen Intelligenz* (Forum: Newspaper of Students and Young Intelligentsia). The series presents a hero who holds no anarchist, Trotzkist, or Maoist tendencies, who is pro-Soviet, and who sees armed revolution as one possible means to an end of national liberation from U.S. imperialism.[10] The most significant GDR text on Guevara is the biography by Josef Lawrezki published in the Soviet Union in 1972, which was translated and published by the FDJ publishing house *Verlag Neues Leben* in 1974. That this edition was printed under license of the FRG Verlag Marxistische Blätter interestingly demonstrates the porosity of national boundaries, official positions notwithstanding.

The biography is both a marker and consolidator of the GDR's official acceptance of Guevara. The publishing house reader Heinz Schnura's 1973 report on this edition echoes the official position on the problems and potentials of Guevara as youth role model: 'Che Guevara's deeds served as a point of discussion for the different streams in the international worker- and youth-movement, especially his theories about the partisan war. At times he was honoured like a saint. The 'left' youth movement carried his images in the demonstrations, and posters with his portrait were to be found everywhere in the rooms of young people. His figure is also known among us. He was in the GDR twice.'[11]

Assessments such as this one helped to create a Guevara appropriate for the GDR. The report links him to socialist organizations that are part of the Soviet tradition rather than to independent, nationalist revolutionary movements of which the Soviets did not approve. A reference to *Der Partisanenkrieg* underscores this link as well because by the 1970s, the Soviet Union completely endorsed the Cuban revolution. Schnura emphasizes Guevara's place in international youth culture, the misguided Western reception of him, and the historical links between the Latin American revolutionary and the GDR, all of which suggest that it was necessary to counter Western versions of Guevara. Tellingly, the text does not suggest that his ideas have opened debates about socialism in the GDR; rather, such debates seemingly occur solely under conditions of nascent socialism. In these ways the report speaks for adding an acceptably nuanced version of the troublesome hero to the GDR catalogue.

Access to Guevara's writings remained circumscribed. *Episoden aus dem Revolutionskrieg* was licensed from Reclam and published in 1981 and the Bolivian diary was not made available until 1987.[12] Even during this period of relative political openness, the reviewers who argued for publication of the latter resorted to emphasizing the GDR-appropriate figure of the Lawrezki biography. The reports also de-emphasized Guevara's contemporary relevance by casting the diaries as artefacts of a past historical moment and a defunct socialist strategy.[13] This publishing history demonstrates that Guevara remained a difficult figure for the GDR.

In addition to being depicted as a programmatic hero in these officially sanctioned narratives, the attractive, masculine figure also functioned as an iconic hero for GDR youth. Although, Alberto 'Korda' Díaz Gutiérrez's well-known 1960 photographic image 'Guerrillero Heroico' remained less acceptable in the GDR than in the FRG, it became part of youth culture on both sides of the Wall. Playwright Heiner Müller's comments in the West German popular magazine *Der Spiegel* highlight the diffuse resistance to official GDR culture that this image expressed.[14] Singer-songwriter Wolf Biermann's *Comandante Che Guevara* also found an audience in both Germanies.[15] His ballad is based on Cuban composer Carlos Puebla's *Hasta Siempre, Comandante* (1965), which this 'singer of the revolution' composed in response to Guevara's departure from Cuba for Congo and Bolivia. Biermann's lyrics are potentially subversive, yet through their focus on imagery they remain largely inexplicit; the popularity of the song across the political spectrum suggests that these lyrics were interpreted variously. The refrain restates the themes of the Spanish original, remaining general in its praise of the political figure through subjective assessment of his character traits. The direct, informal address and the simple rhyme scheme heighten the affective impact: 'What remains is what was good and clear: / That

one always saw you / And saw love, hate, but never fear / Comandante Che Guevara.' In contrast, stanza two suggests an allegorical critique of GDR leadership: 'And you did not become a big shot [*Bonze*]
/ no bigwig [*hohes Tier*] that has his eyes on money / and played the
hero from behind the desk / in impeccable uniform with old medals.'
Stanzas one, three, and four eschew such explicit analysis in favour of
iconizing Guevara as a catalyst for popular struggle. Indeed, stanzas
three and four also draw Guevara away from a more specifically Cuba-
aligned narrative through socialist and religious reference to man not
living by bread alone (*Ja, gerade die Armen dieser Erde, die brauchen mehr
als zu fressen ... das aus Menschen Menschen werden*) and by avoiding
mention of the state leader Fidel, who in the original is aligned with the
people. The last stanza reads: 'The red star on the jacket / the cigar in
the black beard / Jesus Christ with the gun – So your image leads us to
the attack.'[16] Such general, associative representations invite individualized interpretations.

While GDR officials made a virtue of necessity by functionalizing
the legendary Guevara, the opportunity offered by the lesser known
Tamara Bunke was only gradually understood. Tamara's biography
deeply impacted her reception in the GDR and bears repeating here.
Born of German and Russian communist and Jewish parents in exile in
Argentina, a teenaged Heidi Tamara Bunke Bider moved with her family to the Democratic Republic in 1952. As communists who had been
involved in the resistance during and after the War, Nadja and Erich
Bunke gradually, then quickly, gained social positioning; Erich Bunke
also became the secretary of the Cuban Solidarity Committee. The energetic, outspoken Tamara enthusiastically participated in the Marxist-
Leninist program of the new nation through the FDJ and through sports
such as horseback riding and shooting. She was involved in exchange
between Spanish-speaking countries and the GDR, especially in her
capacity as a translator for Latin American delegations. As a teenager,
she convinced officials to allow her to return to her country of birth
and work there for the socialist cause. During the long preparation
period, Bunke instead took an opportunity to fly to Cuba with a group
of Cuban dancers between the founding of revolutionary Cuba in January 1959 and the Berlin Wall's construction in August 1961. GDR government documents and correspondences corroborate that once there
she developed close ties with the Cuban security services and took up
contact with GDR officials.[17] By 1963, Tamara (Tania) Bunke received
orders, probably from Che Guevara whom she had met previously in

the GDR, to train as an agent, a task that involved extended stays in many Western countries. Afterwards, she went undercover in Bolivia, gathering relevant information and otherwise preparing for the arrival of Guevara's cadre. In 1967, Bunke began manoeuvres with them in the jungle and was killed several months prior to the demise of the fighting force.

The well-informed reader may here ask whether Bunke did undercover work for the Cubans, the GDR, and/or the Soviets, especially while working with Guevara in Bolivia. Western reception has focused on this question, usually in conjunction with speculations about Tamara's sexual practices. I will consider the significance of this conflation below. To date these questions about Tamara cannot be definitively answered. This is in part due to the efforts of Bunke's mother, Nadja Bunke, who until her death in 2003 tirelessly and successfully litigated those who suggested that Tamara had such liaisons. In part it is because the post-1989 destruction of Stasi files included many on Bolivia and Cuba and the archival documents currently available are somewhat vague.[18] Ulises Estrada's, Gerd Koenen's, and Ines Langelüddecke's extensively researched scholarship have recently added to the picture, although Koenen's takes some liberties in the service of colourful storytelling.[19] What is clear is that Tamara Bunke's life trajectory did not completely fit the model of a programmatic, fully developed socialist.[20]

For this reason, the GDR state at first treated the figure of Tamara Bunke cautiously. At the mourning ceremony held for her in Berlin in December 1967, the first public event to thematize her life and her death on foreign soil, the keynote speaker, the secretary of the Central Committee (ZK) of the FDJ, Frank Bochow, did not mention her post-Cuba activities.[21] This omission allowed him to avoid publicly acknowledging politically (un)orthodox aspects of Tamara's biography. His reticence was influenced by international security considerations and also reflected the difficulties that GDR officials had in deciding whether and how to craft Bunke into an appropriate hero.[22]

By the early 1970s, this official stance towards Tamara Bunke changed for three primary reasons. One was the effort of Tamara's mother, Nadja Bunke. This well-connected socialist with an impeccable anti-fascist record worked tirelessly to bring her daughter into the GDR public sphere as a heroine on Nadja's terms. It was Nadja Bunke, for instance, who first publicized the site and cause of Tamara's death in a newspaper obituary, to the surprise of some in the GDR government and with the unofficial support of others. Indeed, this announcement helped engender the mourning ceremony. Nadja Bunke, with the particular help of former FDJ functionary Werner Lamberz who knew and liked Tamara, also convinced the GDR newspaper *junge Welt* to make good on its perhaps half-hearted offer to write a series on Tamara Bunke, which the newspaper finally published in 1969. GDR officials were also swayed by Nadja Bunke's argument that the mainstream West press had already come out with several articles, some quite sensationalist, on Tamara Bunke, and that more progressive sources particularly in Latin America, as well as the United States, were reporting on her.[23] As with the case of Guevara, functionaries became convinced that further silence would have jeopardized the GDR's influence on the legend of Tania.

Yet by the early 1970s, Nadja Bunke's efforts also coincided with national interests. Ties between the GDR and Cuba were strengthening, encouraged by the tighter Soviet-Cuban relationship and the new First Secretary Erich Honecker's interest in the island.[24] Steps were therefore undertaken to bring Cuba closer to the hearts and minds of the GDR people. In 1972 and 1974, respectively, Castro and Honecker first paid each other effusive and well-publicized state visits. The Cuban leader found lasting favour among many German citizens, who were impressed by this imposing figure in informal fatigues who demonstrated his interest in their daily lives by exploring on his own and peppering them with questions.[25] A luxurious, large-format, coffee-table volume and newsreels documenting Honecker's trip to Cuba advertised it in the GDR.[26] Youth, educational, and work exchanges between the countries were increased. A GDR/Cuban heroine such as Tamara Bunke fit well into this new foreign policy agenda.

Thirdly, the 1970s saw an increased demand for effective youth heroes. Interest in the anti-capitalist and anti-fascist heroes who had fought in the Russian revolution and the First and Second World Wars waned as these events faded into the past. Heroes of socialist labour always held somewhat less of an attraction. Champions of technological advancement were more engaging, but also increasingly encouraged an unflattering comparison of the scientific advancements of the socialist and capitalist spheres. Furthermore, cosmonauts such as Juri Galgarin, Walentina Tereschkowa, and Sigmund Jähn, as well as sports heroes such as 'Täve' Schur and Toni Sailor, although popular, were squeaky clean to a fault.[27] Figures such as Che Guevara, in contrast, were intriguing insofar as the incompatibility of their political goals and activities with the goals and activities of the GDR and the Soviet bloc could be elided. In this context, the life of Tamara Bunke increasingly seemed appropriate as a basis upon which to construct a heroic figure. A letter to Comrade Markowski of the Political Agitation Section of the SED dated 1 August 1968 states: 'The material [about Tamara Bunke (probably garnered from or sent by Nadja Bunke)] contains a wealth of possibilities that, correctly worked up and based on a clear, political line and message that adheres to the politics of our party, can be used very well for the patriotic and ~~revolutionary~~ class-oriented [sic] upbringing of our youth.'[28] The replacement of the word 'revolutionary' with 'class-oriented' in this positive assessment of the relevance of the heroine metonymizes the translation necessary for the GDR context.

These factors paved the way for Tania the Guerrilla to emerge into the GDR public eye; this entrance was transnationally shaped. While for the Cubans, Tania was primarily a female revolutionary with internationalist goals, the Germans were intrigued by Tania's GDR connections.[29] By 1968, the Cuban journalists Marta Rojas and Mirta Rodríguez Calderón, with the support of the Federation of Cuban Women and the Cuban Communist Party, planned a special issue for the journal *Mujeres* (Women) in celebration of the one year anniversary of Tamara's death. Nadja and Erich were interviewed in the GDR by the wife of the Cuban ambassador and were then invited to Cuba. The project developed into a book and by 1970 Wolfgang Kohlhaase and Konrad Wolf, already important DEFA filmmakers, grew interested in the story. They immediately asked Nadja to translate large sections of the book for a film project.[30] However, neither the GDR government nor the Party actively supported the project and the film was never produced.[31] At first there were no plans to publish Nadja's translation, called *Tania La Guerrillera*, after the titular Cuban text; indeed, DEFA was to have the exclusive rights. Nadja was certainly involved in altering this decision in order to disseminate what she saw as the one unique and true depiction of her daughter among a German readership.[32] It seems that after altercations with Nadja Bunke about his draft introduction to her translation, the well-known writer Eberhard Panitz was commissioned by Werner Lamberz to write another book on Tania, *Der Weg zum Rio Grande*. This shorter, more accessible text was meant as a pedagogical tool that would bring the tale close to GDR youth on GDR terms.[33] Tamara had been Panitz's tour guide on his visit to Cuba to gather material for another project, and Panitz also made extensive use of Nadja's translation. As was the case with nearly all of the works about her daughter, Nadja Bunke objected heartily to Panitz's biographical narrative and took her complaints to the highest levels.[34] These three sources – the thirteen-part *junge Welt* newspaper series and the two books – were the significant public sources of information about Tamara Bunke's life and death available in the GDR.[35]

Tamara Bunke was constructed as a strong-willed, deeply socialist youth who undertook adventurous activities in politically semi-non-aligned or neutral states. According to this narrative, the hero channelled her boundless passion and energy into the fulfilment of socialist goals of international significance; every one of her actions was a means to a socialist end. The specificity of her dramatic life is downplayed, while her attributes and skill set were to be translated into the GDR context and emulated by the youth. A celebratory text, 'Tamara Bunke,' from the factory school in Pulsnitz explains how the hero should function for its students: '[The] life and fate of Tamara Bunke are extraordinary and not repeatable. Why then should precisely Tamara be a model and example for us? Because Tamara as a personality possessed characteristics and behaviours that are valuable and exemplary to a high degree ... Because Tamara modeled for us that also a young and modern person of our times can be many things: passionate and energetic as Communist and Revolutionary.'[36]

As this public statement underscores, officially, Tamara Bunke had value precisely to the extent that a translation of her specific life to that of an exemplary programmatic GDR hero was possible. She was to function as a model for the building of the socialist nation through hard work, obedience to authority, and self-discipline. As the West German writer Cordt Schnibben puts it: 'The SED and the FDJ had made a state-sanctioned Ulrike Meinhof from the corpse, a noble literary heroine, a female revolutionary to idolize, but not to copy in any way. Be like Tania, but don't dream, don't run away and don't run around in the jungle.'[37] Unofficially, it was precisely the ruptures in this programmatic narrative that enabled Bunke's effectiveness as a hero for youths.

A completely programmatic hero would no doubt have been doomed to neglect alongside so many others. Tamara, however, was popular. In a society in which the membership of an organization often influenced its naming, more than 40 GDR schools, brigades, youth groups, and other organizations bore her name by 1980.[38] Nadja Bunke's records indicate that there were more than 200 by 1989.[39] In informal interviews, Eastern German readers, teachers, librarians, authors, and former FDJ functionaries emphasized that inaugurations employing more marginal public figures such as Tamara Bunke more frequently stemmed from popu-

lar initiative than christenings involving mainstream figures such as
Marx or Thälmann. They also believe that Tania was an important figure for many citizens. Moreover, the two biographies were bestsellers,
although they were not required reading.[40] Why?

A prime reason is their representation of a symbolically peripatetic
lifestyle. GDR cultural production has long been understood as a com-
pensatory public sphere and a substitute for de facto emigration;[41] its
relation to *Reiselust* (the desire to travel without a particular political or
social cause) has seldom been considered. GDR officials and scholars
often explained the popularity of travelogues as the desire for knowledge about the world.[42] Post 1989, Eastern German researchers suggest
that they allowed vicarious travel.[43] Film scholars believe that much
DEFA film functioned similarly.[44] The public read officially sanctioned
narratives, and they wandered between the lines.

The GDR system could not and did not sate the Reiselust of its citizens. For instance, in a 1970 comparative study, GDR students ranked
travel third in a list of interests, a score nearly four times higher than
the FRG ranking.[45] Although the rubric was surely variously interpreted, this statistic points to a fascination with touring. Such desires
were not philosophically or pragmatically tenable. The official stance
contended that in a non-alienated society, free time was solely recreational, a recovery rather than an escape from work; recreational travel
was even more superfluous. Moreover, tourist mentalities endangered
the existing social structure because they valued spontaneity, mobility, adventure, and pleasure over a work ethic shaped by order, thrifti-
ness, and self-discipline.[46] Touring threatened to focus citizen interest
beyond national goals and boundaries and energies on personal enjoyment rather than social betterment. Finally, travel was a heavy public
expense. The unfavourable currency-exchange rate made international
travel particularly costly. Even visits between socialist countries were
difficult, not only due to restrictive border regulations, but also due to
lack of infrastructure because the goods and services not dedicated for
export were centrally distributed to meet the demands of inhabitants
rather than the desires of visitors. Travel also decreased the hours of
productive labour. Although its agenda softened gradually in response
to public demand, real-existing socialism was not conducive to tourism.

Thus, Reiselust troubled GDR national identity. The state undertook
steps to mould these desires, measures that also increased popular
acceptance of the circumscribed GDR borders. As I have demonstrated,
it cast other socialist nations as articulations of extended socialist Hei-

mat. Travel restrictions were couched as a national valour that protected citizenry from capitalist influences. Moreover, depictions of possible travel sites other than the Soviet Union and a few eastern European nations discouraged fantasies of first-hand inspection. Countries were treated largely in materialist terms emphasizing demographics, natural resources, production, and other statistics, as well as domestic and foreign policy.[47] The GDR represented poorer, socialist countries, in Latin America for example, as countries similar to the GDR in theory where life was much harder in practice.

Such packaging cast the Democratic Republic in a favourable light. In contrast to fledgling socialist nations, it was economically superior and its living standards compared quite well. Furthermore, although GDR support of these nations through trade and aid was in fact primarily pragmatic – creating foreign markets, garnering raw materials, stabilizing socialism globally, and appeasing the Soviet Union – it was presented to citizens as primarily altruistic. For instance, newspaper articles and *Die Wochenschau* television reports focused on GDR development assistance to these countries. In contrast, the Federal Republic's international policies, including development programs, were criticized as self-serving, its higher living standards enabled by such unjust practices. The GDR was cast as morally and socially superior to such capitalist nations.

The information disseminated about foreign countries was aimed at increasing popular understandings of their socio-economic concerns and geopolitical positionings, at sating interest in travelling to these countries, and at improving attitudes towards GDR life. Bolstered in their geographical rootedness (*Bodenständigkeit*), GDR citizens should not have thought of other nations as nice to visit, and they certainly should not have wanted to live there. Narratives of Bunke did not so much idealize these foreign places as mythologize social and transnational mobility.

The biographical books on Tamara, *Der Weg zum Rio Grande* and *Tania la Guerrillera*, negotiate between restrictions and desires while furthering domestically appropriate forms of internationalism. Both overtly insist on Bunke's adherence to official orders, stress her socialist credentials as enabling factor in her mobility, and de-emphasize the sensual aspects of foreign sites.[48] For instance, the official primary reader report (*Hauptgutachten*) underscores *Der Weg zum Rio Grande*'s pedagogical value: 'Here a true model for our youth has been created, they can identify with the revolutionary patriotism, the courage, the resoluteness, and the willingness to sacrifice of the partisan and female scout Tanja.'[49] However, the popularity of the texts among a broad range of youth indicate that they were read as more than tales of a programmatic hero. These narratives enabled role play beyond approved bounds and the vicarious redefinition of practices according to individual perspectives.

In offering such interpretive possibilities, these biographical texts grant mobility diverse implications. They suggest that categories rest on subjective determinations along a dialectical spectrum. The negative figure of the tourist seeking to tame and consume exotic pleasures on his or her own terms and the positive figure of the traveller visiting for constructive purposes and seeking parity in communication with the visited mutually inform. Similarly, revolutionary tourism and revolutionary travel both describe the practice of visiting revolutionary sites – classically a fledgling, socialist Russia, here revolutionary Cuba; the political convictions of the visitors determine whether the event is tourism or travel. In the Tamara texts, touring categories function, fail, overlap, and destabilize according to the motivations and positionings of the protagonists and the readers.

These works focus on the life of Tamara Bunke, whose operative name is Tania. In what follows, I will use Tamara to refer to the first-person texts written in the narrative voice of the young Bunke and Tania to refer to the first-person texts written as an undercover personality or as a guerrilla fighter. Similarly, Tamara refers to the character representing Tamara Bunke, Tania refers to the character engaged in clandestine operations. This nomenclature evokes the multiplicity of roles presented in the texts.

The narratives emphasize how Tamara's and Tania's actions fulfil her socialist duty, rather than personal adventurism. The many detailed descriptions of her activities sketch only those elements of her surroundings necessary for the reader to understand the actions performed. The description of the actions themselves is stylistically sober, relying on a continuous flow of simple subject-verb-object, largely unadorned with descriptors that would encourage affective readings by appealing to the senses. This austerity contrasts with effusiveness in descriptions of the political situation and the heroic attitudes of the young woman. The hardship to be endured and the revolutionary goals to be met are of primary import; there is little suspense despite the subject matter that would seem to lend itself to it.

Yet both texts simultaneously enable, even encourage, resistant readings. *Tania la Guerrillera* employs a pastiche of commentaries from various actors in Tamara's and Tania's life. While this strategy yields a multifaceted, socially oriented sketch of the heroine, its shifting perspectives, the breaks in narrative flow between the often short reminiscences, and the temporal shifts between periods in her life also create an aura of mystery around the main protagonist, whom the text does not fully capture. Readers are thereby enticed into further imaginings of her and her experiences abroad. This text created by the Cubans with the help of Nadja and Erich Bunke emphasizes in text and paratext the role of Tania in the continuation of armed revolutionary struggle. The direct translation by Nadja Bunke mitigates this potentially politically thorny message through another paratextual note intimating that although socialist struggle in the third world may legitimately take different shapes, Guevara's and Bunke's noble efforts were unsuccessful because they lacked popular support in Bolivia. Because the German edition is singularly additive, however, it enables readers to access and hence to support the Cuban assessment in the main text.

In contrast to the pastiche in *Tania*, *Der Weg zum Rio Grande* overtly offers a more unified narrative perspective. Drawn largely from information and documentation in the *Tania* text, this shorter, 'biographical' report alternates between the narrative voices of Eberhard Panitz, and the first-person texts by Panitz, Tamara, and Tania. The predominance of first-person texts is unusual in GDR biographies, as mentioned earlier even the Che biography published in the Soviet Union seldom employs Guevara's words. In *Der Weg*, the narrative voice of Panitz frames the first-person texts to overtly encourage a particular understanding. Moreover, the flow between the voices is rather smooth and temporally linear.

Nevertheless, the very use of these different perspectives and the resultant juxtapositions between the 'authentic' first-person texts and these narrative frames rupture the flow of the plot and encourage resistant readings. Indeed, especially the Panitz text invites readings that open up the overtly unified narrative in a manner reminiscent of the Brechtian *Lehrstück*. Audience and actors are to slip in and out of roles in these didactic plays, enabling them to experience social dynamics from various perspectives. Because these roles include various stages of socialist development, players learn to think critically about their own lives and their world.[50] *Der Weg* invites readers to slip into multiple roles of Tamara and Tania and to engage with many aspects of socialist struggle. As suggested by the popularity of the text, its invitation to role play also offers vicarious sensual pleasures and alternative lifestyles even in tension with socialist aims.

Writing fictive personalities in the first person also invites such role play in reading. Some of the first-person texts are penned from within existing identities; others inscribe identities into being. Readers encounter letters composed by Tania as one of her undercover personalities, biographies by Tania as another of her undercover personalities, and Tania's reporting in her own voice about the difficulties of travelling under false identities. As Tamara writes herself undercover, the readers are invited to read themselves undercover – imitating her performance and vicariously living as Tamara and Tania in the process. Through such role playing, readers can also more fully experience their adventurous activities, including constructing for themselves the motives and pleasures that the texts do not overtly articulate.

Such role playing furthers vicarious access to capitalist touring sites. Although in other sections of the texts, the narrative voices of the authors and the protagonists often corroborate each other, capitalist countries are described in Tania's own words; they are accessible solely via her perspective. Tania's descriptions overtly deny readers surplus pleasures by leaving the sensual pleasures of capitalism and foreign sites unarticulated. In this way, readers who do not role play are cut off from any non-programmatic potential pleasures. For example, Tamara's description of her first days in Bolivia depict tourist sites only in relation to her revolutionary aims: 'In the first days I visited, as appropriate for a tourist, museums and exhibitions; in doing so I made the acquaintance of the painter Moisés Chile Barrientos, a relative of the Bolivian president, in the archeological museum Tiahuanacu.'[51] A role-playing reader can best imagine the touring pleasures experienced, even as this possibility is overtly thwarted by the paucity of the textual description.

Reproduced photographs of Tania undercover in capitalist lands also function both to entice readers and remind them of the mobility possible under the aegis of service to state. The photos are composed as traditional tourist shots. In each, the revolutionary tourist/revolutionary traveller stands in the foreground against various backgrounds of touristic importance. Tania is the mediator between the reading viewers and these sites. Her presence justifies and thus enables their photographic reproduction while simultaneously limiting their representation. She may turn and enter the forbidden lands, having earned government sanction through her Latin American ties and her made-in-the-GDR socialist convictions. Identificatory viewings and readings thus offer the most complete access to programmatic and subversive revolutionary touring pleasures in and in-between the images and lines of these popular, pedagogical texts.

As the narrative of Tania engaged issues of travel freedom, so it brought concerns of sexuality to the fore. Travel and sexual freedoms have historically been linked, and the FRG and the GDR are no exception. The 1960s and 1970s saw a series of often disparaging or alarmed FRG studies on youth travel and sexual practices; many FRG youth found tourism attractive because of the sexual and social possibilities it offered. In the GDR, Protestantism-based sexual norms were justified through a conservative reading of socialism; many GDR youth, influenced by shifting sexual standards among their FRG counterparts, bridled under these restrictions. Still, for GDR society, sexual liberties were less disruptive than travel liberties; GDR cultural production often employed sexuality as a cipher for concerns such as travel, whether to censor or address these concerns.[52] For instance, Joachim Hasler's youth musical *Heisser Sommer* (1968) uses sexuality to obliquely comment on GDR desertion. This tale of romantic intrigue and wanderlust argues that monogamy, fidelity, and honesty lead to happiness and fulfilment, both in love and in a young citizen's relationship to country. As I will demonstrate below, the 1970s youth film *Für die Liebe noch zu mager?* resolves wanderlust through sexuality, Cuba, Guevara, and Bunke. The biographies, in contrast, offered both travel and sexual freedoms enabled by revolutionary consciousness. The heroine could function both as a socialist role model and as a figure through whom subversive desires could be vicariously lived.

Overtly, the texts depict Tania and Tamara as sexually pure. Her alignment with national causes necessitates this representation. She stands in a tradition of female revolutionaries free of sexual desire due to complete loyalty to the cause and heroines whose strength depends on chastity. This tradition is profoundly gendered. An example of this is Guevara himself. Although Che's writings call for sexual restraint among revolutionaries, he was known to be a poor practitioner. Nevertheless, as with most male public figures, active sexuality did not harm his stature, and in some ways added to his cultural capitalThe Tania biographies achieve this depiction not by denying the sexual practices of the female partisan, but by legitimating them within the logic of revolutionary socialism. The transnational work *Tania la Guerrillera* achieves this by de-emphasizing these practices, a strategy that also

works against traditional stereotypes of Cuban sexuality. Its protagonist resembles an older generation of GDR socialist heroes with only
marginal appeal to a younger generation. Panitz's biography takes a
somewhat different tack. It highlights particularly Tania's unconven-
tional sexuality as part of its overall project of encouraging reader identification with the GDR. This liberal treatment resonated with youthful
interest in changing sexual norms.

The texts manage this seemingly impossible task of simultaneously
presenting Tania as sexually pure and sexually active by constructing
her without her own sexual desire; her sexual practice is driven by –
and sanctioned by – her revolutionary fervour. For instance, each of
the texts explains Tania's decision to marry a conservative Bolivian as
a means to obtain Bolivian citizenship.[53] Each negates conjugal duties
by enclosing the term husband (*Ehemann*) and marriage (*Ehe*) in quotes.
The term marriage here defines the duty of the revolutionary wedded
to her cause, while the quotes function as a grammatical chastity belt
protecting her sexual virtue. In another example, a unique and suggestive dash reminiscent of Kleist's *Marquise von O* creates narrative
modesty. Tania's undercover colleague, Mercy, is quoted as follows: 'I
watched [Tamara and her fiancé] leaving the movie house, they went
by foot in the direction of her house; during this walk, she was the
active one. The determining one. On January 7th she left the house at
8:30 AM ...'[54]

'The active one. The determining one' – this description demonstrates another narrative strategy. Here the female protagonist inhabits
the masculine role in the sexual situation. This masculine gendering of
her sexual practice within the heteronormative logic of the text keeps
Tania symbolically pure: her body remains symbolically impregnable,
impermeable. Moreover, her sexual actions are driven by the socialist
masculine (the mind and reason), not the capitalist feminine (the cor-
poreal and desire). Tania wields her sexuality purely as a revolutionary
weapon and her decisions are based on a pure revolutionary passion.

In these ways, the texts expand the acceptable scope of sexual activity
by circumscribing the meaning of such activity. This programmatic definition grants Tania more freedoms than other female figures. Tania's
reports remind readers that in capitalist systems, unaccompanied
women in the public sphere are policed and must adhere to oppressive
norms of femininity. In contrast, her position as a revolutionary garners
her liberties that female citizens of capitalist nations and less exemplary
GDR citizens do not have. At the same time, the narrow definition of

sexuality officially negates certain facets of this sexuality, notably individual female desire.

In the context of a conservative GDR, Tania's and to a lesser extent Tamara's travel and sexual practices are programmatic and subversive. The Tania of both texts has nearly unlimited access to the public sphere. She also takes and leaves sexual partners at will; even her marital negotiations include stipulations ensuring her continued autonomy and mobility. Such a model fit uneasily with the (in many ways) traditional GDR views on sexual relations and marriage. Within the textual constraints outlined, such representations of non-normative practices could thus offer vicarious resistance to stifling social standards. For young GDR readers in particular, these narratives of travel and sexual freedoms modelled revolutionary pleasures that both intervened in GDR norms and that could be read along an interactive spectrum from programmatic to subversive according to the personal and political desire of these readers.

These are the GDR narratives that focus on Guevara and Bunke; in other texts the youthful figures emerge intermittently, yet also with semantic force. The DEFA feature *Für die Liebe noch zu mager?* (1974) employs them in conjunction with a distant vision of Cuba to intervene in contemporary national concerns.[55] As the Tania biographies do to some extent, the film communicates politically appropriate pedagogical messages as well as critical gestures. Such social criticism was enabled by the period of relative artistic liberty in which the film was produced, and responded to the recognition that programmatic productions were drawing small audiences and thus were having little social impact. The strategy for *Für die Liebe* was to persuade, rather than preach.[56] It wooed its young audience by mimetically representing their quotidian interests and gently offering alternatives such as international socialism.[57]

Für die Liebe noch zu mager? portrays the transformation of the teen-aged 'ugly duckling' Susanne into a socialist woman. Susanne effects this development by learning to articulate personal desires, which consist largely in defining her sexual desires and their place within a fully developed socialist personality. This growth occurs around her interest in, courtship of, and relationship with her somewhat older neighbour, the outsider Lutz. Through their relationship, Lutz is temporarily drawn away from his socially inappropriate interests. In the end, however, he disappears on a train, symbolically rejecting his country, while Susanne turns her back on him and her face towards her adult future in the GDR. Two minor protagonists are foils for the main protagonists. Susanne's colleague Daisy is the negative example of femininity without socialist values. Overly focused on her own needs, Daisy relies on the sexual attentions of men for her self-esteem and suffers accordingly. The 'ugly duckling' Martin confirms Susanne's desirability for the viewers through his courtship and offers a relationship for her to experience and reject.

Several extra-national elements further the pedagogical strategy of this female coming-of-age film.[58] Publicity for it emphasized that the popular music groups the Klaus Renft Combo and Zsuzsa Koncz and the Illés-Ensemble wrote and performed the soundtrack. Particularly the choice to use Illés, a somewhat politically problematic band from Hungary, a socialist brother country with a reputation for openness, was meant to draw audiences.[59] The use of Cuba, Che Guevara, and Tamara Bunke are other examples of *Für die Liebe*'s transnational scope.[60] The film does not treat these foreign elements as topics of inquiry on their own terms, despite the frequent use of explicitly pedagogical scenes in DEFA films that, used in this feature, would have made such messages easy to deliver.[61] Instead, the narrative capitalizes on the cult factor that Che and Tamara had among GDR youth to further its own agenda, while simultaneously avoiding potentially thorny explanations of Latin American revolutionary politics. These extra-national elements primarily speak to youth concerns of social alienation, the 'desert island syndrome' of the GDR, and the related desire for travel or escape.

The Latin American elements resonate variously with GDR concerns and aim to increase GDR youth identification with their Germany. These transnational themes were incompletely defined in official logics. This facilitated their use as tropes of hushed debates closer to home. They increase the GDR's cultural capital by aligning it with the popular, exotic, socialist narrative of Cuba and the heroes Guevara and Bunke. And they enhance the relevance of the German project by suggesting that its socialist work is a direct translation of that in Latin America. The main female protagonist performs much of this translation. Bunke becomes Susanne's role model in her quest to win Lutz for herself and, symbolically, for her society. Lutz's desire for international travel and adventure both mimetically represents desires for more direct participation in the international socialist project and substitutes for less socially acceptable voyage and escape fantasies.

Susanne and Lutz represent two youth types, which is highlighted in their relationship towards free time and travel. Susanne has little interest in either. She does not even consider her volunteer first-aid training to be a free-time activity because such are the duties of society members. The film suggests, however, that the young woman must find a self outside these tasks as well. Her generalized dissatisfaction is explained as stemming from a lack of socialistically oriented individuation. The bohemian Lutz earns his money as an independent handyman – unusual in the GDR – and spends his free time drinking, motorcycling, womanizing, and dreaming of foreign lands. Less than condemning this lifestyle, the film suggests its limitations by depicting it as solitary. Only Lutz's irresponsible attitude towards intimate relationships is directly criticized, most comically when a guard mistakes Lutz for a sexual deviant and allows his dog to rip the seat out of his Levis.[62]

Notwithstanding Susanne's proclivity for the fighting heroine, these protagonists are gendered normatively. The young woman finds her adult self by sublimating her dissatisfaction into desire for, competition for, and a romantic relationship with Lutz.[63] Because her project is bound up with his integration into the GDR society, Susanne's development is a transfer of social aims into personal aims. She represents every good socialist woman whose responsibility it becomes to convert male misfits into upstanding citizens through interpersonal contact on their own time. In contrast, even while the film implies that Lutz's travel plan is doomed, it grants him his chance to escape the confines of the small town and the small nation on his own terms.

The trajectories of both of these identificatory figures are furthered by allusions to Cuba and Cuban heroes. In part, Lutz's nonconformist values, lifestyle, and appearance connote a 'rebel without a cause' and the hippie movement. Both individualistic philosophies foreground personal fulfilment, disavow social responsibility, and incorporate versions of revolutionary tourism, for instance, travel to the global South in protest of policies at home and in search of unspoiled and authentic cultures.[64] Such attitudes were anathema to the GDR system, and two strategies meant to avoid censorship were to focus the narrative and its publicity on Susanne and to depoliticize Lutz's character by marking him as non-normative by coincidence – a 'Spinner'[65] – in order to allay official interpretations of him as representative of generalized GDR youth discontentment.[66] A third strategy was to emphasize Lutz's individual peripateticism in relation to acceptable aims and suitable locations, notably Cuba. Moreover, Lutz's subversive escapism is also expressed through his sexual practices, the latter of which then become Susanne's task to tame.

A scene on the lawn of the apartment house in which they both live demonstrates how non-conformism is triangulated through travel, sexuality, and Cuba. Lutz and Susanne are working outside when Daisy pays Susanne a visit. In response to Daisy's assertion that she and Lutz had met previously at a club in the nearby village of Seifersdorf, the young man thoughtfully mouths the name, then states abruptly:

Do you know how hot it is in Cuba? 40 degrees in the shade. Man, salt stains
on your shirt from sweat and thirst, *bestial* thirst. But the second day is
decisive. If you don't fall over then, people, then ...
DAISY: Incorrigible fool
LUTZ: Seriously, ZEMA is building a sugar factory there.
SUSANNE: Since when do you work at ZEMA?
LUTZ: Just wait, it takes forever for such a factory to be built. This is missing,
then that, and then they have to wait for the next steamship. Cuba is far
away.
SUSANNE: Small cooling off at 40 degrees in the shade?[67]

Susanne mists Lutz with a garden hose. In retaliation, he chases and sprays her with a full stream of water from the hose he now holds erect at his hip. Susanne laughs delightedly while Daisy eyes Lutz angrily.

Lutz's narrative articulates desires for mobility and an exotic elsewhere and connotes escape from national confines, all within a politically acceptable framework. Travel seems most easily achieved from within the system, for instance through employment abroad in noble joint-development projects. Opportunities of a different sort are suggested when Susanne later receives a performance award at her factory; viewers knew that these variously enabled international travel.[68] Lutz's description of the necessarily slow production tempo in Cuba normalizes the *Aussteigermentalität* (dropout mentality) of 1970s youth. Lutz's own pace suits this brother socialist context; there he can be a fulfilled, productive part of society. This pan-socialist link simultaneously flatters the GDR. Production bottlenecks are normalized through their depiction as an international phenomenon, while the indirect comparison suggests that the material conditions in the GDR are superior. Supply side shortfalls resonated with material shortages in the domestic realm, yet because Cuba awaits technical equipment from Germany, the latter here becomes the stronger of the two partners and in this sense is the more normatively desirable nation in which to live.

The sensuality of Lutz's description and the sexual undertones of scenes such as this make his fantasies even more politically palatable. He is driven by imagination and libido rather than by conscious, political choice. His sexual escapades are aligned with these fantasies; he describes the heat and 'bestial' thirst one experiences in Cuba rather than addressing his libertinage with Daisy in the GDR. Susanne's response works to bring a socially acceptable life in Cuba into the GDR realm. Her 'small cooling off' symbolically resolves larger material conditions that might limit production – incapacitating heat and more individual incapacitation Lutz's attitude. Her actions further the transformation of Lutz's wanderlust into sexual desire by redirecting his interest in conquering new lands into conquering new women. The chase scene grants the young man at least temporary release as he soaks the ecstatic Susanne.

Lutz's potentially subversive desires are further disciplined into a steady relationship with Susanne. The scene in which she first succeeds in drawing his sexual interest and the two consummate their desire exemplifies how romantic liaison circumscribes transnational yearnings. A hothouse setting forefronts the availability of the tangibly exotic within GDR borders. The recorded voice of a tour guide emphasizes that the exotic jungle hearkens from the monarchy, but now belongs to all citizens. It is cared for in the tradition of the explorer and collector Alexander von Humboldt, who is also part of the socialist cultural heritage (*Erbe*). Here, the GDR stands in an international tradition, is its patron, and symbolically contains it. The unfolding events between the two young people collapse the foreign exotic into the sexual. While at first Lutz rhapsodizes on the distant origins of his lush surroundings, gradually this tropical setting and the fantasies they evoke help ignite his sexual desire for Susanne and are transformed into sexual practices in the domestic here and now.

That only Lutz's personal goals relate to international travel is one of the many ways in which the narrative is normatively gendered. Only one scene suggests travel or escape for Susanne. After first being thwarted in her courtship, long shots capture the teenager walking along the train tracks that head into the distance as the sun rises. The extra-diegetic lyrics underscore the message: 'At some time or other everybody wants out of his skin' (*Irgendwann will jedermann raus aus seiner Haut*). Yet this evocative sequence is channelled into a more socially appropriate message with the next scene, which finds Susanne in the cab of a locomotive with her father, the driver; her destination turns out to be a return home to the wisdom of the older generation. The comment of her father that women generally want more than the society has to offer only further limits Susanne's wishes by normalizing them without suggesting a solution.

In contrast to Lutz, Susanne seeks to structure her personal life within the Democratic Republic. Official directives increasingly acknowledged the importance of leisure in real-existing socialism and *Für die Liebe* reflects and intervenes in this tension by addressing youth alienation through her. In accordance with its pedagogical strategy, the film depicts a youth culture of free time based in drinking, pop music, and courtship as part of GDR society, while suggesting its hollowness and negative consequences. Susanne's experience of it as painful highlights this assessment that is demonstrated in other ways as well. The stereotypically paternal doctor figure who treats Martin after a dancehall fight emphasizes the irresponsibility of such brawls. Daisy's unwanted pregnancy results from a one-night stand after a night of clubbing. The socializing at a private Datscha is denigrated when one popular and smiling young woman confides to Susanne that such parties are dull and excessively labour intensive.

Its remove from adult oversight gives the bourgeois space of the Datscha particular cultural capital and subversive potential; a circumscribed representation of Che Guevara adds to this. The opening shot of the party is a close-up, eye-level take of the Korda image, illuminated by a music-driven barrage of multicoloured strobe lights, which introduces the event as fringe. The camera offers Guevara as icon, while the narrative disciplines its cultural meanings through Susanne. Simultaneously bored by and uncomfortable at the party, the young woman at first avoids social interaction, including Martin's pseudo-intellectual exposition on Freud that becomes a courting exercise. Instead, she is drawn to the Che image, regarding it while a young man works on the lights display.

ROLF: Something's wrong with the low base filter.
SUSANNE: Who is that there on the picture?
ROLF: Tell me that you really don't know who he is. Give me the pliers, will you?
SUSANNE: Fidel Castro
ROLF: Nearly right. Listen; drum. The green is too weak. You really don't know who he is? Never heard anything about Che Guevara? Now again – too little green![69]

Despite his surprise that implies that Susanne should know about Guevara, the youth offers only Che's name in clarification. Rather than sharing information, he focuses on increasing the green colour of hope on the visage of the hero. Here, Guevara remains based on individual interpretation of a contemporary youth-culture icon. Moreover, the dialogue between Rolf and Susanne maps the politically problematic figure of Guevara onto the politically appropriate figure of Fidel Castro. In these ways, the film grants the youth their revolutionary, transnational hero in a form compatible with GDR domestic and international agendas.

While Che remains iconographic, Tamara Bunke's narrative is briefly but explicitly articulated. Her activities in Latin America serve as the impetus for socialist development at home. Susanne's reading of Tamara and Che's relationship catalyses her socio-sexual awakening. Not interested in sexualized hero worship of Che, Susanne is primarily impressed by Tamara's courage, as is clear from the following dialogue that takes place with Martin in the morning hours following the Datscha party. The two nestle side by side in a hilltop forest clearing overlooking their village:

SUSANNE: How does a girl from the GDR get to Bolivia?
MARTIN: She was in Cuba first
SUSANNE: I wonder whether she loved him, the bearded one in the picture?
MARTIN: Perhaps, but not like that.
SUSANNE: Definitely, most definitely. Man, from the GDR to Bolivia. She was daring, a female partisan among so many men!
MARTIN: They wanted to cross the river. They had wounded and sick along. And as they went through the water, the soldiers shot. It was an ambush.[70]

As Martin speaks his last lines, Susanne removes her belt with resolve; the word 'ambush' is greeted by her demanding kiss. Through this conflation of Bunke and Guevara's Bolivian project and Susanne and Martin's courtship, revolution is domesticated and sexualized and domestic sexuality is revolutionized. The double signification of the ambush to describe both Bunke's death and Susanne's sexual advances elides the demise in Latin America by focusing on the seduction in the GDR. This resignification also effaces the failure of the revolutionaries in the Bolivian jungle by focusing attention on Susanne's success in the GDR woods. Overall, it translates international revolution into nationally appropriate activity.

The meaning of international travel in this scene highlights its gendering. As did Lutz's tale of Cuba, this exchange offers the audience vicarious travel sanctioned by the international socialist system. Here as well, border crossing enriches the socialist landscape in the cultural imaginary. However, unlike her male counterpart Lutz, Susanne is not directly concerned with travel itself. Instead, Bunke's mobility is primarily of interest to her because it is symptomatic of the resolve of this female heroine, an attitude and life practice that fascinates Susanne because it enables non-normative actions, such as sexual forthrightness in the GDR context.

Susanne's interests are femininely gendered; so too are her fears. She desires sexual agency and is concerned with sexual integrity. Until this point in the narrative, the adolescent has been exposed to conflicting messages regarding proper gender behaviour, and neither she nor Daisy has been able to define the terms of her sexuality. This scene implies that socialist belief systems protected, enabled, and shaped Tamara's passions. Socialism also granted the heroine the conditions under which she could perform revolutionary work and the necessary characteristics for it, which included a sort of revolutionary love. From this moment in the film, the national, yet international, revolutionary figure Tamara Bunke becomes an identificatory model after which Susanne fashions herself. By emulating Bunke's revolutionary determination, Susanne incorporates sexuality into a normative, socialist life. This development takes place within a domestic context that, the narrative newly suggests, may support it.

This revolutionary passion is distinct from the normative sexuality in the youth group that *Für die Liebe* depicts. Rather than being about nonproductive pleasure, irrationality, or private desires, Susanne's passion unites personal and social aims. She cannot keep her eyes closed while Martin kisses her. Her gaze suggests an adherence to rationality and conscious choice, a goal-oriented, controlled sexuality rather than a limit (and therefore limited) experience. Keeping her eyes open, Susanne decides against settling for Martin instead of Lutz. Her parting from Martin through the trees and down the hill towards the valley town below is reminiscent of well-known images of Cuban guerrilla fighters in the Sierra Maestra mountains. Susanne's newly formulated desire merges traditional socialist attitudes with her newfound conception of revolutionary passion in the personal and the public spheres.

This attitude and the challenges it involves are underscored in the scenes that follow. First, an unenthusiastic Susanne is photographed

and decorated for her factory work to a score with lyrics that, as elsewhere in the tale, articulate her thoughts. Here they express her dark
assessment of the pretentiousness of the situation and her corresponding feelings of humiliation and frustration: 'Does the city only need
my hands? Doesn't this city also need my courage? My courage? My
courage? Smile! Quickly tried. Photographed. Don't you all look at
me! Close your eyes! I'm in the limelight. I'm not a joke. Close your
eyes, man!' Then, in the next factory scene in which she supports her
colleague Daisy against the moralistic criticisms of her co-workers the
sound over vocals croon: 'You all look here! ... Anger tastes good. Look
at me! Sometimes new is good. Anger becomes me. Wake up, man!'[71]
From the decisive struggle in the mountains forward, Susanne dares to
follow in the footsteps of her GDR–Latin American role model, using
her own newly modelled courage in the fulfilment of personal goals
that are individual articulations of national goals.

Tamara orients Susanne on her own path to maturity, yet her personal romantic desires align with social demands. Susanne's actions
stand in a GDR tradition of works such as *Katzgraben* and *Bürgermeister
Anna* in which good socialist women turn men into good socialist men.
Lutz finds her newfound confidence attractive; he decides she is no
longer 'too thin for love.' In tying him to her, Susanne also ties him to
a productive GDR life. Romantic scenes depict Lutz working diligently
while the young woman watches contentedly. In contrast to Susanne's
domestification and socialization of the Latin American adventure, the
perpetually immature Lutz continues to idealize Cuba as an individual
utopia. When the ill-prepared traveller waves from a departing train in
one of the last scenes, it is clear that he will not reach his fantasy. On the
other hand, Susanne revels soberly in engaging her newly articulated,
revolutionary direction within the circumscribed intranational space of
the GDR.

Guevara and Bunke functioned variously as heroes for GDR youth.
Their links to the far away, tropical island of Cuba increased their cultural capital, particularly as the establishment attempted to increase
youth identification with GDR socialism by bringing these figures who
were so conveniently linked to a socialist brotherland into public discourse. While Guevara was represented primarily iconographically as a
means of circumscribing his troublesome political message, Bunke was
more completely articulated as a programmatic hero. Yet particularly in
the case of Bunke, the significant texts enable, even encourage, resistant reading. Thus, Tania functioned as a programmatic revolutionary

hero, a radical innovator for GDR touring culture, and an inspiration for socialist citizenship. Her biographical narratives invited GDR youth to construct citizenship differently than did their government. Imagining themselves as revolutionary tourists and travellers in foreign lands, these youth could develop desires whose degree of accordance with GDR norms depended more on the attitudes of the youth than on state demands.

Tamara Bunke and Che Guevara in the FRG

German narratives of Bunke and Guevara exemplify how present circumstances impact historiography. GDR archives are open to researchers due to national programs meant to further the 'working through' of Nazi Germany and the GDR (*Vergangenheitsbewältigung*); FRG and U.S. archives are not as accessible. Thus while official GDR reception and deployment of Bunke and Guevara can be reconstructed with some assurance, similar investigations about the FRG and United States remain somewhat speculative. This situation strongly influences the results of research, beginning with the very questions posed and the methods of investigation employed.[72]

Tamara Bunke was not particularly significant for the FRG, even for much of the left. For instance, Helke Sander's documentary-style feature film on the West Berlin women's movement, *Der subjektive Faktor* (1981), employs an image of Che, not of Tamara, in the pivotal scene in which the women begin organizing.[73] The female internationalist was problematically positioned between Cold War camps. Her links to the Soviet bloc made her suspect among those who criticized it; her own rebuff of the GDR made her suspect among those who supported it.[74] Bunke's popularity was also impacted by the FRG's mainstream press, whose reception was markedly chauvinistic.[75] Jenni Calder encapsulates the sentiment: 'What is so striking is that is appears too difficult to accept her membership in the guerilla band as being no more curious or remarkable than that of any other member. In an extreme situation, the implication is that the heroic woman is a freak, sinister, untrustworthy and promiscuous. The imitation of men is acceptable, so long as the imitative nature is clear. The actual assumption of 'male' qualities and actions is much more dubious. The heroic woman, the adjective derived from heroine, not hero, is more acceptably the woman who acts as a supportive limb to the true hero, who suffers with and for him.'[76]

In the East, readers embraced armed female heroes. In the West, as Calder points out, Bunke's gender bending was unsettling for a culture whose very legislation discriminated against women, and that was struggling with the new social movements, including feminism. In the FRG, it was therefore precisely the radical women's movement that most appreciated Bunke. They found in her a female role model who disrupted sexual and gender stereotypes.[77] Their publications offer little more than a recapitulation of the GDR texts; their cultural contribution is the positive staging of Tamara in the Federal Republic. Consider, for example, Regina Scheer's article that places Bunke with powerful public figures in a volume whose title roughly translates as Wild Women: Furies, Hussies, and Women with Weapons.[78] Such company stands out precisely in its resistance to the mainstream, a mainstream that did not yet have space for women in masculine roles.

Che is quite a different story. Much has been written about Guevara and his reception in the FRG. Among left-leaning youth, he was and is an icon. They had some opportunity to imbue this figure with self-designed meanings based on various informational sources. This is not to suggest that many sought extensive knowledge about Guevara, nor that FRG and U.S. governments did not take notice. Indeed, as my discussion of the West Berlin anti-authoritarians suggests, Guevara's role was of primary significance among politicized youth who were critical of both the Soviet and U.S. blocs, and his symbolic value as an oppositional figure was threatening to many governments. In what follows I will focus on the as-yet-unexamined importance of Guevara as a revolutionary tourist/revolutionary traveller for left-leaning FRG youth. Guevara embodied travel in both Germanies; in the FRG, his post-war touring negotiated a thorny network of concerns around fascism, internationalism, and consumer culture.

Although Germans have long understood themselves as travel *Weltmeister*, large-scale FRG tourism developed with the economic miracle and the Cold War.[79] Citizen-producers increasingly identified as consumers, and travel to poorer nations furthered the emulation of the richer consuming classes.[80] Many on the left criticized mass tourism in particular, arguing that it divided work and play, reinscribed the hold of the culture industry, and was a neocolonial impulse, a return of a repressed desire for *Lebensraum*.[81]

Their own interest in visiting foreign countries was difficult to square with such critique. The notion of 'revolutionary travel' was one response; interestingly, critics included Hans Magnus Enzensberger,

whose writings had repopularized the term. It suggested escape from
the mainstream and even the left establishment. For many left-leaning youth, the independently minded Che Guevara was a practitioner
through whom they could vicariously live out their own desires for
travel while retaining their critical stances in relation to the Federal
Republic. This paradigm has longevity. Horst-Eckart Gross's 1989
introduction to a collection of Ernesto Che Guevara's writings on internationalism addresses the critique developed decades earlier, asserting
that 'the young Guevara did not roam through Latin America in order
to "check off" countries and sights of interest, rather, he made the effort
not only to investigate the situation of the poor and the poorest people,
but also to question the ways of thinking and self-understandings of
the people.'[82] Gross's emphatic assertion that Guevara was not an 'it's-
Tuesday-it-must-be-Bolivia' tourist evidences precisely the discomfort
of this German critical intellectual with such understandings of the
guerrilla leader. Gross is at pains to cast Guevara's travelling practices
in accordance with travel norms of the FRG left. Guevara's 'desires for
adventure and travel' are justified because they serve the revolution.

Yet there are even bigger stakes involved here. To define revolutionary tourism/travel was to define possibilities for populist nation building. If Guevara's attempts to spark armed revolution in Bolivia were
but a self-serving project of a foreign adventurer, as the Soviet-aligned
Bolivian Communist Party asserted, then a central standpoint of critical FRG leftists – grassroots solidarity – was called into question. Hans
Magnus Enzensberger was correct and Peter Weiss incorrect – international solidarity across the North-South national, class, and cultural
divide was impossible. This was a significant problem; for the West
Berlin anti-authoritarians, for instance, such a stance would jeopardize
their hopes of sparking multiple Vietnams in first-world metropoles.
Whether they recognized it consciously, for many in the FRG left the
possibility of progressive revolutionary tourism was not only about the
pleasures of travel but stood in for the possibility of international solidarity with the third world and the possibility of concomitant revolutionary change in the Federal Republic.

Interest and identification with Guevara as revolutionary traveller
took many forms. For instance, as I have shown, the anti-authoritarians,
who were interested – however fancifully – in sparking the emergence
of an independent West Berlin, studied Guevara's publications for relevant strategy. Their working group 'Third World/Metropolis' analysed
Guevara's guerrilla activities in the Bolivian jungles, as recounted in

left-leaning journals and the daily news. Members criticized and lauded
these actions as if they themselves were expertly positioned in relation
to guerrilla fighting, as if they were in Bolivia themselves. Published
in the FRG in 1968, Guevara's *Bolivianisches Tagebuch* (*Bolivian Diary*)
had a considerable influence among many of the left. The popularity
of this first-hand account suggests attention to the personal experience
of Guevara in Bolivia. Its day-to-day recounting furthers identification
with Guevara, encouraging its readership to imagine itself in revolutionary struggle abroad.

The more mainstream press was also interested in Guevara as revolutionary tourist. A lengthy 1968 series in the news and culture magazine *Der Spiegel* illustrates this phenomenon. These lead articles suggest
ways in which Guevara resonated with its young readers in particular.
The series title, Che Guevara: Erlöser von dem Dschungel (Che Guevara: Saviour from the Jungle), casts Guevara as an exotic, quasi-mysti-
cal hero.[83] Such a representation draws on two notions popular among
critical youth: the power of the irrational, particularly as defined by
Herbert Marcuse, Wilhelm Reich, and Carl Jung; and the revolutionary
potential of third-world inhabitants who have not been debilitated by
late industrial capitalism.

Several of the photographic images of the series encourage identification with Guevara by emphasizing similarities between him and
Der Spiegel's high-school and university readers. Guevara's student
roots are highlighted, as well as the relationship between institutions
of higher learning and the revolutionary project. A formal photograph
of Guevara in coat and tie bears the caption 'Student Guevara: "Our
Continent's Revolution."' (Student Guevara: 'Die Revolution unseres
Kontinents.')[84] The accompanying text is a segment from a 1966 interview with a well-heeled Guevara working as a guerrilla fighter; a visual
image of this older Che would have been more immediately relevant to
the text. The grouping of the student photo, its caption that links university life and revolutionary vision, and the accompanying text asso-
ciate the work of FRG student activists with Guevara's revolutionary
project. This combination also affirms the significance of student revolt
by conjoining Che's later political impact with his earlier student years.
And, it reminds the FRG audience that Guevara's revolutionary ideas
were not well defined until after he completed his studies.

Another photographic image depicts a Venezuelan university taken
over by government forces after an uprising that involved students
using it as a base. This 'critical university' in Latin America resonated

5.1 The newly revolutionized *Spinnerin* Susanne tames the *Spinner* Lutz in
Für die Liebe noch zu mager? Photo (18774) by Uwe Fleischer. Used with the
kind permission of the BA-FA.

with German readers. The timing, July 1968, was shortly after the similar formation of 'critical universities' in the Federal Republic that was
part of the most violent period of the student movement proper. A
photo of a thoughtful, unkempt Guevara in a cardigan sweater entitled 'Guerrilla Leader Guevara: "All that is great arises from chaos"'
is reproduced on the same page.[85] This phrasing resonates with contemporary concerns about authoritarian leaders arising from political
'chaos,' as seemingly had occurred in the Weimar Republic. This magazine spread that casts the university as revolutionary and the revolutionary Guevara as scholarly associates the project of the FRG critical
universities and that of the revolutionary Argentine. In these ways, the
series links Guevara to students of the global North.

   Der Spiegel also casts Che in the role of revolutionary tourist. One
photographic image depicting a young Guevara on a raft on the Ama-

5.2 Che Guevara as a student. *Der Spiegel*, no. 31 (1968), p. 62.

zon River is entitled 'Südamerika-Tramp' (A tramp in South America).[86] Another two depicting Guevara on state visits to Russia and China are labelled 'Tourist Guevara, Premier Chruschtschow "The Revolution of the Russians"' and 'Tourist Guevara, Party Leader Mao … is the biggest swindle of all time.'[87] Importantly, the accompanying texts stand in tension with the captioned visual representations of Guevara as pleasure-seeking traveller. The narrative of Guevara's voyage as a youth couches this journey as an attempt to overcome physical ailments. The text accompanying the 'Tourist Guevara' images are the words of Guevara in his role as government official analysing the relationships of Soviet- and Chinese-style communism to Cuban political organization. Guevara's physical presence in these foreign countries seemingly enabled him a more thorough understanding of the situations there. The photos primarily address the desires of readers for pleasure travel; the text primarily feeds demands that such travel fulfils useful or revolutionary aims. The resultant Guevara is a revolutionary tourist and traveller, a

5.3 Che Guevara as Südamerika-Tramp (a tramp in South America). *Der Spiegel*, no. 32 (1968), p. 45.

figure whose precise definition remains dialectical.

A caption under the photographic image of his guerrilla forces articulates similar definitional tensions from a more Latin American political perspective: 'Guevara Partisans at the Rio Grande: "Foreign Adventurers from Cuba."'[88] The accompanying text clarifies that the quote is the description of Guevara's group by the Bolivian Communist Party leader. It suggests that by defining Guevara as revolutionary tourist in this way, Party leader Monje sought to convince the Bolivian people, the organized communist parties, and the rest of the world that the Argentine/Cuban Guevara and his revolutionaries did not belong in Bolivia.

The *Der Spiegel* series reflects and furthers the then lively debate on international solidarity. Its construction of Guevara as revolutionary student and revolutionary tourist suggests that in these roles Guevara appealed to FRG students. He offered an alternative for adventurous FRG youth who were critical of what they saw as the Federal Republic's consumerist, neocolonialist mass tourism, a practice that they saw as emblematic of misguided nationalist attitudes. Che's revolutionary touring was understood to have combined pleasure with progressive political chang

Conclusion

To numerous Germans, Guevara and Bunke practiced critical nation building at odds with the dominant models. They placed themselves voluntarily at the service of nascent grassroots movements that sought national independence based on democratic socialism. For many of the German left, Guevara recalled the revolutionary Cuba of the 1960s, a Cuba as non-aligned as it would ever be. Guevara's departure from an independent, yet increasingly aligned Cuba was read as idealistic, even utopian adherence to his political goals. This action was certainly attractive to those of the Federal Republic who chafed under their lack of autonomy in relation to the United States and their own government. Similarly, Bunke's fidelity to 1960s revolutionary Cuba and her subsequent choice to support grassroots revolution elsewhere in Latin America was read by critical GDR citizens in particular as demonstrating her adherence to grassroots revolution unencumbered by Soviet pressures. These Latin American revolutionaries transporting the seeds of the Cuban revolution elsewhere were identificatory figures, particularly for youth dissatisfied with the opportunities for travel that their countries offered. This dissatisfaction exemplified frustrations with the roles that youth found and the freedoms they did not find in their Germanies. These revolutionaries struggling abroad for grassroots reinterpretations of 'nation' stood for the possibility of reinterpretations of nation generally and the German nations in particular.

Epilogue

Si, se puede! Southerners credit themselves with the legendary exhortation of U.S. President Barack Hussein Obama's 'Yes, we can!' political campaign. When dreaming in Cuban, the capacity of these particular Southerners to *arreglar todo* (find solutions for every problem and ways around every obstacle) has long increased their global appeal and garnered respect from even their most ardent detractors.

Cuba in the German Imaginary has told one story of the geopolitical and cultural significance of the island. This study about the South's influence on the North has detailed German projections of Cuba in relation to themselves and their German neighbours. The Caribbean nation has held many special meanings. The Soviet Union encouraged the Democratic Republic's ties with the real-existing socialist island in the U.S.-dominated hemisphere. For the GDR government, Cuba promised legitimation well beyond recognition of their fledgling German sovereignty. While culture and media encouraged popular support for their policies towards Cuba and for the island itself, the embrace of Cuba by citizens and intellectuals demonstrated significances far in excess of official perspectives. Meanwhile, the FRG government adhered to the policies of their Marshall Plan provider and NATO partner that restrained trade with and recognition of Cuba. As in the United States itself, such prohibitions inversely affected popular attention; interest in the island grew. In the 1960s Germanies and in many other nations, Cuba seemed to embody leftist ideals not found domestically.[1] For critical citizens on both sides of the Wall, examples such as Cuba made socialist projects on the national and the global scale palatable and even noble; the Cuban revolution sometimes came to be imagined as an alternative to their situation at home. The ties of enmity across the Florida

E.1 The interior of Tropical Island. Photograph by Jennifer R. Hosek.
(See page 13.)

straits also intrigued Germans for whom the United States was saviour or sire. As this study has shown, distinctions were shaped not only
temporally, but spatially; meanings in East and West were often markedly distinct. At the same time, the scholarly emphasis on differences
between the blocs is also a Cold War product and interconnections have
often been underestimated. The refractive scrutiny of this examination
that has sighted the Germanies through Cuba has therefore sought to
expose the spectrum of commonalities and shared discourses that continue to today, as well as to illuminate seldom articulated narratives
about a less than unified post-1990 Germany.

Our infatuations with Cuba seem eternally complex and multiply specific. This study considered post–Second World War German representations of Cuba for their messages about German self-understandings.
A good case study is defined by its transferability and I propose that
the structure of this analysis could be fruitfully employed for study
of other instances of cultural influence between unequally positioned

interlocutors. Two sketched examples – one general and one specific – suggest potentials for expansion beyond the German case.

Broadly speaking, Canadian popular sentiment favours a narrative in which Canadian foreign policy opposes U.S. policies towards Cuba. The story goes that Canadian policy respects national sovereignty abroad and/or that constructive engagement with the island is more effective than the U.S. stance. Yet, scholars such as Robert Wright have shown that from the very early 1960s, Canada's policy fell into line with U.S. preferences. Using recently declassified documents to support contemporary educated suspicions, Wright argues that the United States encouraged Canada to pay limited heed to the U.S. embargo and employ its relations with Cuba to keep a North American listening post there.[2] This Canadian situation parallels German cases in that popular mythologies of official practices shore up preferred notions of national identity. Moreover, governmental policies that further on-the-ground exchanges mean that as fantasy and as entity, Cuba shapes Canadian identities in ways that go far beyond expressions of foreign policy. Tangible Cuba connections in relation to the United States range from symbolic separation through snowbird getaways free of the 'ugly American' to the embrace of a Canadian identity putatively more rational and fair-minded. Over decades of exchange, these connections increasingly include personal and interpersonal ties that also lastingly alter Canadian self-perceptions.[3]

German-Cuban, Canadian-Cuban, U.S.-Cuban relationships are multifaceted and multiply distinct. Yet the following anecdote involving the United States is another example of the enormity of Cuba on the global stage and the transferability of this case study:

The California Palace of the Legion of Honor in San Francisco hosted Havana Deco Night as a special event of their 2004 Art Deco exhibit. Mitzi Mogul, self-styled historic consultant and member of the Art Deco Society of Los Angeles held the slide show and lecture entitled 'Cocktail Time in Cuba: An Exploration of the Architecture and Social Customs of the Deco Era in Havana.'[4] Mogul regaled her audience (myself included) with images of deco buildings captured during her visit to the island, augmenting the visual spectacle with an exuberant first-hand report on Havana's crumbling opulence and historical anecdotes featuring demon rum in its many alluring guises. This performance serviced her audience, allowing them to vicariously partake of Cuba's former splendour. Despite her 'attempt to keep politics out of it,' Mogul had harsh words for the U.S. government, whose embargo, she lamented, stands in the way of preserving the architectural wonders of this golden age of Cuban culture. The evening continued with live Cuban music of the period. Guests in full flapper regalia sipped martinis at the mojito bar and danced the tango, the rumba, and the salsa. Performers in showgirl attire wove their way through the dense crowd. As the band leader introduced the mostly Californian musicians, he also lambasted the U.S. embargo. Sustained applause filled the room.

This Havana Deco Night was a domestic national fantasy that symbolically reworked the power matrix in which these largely white, U.S., bourgeois actors play. Their fastidious, vintage costuming indicated their fervour for the 1920s high society of leisure in whose performance they were evidently practiced. This 'class drag' reminded me of the 'ethnic drag' that Sieg finds in FRG culture. As Sieg's German *Indianer* obfuscate their own national legacies by performing natives oppressed by white U.S. invaders, these flappers performing Great Gatsby fantasies of a golden age eschew culpability for the political and economic influences that enabled such lifestyles in the past and that continue to support inequity in the present. Their drag of an idle class passes as creative anachronism in a U.S. culture whose members nearly all identify as part of the labouring middle.

The applause was enabled by a selective fantasy in which this phantasmagoric 1920s Cuba was disassociated from contemporary neoimperialist practices of the global North. The band played Caribbean rhythms while the cosmopolitan crowd flaunted mainland accoutrements and gin trumped rum. This performance of a night at a U.S. speakeasy chanced to be staged in the devil's playground just off Florida where a plethora of vices could be openly enjoyed. The fantasy island backdrop enabled a *Buena Vista*-esque beneficence, while erasures of historico-cultural specificity elided the transnationally organized oppressions that engendered 1920s Havana. The Caribbean capital seemed the tropical extension of U.S. cocktail society and Cuba's quintessential architecture art deco.

In a morning-after of widespread Northern disillusionment with organized socialism, Cuba's utopian promise is shifting. Not an absence, but a condition, the 'post' of the post–Cold War is nowhere felt more strongly than in the global South, where many hot wars and aid programs have summarily ended while bilateral relations offer even more one-sided ties. Yet a global taste for an End of Utopia has not arrived. What roles will other nations seek to have Cuba play, what will they project onto this island in future decades? And what roles will Cuba seek to play in these infatuations? How will it shape itself domestically and project itself abroad? Many argue that these answers depend on the stability of Cuba's leadership. Others suggest that even with U.S. support for domestic dissent on the island, popular support for large-scale change is low.

Undoubtedly, Cuba is transnationalizing differently in this 'post.' I have touched on its early efforts at cultural self-representation in the Germanies; efforts that in the 1960s were minimal. As the Kuba Welle suggests, since the 1990s, Cuba has increasingly marketed itself as a multifaceted travel site that elides sex tourism through articulation of tourisms of solidarity and nostalgia. Many of its recent feature films revolve around visitors, a theme promoted by their affluent foreign co-producers. Fernando Pérez's *La vida es silbar* (*Life is to Whistle*, Cuba-Spain, 1998) and Daniel Díaz Torres's *Hacerse el sueco* (*Playing Swede*, Cuba-Spain-Germany, 2001) problematize tensions and desires surrounding Europeans on the island. Countless low-budget documentaries, such as Birgit Hein's *La Moderna Poesia* (2000) and Torsten Schulz's *Kuba Sigrid* (1997) and *Techno Salsa* (2000), engage the island through the cameras of interested and critical Germans with long solidarian relationships. Recent emphasis on the historical connections between Russia and Cuba function strategically to strengthen their contemporary ties in newly cast renditions of favoured travel site and hemispheric gateway.

It may smack of irony that the cultural capital of pre-revolutionary Cuba shores up the current system by reinforcing transnational interest in the island such as that evidenced during Havana Deco Night. Films like Sylvio Heufelder's *Havana Feelings* (Cuba-Germany, 2002) and Florian Borchmeyer's *Havanna – Die neue Kunst Ruinen zu bauen* (Germany, 2007) mythologize remnants of Batista's legacy yet also boost interest in Cuba today. The much-feted reconstruction of Old Havana foregrounds the colonial period; the revolutionary government accords its director Eusebio Leal Spengler great financial and planning liberties on this enormous project that makes Cuba's pre-revolutionary history more tangible and marketable as well as liveable. The commemoration of events such as Alexander von Humboldt's landing on the island, supported by the Goethe Institute and the German embassy in Cuba, may suggest tentative mutual warming of relations strategically expressed in pre-revolutionary terms.

Post–peaceful coexistence does not herald the End of Utopia or History. Indeed, a U.S.-centric empire seems to be birthing an oppositional phoenix of pragmatic utopianism in which entities such as the 'enormous' island nation figure more strongly. Even in the North, from this side of the false security of the 1990s and its promised and delusory peace dividends, cynicism seems a short-sighted indulgence that would enable hegemonic actors to define globalization. In the face of such pressures, a puny Caribbean nation that drills for oil in Goliath's backyard and makes alliances with the rising left in mainland Latin America may be all the more endearing. The final comments of the Art Deco event organizer recall for me the politically destabilizing reception of *Buena Vista* in the United States. For all the limitations of this night, it is precisely in its masquerade as Art Deco Havana that contemporary Cuba was insinuated into a venue as established as the San Francisco Palace of the Legion of Honor. Whatever the future, Cuba's waves will be transnational.

My German Romance: Writing from Havana

VICTOR FOWLER

When I was about ten, Cuban television was overloaded with all kinds of productions from the now extinct 'socialist countries,' a situation that continued until the beginning of the nineties when the USSR disappeared and the Bloc imploded. It is important to understand the meaning of this to a country like Cuba where a revolution took place in 1959 and the ties to the United States were broken, not only political and economic, but cultural ones too.

I speak of culture as our window to the world, the common language to approach the other, air circulating through the lungs that frees or suffocates, a collective and individual mechanism of endurance, strength, and resistance.

When in Western Germany in 2002, I tried to obtain episodes of *Ferdinand Clown*, a TV show from my boyhood. Nobody could help me. I spoke about a character of the East, about a memory that they don't have. It was shocking to experience how memory is erased. A young Cuban émigré living in Spain has a blog space to talk about childhood cartoons and there I could read about Ferdinand: Jiri Vstala (still alive, I think) was born in Liberec, Czechoslovakia. One visitor writes: 'After the fall of communism the actor Jiri Vrstala was hunted fiercely ... and accused of traumatizing many children in the socialist camp. His sentence has been to see his own TV program for life.' Another writes: 'I remember his joy and his wave goodbye; that unique way of saying goodbye, with the hand offering trust and affection, while the cart moved away. It was like kind of an infantile final blessing.'

Culture is our lungs, remember. On this journey to Germany I also tried to find the variety TV program *Ein Kessel Buntes*, also from the East. We saw it as part of Cuban TV, during my boyhood too, and were desperate for these minutes of fresh air. Now I read that it was conceived to compete with similar programs on West German television, but in those times it was only freedom to me: there we saw (in this, our only window to the music of the West) musicians like Barry White, Boney M, Tina Turner, Rafaela Carrá, and Lionel Hampton. Side by side with this, we could enjoy the rock style of bands from the East like Karat or Puhdys, the international pop style and permanent smile of Chris Doerk, and – calming our ignorance about The Beatles – we had the joyful country sound of Dean Reed, a Westerner after all. Not in vain; his LP of many songs in English was widely sold in Cuba; in other words, you heard the sound, watched the style, and didn't pay attention to the meaning of the lyrics. Please, be generous and consider that we are speaking about (and from) Cuba in the seventies and beginning of the eighties: a space not closely tied to the United States, the main cultural provider of world visions before the revolution. A contemporary Cuban essayist, Iván de la Nuez, has proposed what may be the best definition of our situation: 'A fragment at the shores of the World.'

More than this, culture was involved in an extended battle against all forms of 'imperialism.' In this context, to enjoy Karat or Puhdys (even just the sounds and long hair) was a form of resistance. We didn't have *Rolling Stone* magazine or anything of the like. Beyond the official propaganda, we didn't have clear ideas about the life of young people in the West; few people from those countries travelled to Cuba in those times (the seventies of the past century), magazines could not be acquired, a few musicians were broadcast, no TV programs were broadcast, and only a few carefully vetted films from the West could be seen.

I was born in 1960, one year after the Triumph of the Revolution, and have been depicting a personal history of love that on many levels is the history of my generation. How could we have any idea about what it was to live in capitalism? Official propaganda, the educational system, and the books we could buy repeated that 'the past' was infamous and the future 'luminous.' The outside was ugly and anti-human; the inside radiant and oriented to allow the expression of the best qualities of each.

Other than our own, we only had access to a handful of cultural magazines coming from the socialist countries; central to them and one of my favourites was *Kontact*, a small, colourful publication made by the GDR's Union of Young Communists. There you could find examples of 'modernity' and, in the last section, two or three pages were filled with addresses of young people from different parts of the world (many of them from Great Britain, France, Italy, United States) looking for friendship. What kind of imagination about the world is necessary to write a letter to a stranger? Oh, the Germans, they seemed so liberated to me! In 1981 the bestselling title in Cuban bookstores was Siegfried Schnabl's 1969 *Man and Woman Intimately* (*Mann und Frau intim*), a bestseller in East Germany. Everyone wanted to read the book. For the first time in the Cuban revolution (and in Cuban history too) there was a book written by a scientist, an authority in psychology, in which sexual choices were considered a private matter and homosexual behaviour deemed normal. And this was only part of the German contribution to Cuban life; at the beginning of the seventies the teaching of mathematics was transformed by what we in those days called the 'German mathematics.' The pedagogical science textbook written by Lothar Klinberg came from East Germany too.

Sexuality, mathematics, and didacticism... to which we need to add the stories of thousands of Cubans (my father was one) who visited the GDR to study, work, or for other reasons. They returned deeply impressed by characteristics of the Germans – maybe it sounds cliché, but characteristics like hard work, order, discipline, seriousness and rigour. Alongside this, they carried a memory of liberal sexual behaviour and a society with an abundance of consumer goods. It is not necessary to remark that this was exactly the opposite of life in Cuban society.

A comment from the musicologist Olavo Alén, who studied there, moves us to a most thoughtful problematic:

> The Germans always have to find an order in everything. They are the beings of the Earth least prepared to live in chaos. The Cubans are prepared to live in chaos. (56)

If we are prepared to live in chaos and they don't, how do they look at us and what do they see in our faces and history? What kinds of answers are offered? A story in our oral tradition relates that Hitler asked for a planisphere when, in 1940, Cuba declared war on the Nazis; he put a finger over the island and answered mockingly: 'Cuba, where's that?'

In that 2002 I stayed almost four months as a fellowship holder in Munich's Villa Waldberta. I travelled to Berlin, where I saw a little Romanian girl playing wonderful violin asking for money and, in the mathematical centre, Alexanderplatz, an old man (surely a soldier and hero of the Second World War) drunk and selling his medals. I visited the famous Checkpoint Charlie (a copy of the original, simultaneously for tourism and celebration), took pictures standing in front of remains of the Wall, and took more pictures at the monument to Karl Marx and Friedrich Engels. In my country both leaders of socialism were venerated as sacred personalities; here young people of the new Germany had painted graffiti over the statues: phrases of love mainly. I was at the newly appointed buildings in Berlin, at the Reichstag, the Jewish Synagogue, one neighbourhood in which – along the outside wall of many apartments – the names of Jewish residents deported to concentration camps and killed there have been engraved. The night of 1 May, very late, a big riot was broadcast and I saw the police charge against the demonstrators. The next morning, sleep-deprived, frazzled, I took the metro to the university and missed my stop; I woke up surrounded by ugly buildings, big blocks of grey cement and I thought that Havana – through some kind of magical teleportation – was in front of my eyes, but we were crossing a zone of East Berlin with buildings in the same style. The dream came to an end and my country of the future was the country of the past.

Before the end of the Wall, I had heard of Stasi on a few isolated occasions. It was later when I heard, for the first time, the unthinkable range of surveillance that Stasi had over the lives of ordinary people. The combination of political structures and the perpetual work of the ideological apparatus elaborates an immense veil, so it is almost impossible to see more than what it is permitted to see. In the summer of 1989 I saw on TV the popular protests in East Germany and the placards, at least in the beginning, showed only two petitions to the authorities: freedom of the press and the right to travel without restriction. This was just the same anguish that my country had had during all these years of socialism, the most evident examples of the structural weakness of the system. A system that, in other points, is strong even now when it is living its deepest crisis.

In a society like the Cuban, where cultural circulation is centralized in the hands of the state, to enter another culture is an act that depends on a combination of personal will and the opportunities that this same state offers. In this world order, cultural production fuses with political discourses, travellers' tales, and objects that arrive from the country that we are trying to know: *the things*. And profoundly important to this discourse is the degree of our own poverty. All of these shape the fabric or image that reveals the other and the process is extended, absolute, it embraces all corners and levels of the country (the space) and the totality of life (the time). There is nowhere to hide from it and there are no alternative sources to feed a different point of view; it is a process in which economic conditions and political work manufacture an ideological construction; the cultural products are doubly filtered and even the stories of the travellers (that moved, for instance, from Cuban poverty towards East German's opulence) are twice contaminated: by the conditions of underdevelopment from which they leave and for all that is chosen for them not to see at their destination. In this way, even the most reliable sources, people, introduce their most primary daily necessities in their travellers' tales and so offer deformed and sweet memories, without repression or conflicts. At the same time, we saw many sectors of Cuban industry working with enormous and modern German machinery, so the representation that we had of that country was determined by the perfect thing, the modern thing, and the monumental.

In constructing images of the other, a bonbon is as important as a political speech, a movie of as much value as a new factory, the tales of a witness as decisive as the signature of an official treaty. It is the sum of all these influences that feeds popular expectations about the future and that plants ideas of what we want to be or to whom we want to look. No doubt, especially at that time, ideology was a strange game of mirrors in which, when looking at ourselves, we saw a mostly a blurred image of the other.

Works Cited

Alvarez Gutiérrez, Luis. 'Un proyecto de colonización alemana para la Isla de Cuba en 1871.' In *Cuba, la perla de las Antillas. Actas de las I Jornadas sobre 'Cuba y su historia,'* edited by C. Naranjo and T. Mallo, 109–20. Madrid: Ediciones Doce Calles, Consejo Superior de Investigaciones Científicas, 1994.
Armíldez de Toledo, C. *Noticias de Estadística de la Isla de Cuba.* Havana: Imprenta del Gobierno, 1864.
Berschin, Helmut, Vales Bermúdez, and José Francisco. '"La matemática lengua alemana": ¿Es qué José Martí sabía alemán?' http://jose-marti.org/jose_marti/articulos/articulospermanentes/berschin-vales/01matematicalenguaalemana.htm.
Jacobs, Frank. 'East Germany Lives On – As a Tiny Caribbean Island.' http://bigthink.com/ideas/21128 (accessed 20 February 2007).
Lezama Lima, José. *Analecta del reloj.* Havana: Editorial Orígenes, 1953.
– *La expresión americana.* Havana: Editorial Letras Cubanas, 1993.
– *La polémica filosófica cubana*, vol. 2. Colección Biblioteca de Clásicos Cubanos

11, 700. Havana: Ediciones Imagen Contemporánea, 2000.

– 'Triunfo de la Revolución Cubana.' In *Revista de la Biblioteca Nacional José Martí*, vol. XXIX, no.2 (May–August 1988): 45–6.

Luzón, José L., José Baila, and Francisco Sardaña. 'Estado, etnias y espacio urbano. La Habana, 1878.' In *Boletín Americanista*, año XXXVII, no. 41, 137–50. Barcelona, 1991. http://www.raco.cat/index.php/BoletinAmericanista/article/viewFile/98573/146170.

Martí, José. *Obras completas, Volumen 16, Poesía*. Havana: Editorial de Ciencias Sociales, 1991.

– *Obras completas, Volumen 19, Viajes – Diarios – Crónicas – Juicios*. Havana: Editorial de Ciencias Sociales, 1991.

Rojas, Rafael. 'Benjamin no llegó a La Habana.' Letras Libres, May 2008. www.letraslibres.com/index.php?art=12938.

Schnabl, Siegfried. *El hombre y la mujer en la intimidad*. Havana: Editorial Científico-Técnica, 1979.

Streich, Michael. *The German Connection with the Spanish American War*. http://www.suite101.com/content/uss-maine-in-havana-harbor-1898-a163540.

Torres Rivera, Alejandro. 'El pensamiento masónico en José Martí: Una contribución al debate desde la masonería patriótica puertorriqueña.' http://www.areitodigital.net/El%20pensamiento%20masonicoJOSE%20MARTI.htm.

Vogel, Wolf-Dieter. *Regresé siendo otra persona. Cubanos y cubanas en la RDA*. Mexico City: Rosa-Luxemburg Stifung, 2009.

Notes

Introduction

1 Upon hearing of Guevara's death, organizers of the 1968 Vietnam Congress in Berlin stamped this phrase – Che lebt! – onto the Dutschke/Salvatore translation of Guevara's Vietnam letter to OSPAAL. Distributed in pamphlet form, this 'Vietnam letter' helped to inaugurate Che as martyr.

2 Bammer, *Partial Visions*; Wallerstein, *Utopistics*.

3 In relation to the global North and Cuba, see Westad, *The Global Cold War*, 158, 180.

4 Hardt and Negri, *Empire*, 334.

5 1947 to 1989 is a widely accepted, generalizing periodization. Stephanson, 'Cold War Origins.'

6 For a definition of third world, see Chandra Talpade Mohanty, Ann Russo, and Lourdes Torres, eds., *Third World Women and the Politics of Feminism* (Bloomington: Indiana University Press, 1991), ix.

7 Amin, *Obsolescent Capitalism*.

8 Larsen, *Reading North by South*. For more on what is often called the Brandt Report, which was updated in 2001, see http://www.stwr.org/special-features/the-brandt-report.html.

9 Anderson, *Imagined Communities*, 7–8.

10 Renan, 'What is a Nation?'

11 Hobsbawm, *Nations and Nationalism since 1780*; Hobsbawm and Ranger, eds., *The Invention of Tradition*.

12 Wildenthal, 'Notes on a History of "Imperial Turns" in Modern Germany.'

13 Glissant, *Poetics of Relation*.

14 Such work remains important although its canonization may contribute to upholding the power structures that it seeks to undercut. When Nina

Berman demonstrates that Edward Said's arguments partake of a larger, older debate on orientalism among Arab scholars, she points to such problems of canonization/marginalization that many have thematized without sufficient result. Berman, *Orientalismus, Kolonialismus und Moderne*, 14, footnote. On this phenomenon in relation to theories of nation, see for example, Grewal and Kaplan, 'Transnational Feminist Cultural Studies.' In relation to philosophy and critical theory, see for example, Bordo, *Unbearable Weight*. In relation to race, literary theory, and the literary canon, see for example, Christian, 'The Race for Theory.' Such problems of voice are exacerbated by mythologies of individualism that remain undertheorized in contemporary critical theory.

15 Ashcroft, Griffiths, and Tiffin, *The Post-Colonial Studies Reader*.
16 McClintock, *Imperial Leather*.
17 Obeyesekere, 'British Cannibals.'
18 Pratt, *Imperial Eyes*.
19 Friedrichsmeyer, Lennox, and Zantop, eds., *The Imperialist Imagination*.
20 Pratt, *Imperial Eyes*, 6.
21 McClintock, 'The Angel of Progress.'
22 The term 'revolutionary fantasies' recalls Susanne Zantop's term 'colonial fantasies,' while denoting the identificatory, solidary, and variously problematic relationships of first world with third world. Zantop, *Colonial Fantasies*.
23 Adelson, 'Imagining Migrants' Literature'; Breger, 'Meine Herren, spielt in meinem Gesicht ein Affe?'
24 Kacandes, 'From Deconstruction to Postcolonialism, 1980 to the Present.'
25 Fachinger, *Rewriting Germany from the Margins*.
26 Hosek, 'Whose Culture, Whose Feminism.'
27 Hong, 'Remarks at the Round Table on Transnationalism.'
28 Lionnet and Shih, 'Introduction.'
29 For example, Speck, 'Deutsche Interessen.'
30 Sieg, *Ethnic Drag*.
31 Friedrichsmeyer, Lennox, and Zantop, 'Introduction.'
32 For example, Herzog, 'Pleasure, Sex, and Politics Belong Together'; Linke, *German Bodies*.
33 See also, Nielsen, 'Aspekte der Faschismuskritik der Antiautoritären Bewegung.' My thinking here has benefited from discussions with Marike Janzen and Jamie Trnka.
34 Teraoka, *East, West, and Others*.
35 Hohendahl, 'Von der Rothaut zum Edelmenschen. Karl Mays Amerikaromane.'

36 Berman, *Orientalismus, Kolonialismus und Moderne.*

37 Zantop, *Colonial Fantasies.*

38 Sieg, *Ethnic Drag.* In this text, I will follow Dominick LaCapra's practice of referring to the Nazi extermination of undesired people both as the Holocaust and the Shoah. The religious roots of the term Holocaust make it inadequate. However, using only Shoah risks casting the extermination as genocide aimed solely against Jewish people. LaCapra, *Representing the Holocaust.* My decision here has benefited from discussions with Max Friedman, Dirk Moses, and Irene Siegel.

39 Melin and Zorach, 'Cuba as Paradise, Paradigm, and Paradox,' 496.

40 Bauschinger and Cocalis, eds., 'Neue Welt'/'Dritte Welt.'

41 Brunner, *Die poetische Insel.*

42 Butler, 'Tourism Development in Small Islands'; Conlin and Baum, 'Introduction.'

43 Bauschinger, 'Wie die Deutschen zu Reiseweltmeistern werden'; Spode, 'Reif für die Insel.'

44 In the 1950s in the FRG, Italy made a qualitative shift in signification from self-education destination to a site of tourist trysts between female Germans and the male Italians that they sought. Schumann, 'Grenzübertritte.' This change resonates with, but is not explained by, the overabundance of single woman in the FRG post war. Such gender bending narratives may have been destabilizing, yet they also may have avoided conjuring German cross-border colonization, an elision that points to the symbolic value of tourism as a practice of domination. 'What travel to Italy began, mass tourism to Mallorca epitomized. In 1955, the Allies allowed the FRG its own airline and by 1956, the first travellers were on their way. The hot, drunken sands of Mallorca became the most important travel destination for German airlines.' Göckeritz, 'Die Bundesbürger entdecken die Urlaubsreise.' Tropical islands frame heterosexual male fantasies of nubile, libidinous women. The FRG soft-porn industry commonly employed island settings in its films that co-opt 1960s notions of sexual revolution. Survey of electronic British Film Institute Film Index International: http://fii.chadwyck.com/home.

45 Angela Piekarski (STA advertising executive), personal interview with the author, Berlin, December 2002.

46 Borris, 'Sonne und Amore'; Opaschowski, *Jugendauslandsreisen.*

47 http://www.tropical-islands.de.

48 Edmond and Smith, eds., *Islands in History and Representation.*

49 For example, Nachbar, *Die Gestohlene Insel,* 206

50 Ette, 'Einleitung'; Kapcia, *Cuba.*

51 Miguel Benavides (Peña in *Preludio 11*), personal interview with the author, Havana, March 2003.
52 Jameson, 'Of Islands and Trenches.'
53 Utopias may then become sites 'that have the possibility of coming to full fruition.' Elliott, *The Shape of Utopia*, cited in Beck, 'Frauen.' The Cuban professor and novelist Guillermo Rodríguez Rivera replaces utopia with 'uchronia,' a social entity that is possible, but not at this time. Guillermo Rodríguez Rivera, personal interview with the author, Havana, February 2003.
54 Mannheim, *Ideology and Utopia*, 173.
55 Jacoby, *The End of Utopia*.
56 Foucault, 'Of Other Spaces.'
57 Laclau and Mouffe, *Hegemony and Socialist Strategy*.
58 Harvey, *Spaces of Hope*.
59 Wallerstein defines utopistics as the 'serious assessment of historical alternatives ... the sober, rational, and realistic evaluation of human social systems, the constraints on what they can be, and the zones open to human creativity. Not the face of the perfect (and inevitable) future, but the face of an alternative, credibly better, and historically possible (but far from certain) future.' Wallerstein, *Utopistics*, 1–2.
60 Mannheim, *Ideology and Utopia*, 187.
61 Bammer, *Partial Visions*.
62 Ferns, *Narrating Utopia*.
63 Retamar, 'The Enormity of Cuba.'
64 Hobsbawm, *The Age of Extremes*, 440.
65 E.g., Butler, *Bodies That Matter*.
66 See note 14.
67 Kontje, *German Orientalisms*.

Chapter One. Contesting the New Berlin Republic through Germany's Cubas

1 'Die hatten keine Ahnung von Sozialismus, die hatten keine Ahnung von der DDR und die kümmerten sich auch nicht darum. Die wollten bloß den "armen Kubanern helfen." Es war ein Abenteuer für sie.' André Lüdtke, personal interview with the author, Berlin, November 2001.
2 'Larger FRG' means Germany from 3 October 1990.
3 'Merger' de-emphasizes the political nature of the unification of the Germanies from 3 October 1990 and bears economic connotations. 'Unification' and 'reunification' emphasize the respective political valence.
4 On the use of Americanization as a way out of fascist ideology see Maase, *BRAVO Amerika*.

5 Brockmann, *Literature and German Reunification*.
6 For an interesting summary of the debate as articulated in *Der Spiegel* in 1993 see Parkes, 'Postmodern Polemics.'
7 Dümcke and Vilmar, *Kolonialisierung der DDR*.
8 Habermas, *Die nachholende Revolution*, 160; Habermas, *Die Normalität einer Berliner Republik*.
9 Grass, *Ein weites Feld*.
10 Herzka, *Kuba*, 149.
11 Jiménez, 'La economía del turismo en Cuba.' Cited in Beier, 'Tourismus,' 375.
12 Krämer, *Der alte Mann und die Insel*, 26.
13 Le Bel, *La Réhabilitation de la Vieille Havane*.
14 The term Kuba Welle, which was commonly found in print media around the time of *Buena Vista Social Club*, was used prior to this in oral parlance to refer to interest in or manifestations of Cuba and Cuban culture. Anthropologist Ruth Behar has mentioned a similar phenomenon in the United States in Behar, 'While Waiting for the Ferry to Cuba.'
15 Beier, 'Tourismus,' 377. See also 'Cuba: Arrivals of Non-Resident Visitors at National Borders, by Country of Residence.'
16 Bert Hoffmann, personal interview with the author, Berlin, June 2002; Joaquín Santana Castillo, personal communication with the author, Havana, February 2003.
17 Travel to Cuba was costly both for the state and for individual citizens. SAPMO-BArch, DY30, IV a 2/20/185.
18 Survey of 'Verzeichnis Lieferbarer Bücher' (German *Books in Print* equivalent), May 2003.
19 Santana Castillo, unpublished manuscript.
20 Letz, 'Im Osten nichts Neues?'
21 Reichardt, *Nie vergessen Solidarität üben!*
22 Cuba Sí members, personal communications with the author, Berlin, March–October 2002.
23 Dominic Boyer, 'Ostalgie and the Politics of the Future in Eastern Germany,' 363.
24 Letz, 'Im Osten nichts Neues?'
25 Ulises Estrada Lescaille, personal interview with the author, Havana, March 2003.
26 Letz, 'Im Osten nichts Neues?'
27 Hollander, 'Political Tourism in Cuba and Nicaragua,' 29.
28 *Cuba Sí* members, personal communications with the author, Berlin, March–October 2002; Tobias Hauser, telephone interview with the author,

Berlin, January 2002; Hoffmann, interview; Santana Castillo, interview.
Tobias Hauser, long-time producer of and projectionist for his travel-
ling slide show *Cuba Real* recalls frequent comparisons made by Eastern
German travellers in the early 1990s. For them, Cubans were coping with
the fall of the Soviet Union better than countries in Eastern Europe. The
Cubans were *pfiggiger* (sharper) and knew that they would become another
Dominican Republic (i.e., overrun by tourism and foreign investors) if
their system collapsed.

29 Factual assertions about marketing strategy in this section stem from
Pernod Ricard's promotional packets and from lengthy discussions with a
Pernod Ricard sales and distribution representative over the first months
of 2002, augmented by Web research. Further interviews have been
thwarted by ongoing court cases with Bacardi.

30 Just-drinks.com, editorial (accessed July 2009).

31 For brief histories of the value of Eastern German products in the
larger FRG and their newest incarnation as retro fashion see Ahbe, 'Der
Dammbruch'; Wedel, 'Jetzt seid ihr alle Spreewaldgurken.'

32 These walls are also, of course, reminiscent of the Havana walls in Wim
Wenders's colour-engineered documentary, *Buena Vista*. Iterations of
the Havana Club website also suggest commercial connections between
the Cuban rum and Wenders's well-known Berlin films *Himmel über
Berlin* (*Wings of Desire*) and *In weiter Ferne, so nah!* (*Faraway, so close!*)

33 Gabriela Fiorentini, personal interview with the author, Berlin, February
2001.

34 Cabezas, 'Discourses of Prostitution.'

35 Fusco, 'Hustling for Dollars.'

36 Kempadoo, 'The Migrant Tightrope'; My own non-exhaustive review
of 'Autobiographical Travel Reports,' http://www.worldsexguide.org
(accessed September 2003).

37 For more on the Bacardi story, see, for example: Gjelten, *Bacardi and the
Long Fight for Cuba*; Morgenthaler, 'Zwischen Rum und Revolution';
Ospina, *Bacardi*; Voss, *Die Bacardis*.

38 This rivalry also mimics the debate on Cuba between Cubans in Cuba
and Cubans and Cuban-Americans in the United States. This U.S.
researcher cannot help but be fascinated by other parallels in the structures of Cuban political and social groupings in the United States and
Germany. In the United States, the Cuban-American population is split
between those who left Cuba for politico-economic reasons, mostly in the
1960s, and those who left Cuba primarily to achieve a better standard of

living in the subsequent decades. In Berlin, a similar division is found in the groups of Cubans and Cuban-Germans. The Deutsch-Kubanische Gesellschaft e.V. (German-Cuban Association) comprises exiles that disagree with the current Cuban regime and believe that they have been defrauded of their property in Cuba. El Caimán e.V. (The Crocodile) comprises those who are not particularly critical of the Cuban government, yet who remain in Germany to enjoy its higher standard of living. The former group seeks to increase its political influence, despite its lack of funds, while the latter is primarily a social organization that is interested in retaining Cuban cultural traditions. El Caimán's membership has a much higher percentage of Cuban-Germans who lived in the GDR. Deutsch-Kubanische Gesellschaft e.V. members, personal communications with the author, Berlin, May–June 2002; El Caimán e.V. members, personal communications with the author, Berlin, May–June 2002. Between 1984 and 1989, at least 30,000 mostly male Cubans were educated and worked in the GDR, primarily as skilled labourers. Krämer, *Der alte*, 156.

39 Halle, *German Film after Germany*.
40 Gemünden, 'Nostalgia for the Nation.'
41 Exceptions are Robert Phillip Kolker and Peter Beicken who read Wenders's extra-national authenticity project as an uncanny *Heimat* journey. Kolker and Beicken, *The Films of Wim Wenders*, 165.
42 Hentzi, 'Buena Vista Social Club,' 50.
43 On this connection more generally, see Benn Michaels, 'Race into Culture.'
44 For an example of the use of familial metaphor in German unification narratives, see the following publication of the federal administration for political education: Lindner, *Die Demokratische Revolution in der DDR 1989/90*, 152–3.
45 Taussig, *Mimesis and Alterity*.
46 Liberal U.S.-Cuban reception of this film has emphasized this point as well. Oteri, 'Tania León Interview' (accessed March 2005).
47 See also Ghosh, 'The Many Uses of Jazz' (accessed March 2005). Members of the conservative U.S.-Cuban community read the film similarly – they ap-plauded the movie after having boycotted the visit of the Cuban musicians themselves. Levine, 'Viva *Buena Vista Social Club*' (accessed March 2005).
48 Appadurai, 'Putting Hierarchy in Its Place.'
49 Andrea Rinke cites a 1992 *Emnid-Institut für Meinungsforschung* opinion poll of 3000 Germans in this regard and demonstrates that such attitudes

are represented in popular culture as well. Rinke, 'From Motzki to Trotzki,' 235, 237.

50 Eason, 'Ry Cooder's Buena Vista Project Scuttled by Cuba Policy,' http://www.mountaintimes.com/mtweekly/2003/0227/cooder.php3 (accessed February 2004).

51 See Agneskirchner, 'Gespräch mit Uli Gaulke.' See also Schölzel, 'Warum drehen Sie Filme über Kuba?' http://www.jungewelt.de/2000/07-18/014.shtml (accessed July 2004).

52 Jeannette Eggert, personal interview with the author, Berlin, June 2003.

53 Naughton, *That Was the Wild East*; Myra Marx Ferree, informal discussions with the author.

54 Review of film reception folder on *Havanna mi amor* at the Hochschule für Film und Fernsehen, Konrad Wolf, Potsdam.

55 Bremme, 'Havanna Mi Amor,' 43.

56 Hosek, 'Postcommunist Spectacle.'

57 Eastern German scholars who specialize in gender analysis have been particularly adamant about pointing to the limitations of this genre and of DEFA's representation of women in general. See Dölling, 'Wir alle lieben Paula, aber uns liegt an Paul.' On the topic in literature, see Dahlke, *Papierboot*.

58 Perhaps the classic example is the six-film series Lebensläufe – Die Geschichte der Kinder von Golzow in einzelnen Porträts, filmed between 1961 and 1980. Gaulke's first documentary film on Cuba, *Quién es el ultimo – Wer ist der Letzte*, was completed in 1997.

59 Schieber, 'Im Dämmerlicht der Perestroika 1980 bis 1989.'

60 Scholars have demonstrated that this communicative strategy is present across genres. On GDR feature films see Feinstein, *The Triumph of the Ordinary*.

61 Eggert and Gaulke see what they term the Western approach of direct questioning to be communicatively ineffective. Furthermore, they consider it disrespectful, because it elides the circumstances of the interviewee and constructs a mythology of freedom of choice and expression that obscures the logics of life in societies with authoritarian regimes. Personal interview with the author, Berlin, December 2001.

62 See, for example, contemporary novels with autobiographical elements such as Hein, *Mein erstes T-Shirt*; Hensel, *Zonenkinder*; Rusch, *Meine Freie Deutsche Jugend*; Simon, *Denn wir sind anders*.

63 I use the term womanism, favoured by African American women, rather than the term feminism because East German women generally objected to the latter, deeming it bourgeois and anti-male. Hosek, 'Whose Culture, Whose Feminism.'

64 See Carstens-Wickham, 'Gender in Cartoons of German Unification';
Cheryl Dueck, 'Gendered Germanies.'

65 'Jetzt muß ich hier weg, jetzt muß ich los,
bevor ich zu einem kleinen, harten Betonklotz werde,
zusammengepreßt von dem Nichts nach hunderttausend
Worten.
Jetzt muß ich hier weg, jetzt muß ich los,
bevor ich zu einem kleinen, kalten Eisklumpen werde,
gefroren nach der einzigen, ständigen Frage:
Wie weiter?
Also packe ich den Rucksack und laufe fort auf der Suche nach uns Menschen.
Also reise ich nach Kuba. Dahin wo die Internationale mit wiegenden Hüf-
ten gesungen wird. Meinen wärmsten Dank an Helene und Karl, die mir
diese Aussicht bereits schenkten, als ich noch im Gefängnis war.'
Viett, *Cuba libre bittersüß*, 5. Throughout this monograph, translations are
my own unless otherwise noted.

66 'Soll er doch kommen, der Kapitalismus, sie werden Kubaner bleiben und
nicht aufgeben, was die Revolution ihnen an Menschenwürde, Freiheit
und Solidarität gegeben hat … Ich fühle mich sehr wohl unter den Compañeros, ihre Zuversicht ist ohne Pathos und wie Balsam auf meinem von
der Niederlagen angegriffenen historischen Optimismus.
Aber ich kann nicht ermessen, wie stark und selbstbewußt die Revolution die Kubaner gemacht hat, wie tief ihre Souveränität individuell und
kollektiv verankert ist. Ich habe nur die Erfahrung einer geschichtlich
Besiegten. Der handstreichartige Sieg des Kapitalismus über den sozialistischen Osten und die bestürzend höfische Demut der Unterlegenen macht
mich vielleicht zu kleinmütig, zu mißtrauisch und verunsichert mich in
meinem Optimismus. Kuba hat andere Erfahrungen. Kubas Revolution ist
aus den Menschen erwachsen, sie haben sie gemacht um ihrer Selbstach-
tung willen, und sie ist das Ergebnis einer fünfhundertjährigen Unterdrü-
ckungs- und Befreiungsgeschichte. Warum sorge ich mich nur immerzu?
Die Compañeros tun es nicht. Ihr Optimismus fasziniert mich. Er ist
oftmals gar nicht politisch geprägt, sondern eine Haltung, die ansteckt, die
fröhlich macht.' Ibid., 52.

67 'Es ist nicht zu verbergen, daß wir Ausländerinnen sind und Dollars
haben. Mein schlechtes Gewissen gegenüber den schon viel länger Wartenden beruhigt sich schnell in der Bequemlichkeit des PKWs und der
Aussicht, in zwei Stunden in Pinar del Rio zu sein. Schleißlich bin ich
unschuldig daran, nicht in Kuba geboren zu sein.' Ibid., 26.

Chapter Two. Extending Solidarian *Heimat*: Cuba and the 1960s Democratic Republic

1 Boa and Palfreyman, *Heimat – A German Dream*.
2 'Und wir lieben die Heimat, die schöne, und wir schützen sie, weil sie dem Volke gehört, weil sie unserem Volke gehört.' Keller, Herbert. 'Junge Pioniere lieben die Nature.' *Frisch auf singt all ihr Musici*. Quoted in Lange, *Heimat*, 17.
3 Blunk, 'The Concept of "Heimat-GDR" in DEFA Feature Films.' Domestic travel books on the GDR exemplify this phenomenon as well.
4 Wickham, *Constructing Heimat in Postwar Germany Longing and Belonging*, 6–9.
5 For example, On the overthrow of Salvador Allende in Chile, *El Golpe Blanco* (*The White Coup*, 1975) and *Im Feuer bestanden* (*Persistence under Fire*, 1978).
6 MacCannell, *Empty Meeting Grounds*.
7 On islands as boundless rather than bounded, see Hau'ofa, 'Our Sea of Islands.'
8 Zimmermann, 'Der Dokumentarfilm der DEFA zwischen Propaganda, Alltagbeobachtung und subversiver Rezeption.' These first-generation GDR documentaries, two of the last of which are Karl Gass's *Schaut auf diese Stadt* (*Look at this City*, 1962) and Heynowski's *Brüder und Schwester* (*Brothers and Sisters*, 1963), depict Western locations from the FRG to Paris to Chile. They focus on revolutionary sites and events, such as demonstrations, and social problems, such as homelessness. This gaze of revolutionary tourism avoids the sweeping panoramas and famous monuments typical of Western travel documentaries. In this filmic revolutionary tourism, travel is undertaken as an enlightenment project for the vicariously travelling viewer.
9 Johannes von Moltke's and Jan Palmowski's work continues this tradition by considering GDR Heimat only in relation the 1950s and to local concerns. Moltke, *No Place Like Home*; Palmowski, 'Building An East German Nation.'
10 *Allgemeine Deutsche Nachrichtenagentur* (*ADN*), 1967 SAPMO-BArch, DY 30, IV a 2/20.
11 Julio A. García Oliveras, personal interview with the author, March 2003; Krämer, 'Von den anfänglichen Hürden, dem Alltag und abrupten Ende einer engen deutsch-kubanischen Liaison'; VEB F.A. Brockhaus, *Compañeros*; Review of *Augenzeuge* newsreels at the Hochschule für Film und Fernsehen Konrad Wolf, Potsdam, 2002.
12 SAPMO-BArch, DY 24, 6954.

13 For example, Fries, 'Kubanische Kalenderblätter'; Marquardt and Marquardt, *Report aus Havanna*; Otto, *Republik der Leidenschaft*; Panitz, *Kubaskizzen*; Rubinstein, 'Meine kubanische Reise'; Scheer, *Von Afrika nach Kuba*; Schubert, *Rote Insel im Atlantik*; Villain, *Frühling auf Kuba*.

14 'Liebe und Moral junger Menschen in der DDR poetisch [zu] gestalten.' The artistic working group Heinrich Greif included director Frank Vogel, writer Paul Wiens, dramaturge Willi Brückner, camera man Günter Ost, and producer Hans-Joachim Funk. In DEFA's early years, the individual role of the director was de-emphasized. Similarly, *Preludio 11* was produced by the working group Roter Kreis, which included director Kurt Maetzig and screenwriter Wolfgang Schreyer. SAPMO-BArch, DR, 117, BA 0015; SAPMO-BArch, DR 117, BA 1945.

15 SAPMO-BArch, DR 117, BA 1945.

16 SAPMO-BArch, DR 117, BA 0015.

17 SAPMO-BArch, DR 117, BA 1945; Rogelio París, personal interview with the author, Havana, February 2003.

18 My thanks to Mario Naito of ICAIC, Caridad Cumaná of the Fundación del Nuevo Cine Latinoamericano, and Renate Goethe and Ute Illing of the HFF Konrad Wolf for their archival work on this question.

19 SAPMO-BArch, DR 117, 1945.

20 'Liebeserklärung an die Menschen Berlins … Wahre Liebe ist ja nicht die alles duldende, die alles verzeihende, sondern die aufrichtige, die fordernde, die Liebe, die auch weiß, daß eine Grenze gesetzt werden muß wenn es notwendig ist.' Progress *Filmblatt* for *Und deine Liebe auch*, 1962. BA-FA, 17552.

21 Various newspaper clippings. BA-FA, 17552.

22 BA-FA, DR 1, MfK-HV Film: 203. Mueller-Stahl did not emigrate to the FRG until 1980, thus, this did not influence the 1967 decision.

23 For example, Crew, ed., *Consuming Germany in the Cold War*.

24 Chanan, *Cuban Cinema*, 167.

25 Alea, '¿Que es lo moderno en el arte?'

26 Kurt Maetzig, telephone interview with the author, Berlin, June 2003; Mesa, 'KinoCuban'; Guillermo Rodríguez Rivera, personal interview with the author, Havana, February 2003.

27 Miguel Benavides (Peña in *Preludio 11*), personal interview with the author, Havana, March 2003; Marco Madrigal, personal interview with the author, March 2003; Maetzig, interview.

28 SAPMO–Barch, DR 117, BA 1948.

29 Maetzig and Schreyer, *Preludio 11*, available for viewing at the BA-FA, Berlin.

30 '[Wir] fassen es als eine Ehrensache auf, gerade jetzt an der "Filmfront" zu kämpfen, so gut es geht, um dadurch auf unsere Weise unseren kubanischen Freunden zu helfen.' Vogel, 'Heisses Pflaster Havanna.'

31 'In diesen Stunden verwischt sich im Hotel "National" die Kulisse mit der Wirklichkeit. Während im Park die Filmszenen gedreht werden, sind auf der anderen Seite des Hotels Schnellfeuergeschütze in Stellung gegangen, und kubanische Miliz und Militäreinheiten haben Posten bezogen ... So ist es in diesen Stunden auch nicht verwunderlich, daß der echte kubanische Milizsoldat sich in strammer Haltung an den falschen deutschen Kapitän wendet, um ihm eine Meldung zu erstatten.' Ibid.

32 Benavides, interview; Antonio Masón, personal interview with the author, Havana, February 2003.

33 Some GDR film critics thematized the parallels between the GDR and Cuba, particularly the emigrant situations and the danger that the United States posed to Cuba and the GDR. For example, Skulski, 'Sechs Mann in einem Boot.'

34 SAPMO-BArch, DY 30, IV a 2/ 20.

35 Benavides, interview; Madrigal, interview; Maetzig, interview.

36 For instance, Sieg argues in the case of Rainer Werner Fassbinder's film *Katzelmacher*, the focus on the positioning, but not the subjectivity, of the foreigner of colour (played by the white director and actor) undercuts its anti-racist agenda. She regrets that 'the story is not really about [the character Jorges] at all.' Sieg, *Ethnic Drag*, 166.

37 'Denn man hat Feuer, wenn man aus Kuba stammt.' Roth, 'Der erste Schnee, die erste Rolle für Aurora.'

38 Zantop, *Colonial Fantasies*.

39 SAPMO-BArch, DR 117, BA 1948.

40 Ibid; SAPMO-BArch, DY 30, IV a 2/20.

41 SAPMO- BArch, DY 30, IV a 2/20/185. Letter dated 19 September 1963 from head of production Hans Mahlich to Progress film distribution.

42 Ibid.

43 'Die Schönheit der Tropeninsel, heißes Spiel von Gitarren und Tamtams, vor allem jedoch bezaubernde Frauen.' Reprinted in H.A., 'Abenteuer in der Schweinebucht.'

44 SAPMO-BArch, DR 117, BA 1948.

45 Various newspaper clippings from the BA-FA *Preludio 11* film folder. Official directives influenced cultural reporting and all public information in the GDR; this internationally ubiquitous phenomenon finds its expression diversely.

46 Madrigal, interview; Mario Naito, personal interview with the author,

Havana, February 2003; París, interview. Analysis of extant film reviews at ICAIC and libraries in Havana.

47 Chanan, *Cuban Cinema*, 166–7.

48 Masón, interview.

49 Angelika Bammer suggests that precisely through their openness and fragmentary nature, 'partial visions' of utopia enable both a critical perspective on the present place and non-prescriptive possibilities for the future. Bammer, *Partial Visions*.

50 Bussmann, 'Die Utopie schlägt den Takt.'

51 Kaufmann, 'Interview mit Irmtraud Morgner.'

52 Barck, *Jedes Buch ein Abenteuer*.

53 GDR publishing histories can be notoriously difficult to decipher without extensive knowledge of the functionaries and authors involved. Geoffrey Westgate's research expertly analyses Morgner's work in relation to this context. Westgate, *Strategies under Surveillance*.

54 For example, Schwarzer, 'Jetzt oder Nie!'

55 Morgner suggests this as well; see Kaufmann, 'Interview mit Irmtraud Morgner,' 1510.

56 For an analysis of Morgner's work in the context of U.S. 1970s feminism, see Bammer, 'Sozialistische Feminismen,' and Hanel, *Literarischer Widerstand zwischen Phantastischem und Alltäglichem*. The latter text includes a contextualization of Morgner as feminist in the GDR and the FRG.

57 See, for example, Diemer, *Patriarchalismus in der DDR*.

58 See, for example, Kaplan and Grewal, 'Transnational Feminist Cultural Studies.'

59 The closing pages suggest that his name is Orpheus in reference to the Greek master musician and Argonaut. In such a reading, Persephone suggests an earthly life force and Orpheus suggests the life-affirming power of music. Morgner's texts are rich with intertextual allusions, most of which are not of direct relevance here.

60 See also Emde, 'Irmtraud Morgner's Postmodern Feminism.'

61 Morgner, *Rumba auf einen Herbst*, 85. Subsequent quotations will refer to this edition. Jeanette Clausen's translation of Irmtraud Morgner's work, *The Life and Adventures of Trobadora Beatrice as Chronicled by Her Minstrel Laura*, includes a version of *Rumba* in *Trobadora*'s intermezzos.

62 Butler, *The Psychic Life of Power*.

63 A thorough analysis of this trope across Morgner's oeuvre can be found in Linklater, '*Und immer zügelloser wird die Lust*.' For a light-hearted and useful contextualization of the notion of Produktivkraft in the GDR, see Soden, 'Sexualität als Produktivkraft?'

64 Third person was the accepted narrative perspective of GDR literary texts;
    many authors, including Morgner, worked to extend the definitions of this
    and other artistic conventions through political action and in their own
    texts.

65 'Fahles, kurzes Gestrüpp wuchs aus dem baumwollenen Firnfeld hinauf
    bis zu einer Hochebene, die mehrfach quer gerissen war. Im Vordergrund
    endete sie an einem bewachsenen Gesims, unter dessen Überhang ein
    Augenkogel undeutlich sichtbar wurde. Im Hintergrund erhob sich am
    Fuße der Brauen der Nasenberg, großporig, fettglänzend, steil ansteigend
    bis zum Gipfel ...

    Ev sah, wie sich der rechte Nasenflügel spannte, dehnte und wieder
    erschlaffte. Die dicken Lider, die an den Rändern mit hellen, gekrümmten
    Wimpern besetzt waren, zuckten ab und zu. Ev beobachtete die gleichför-
    mige Bewegung unter der Hautdecke des Halses, die vereinzelt mit rötlich
    schimmernden kielartigen Haarstiften besteckt war, und das Stoßen im
    Zentrum dieser Bewegung ...

    Der Körper lag starr wie zuvor. Er hatte Ev gegen die Wand gepreßt. Er
    schien aufzuquellen im Schlaf. Wenn er so weiterschlief, schien der Augen-
    blick absehbar, da er sie erdrücken würde.' Morgner, *Rumba auf einen
    Herbst*, 82–3. (My translation seeks to do justice to Morgner's neologisms.)

66 'Eine große, aber durchaus überschaubare Konstruktion', sagte Lutz P. zu
    den Hotelgästen ... Durch die Hauchflecken [auf der Fensterfront] besahen
    sie den Oktoberhimmel. Und sie glaubten undeutlich zu erkennen, was da
    in einer seltsamen Spiegelung über dem See abgebildet und von Lutz P.
    mit einer Definition belegt worden war: Ein Rumpf, klotzig, inselhaft, aber
    bewegt, sowohl im Ganzen als auch an der Oberfläche teilweise bewegt,
    tote und belebte Materie in Symbiose, vor allem Stahl und Menschen, wie
    es schien, die Hohlräume waren mit Beton ausgegossen, an den Stellen,
    wo rohrähnliche Gebilde aus dem Rumpf herausragten, war er, soweit
    man erkennen konnte, mit Bleiplatten belegt, die rohrrähnlichen Gebilde
    trugen drachenkopfartige Verdickungen an ihren Enden und bewegten
    sich steif, und wenn man genau hinsah, erkannte man auch die Decke, die
    das Ungeheuer bis eben noch verhüllt hatte, das bekannt war unter dem
    Fachausdruck: doomsday-machine.

    "Ich war schon fünfmal da," sagte ein junger Mann. "Das letzte Mal vor
    acht Wochen. In Baracoa hab ich ne Freundin." Er zog ein Foto aus seiner
    Hosentasche und zeigte es herum.' Ibid., 9.

67 'Sonnengroßen Staubfleck, der nicht Schwimmen kann. Der immer an der
    gleichen Stelle klebt, bestimmt durch die gleichen Koordinaten.' Ibid., 10.

68 '"Eine große, aber durchaus überschaubare Konstruktion ... Die Abmes-

sungen könnte man vielleicht als riesig bezeichnen," sagte Lutz P., "als riesig oder gewaltig, wie Sie wollen. Aber ein Ingenieur beurteilt eine Machine nicht nach ihren Ausmaßen, sondern nach ihren technischen Daten." Ibid., 8. '"Eine riesige Konstruktion," sagte das Fräulein, "aber man beurteilt eine Maschine ja gottseidank nicht nach ihren Ausmaßen, sondern nach ihren technischen Daten, nicht wahr?"' Ibid., 81.

69 Music is part of this connection; cf. Cardinal, 'Irmtraud Morgner's *Rumba auf einen Herbst.*'

70 'Sie öffnete die Augen und blinzelte in den Himmel. Der war tief wie ein umgestürzter Brunnen, schmal und unheimlich tief, und der Schaft war mit buntem Laub ausgemauert. Oben. Das Mauerwerk war natürlich nicht bis zur Sohle niedergebracht, es reichte vielleicht hundert Buchenjahre hinab oder hundertfünfzig. Die Sohle war blau, je länger Evelyne B. hinuntersah, desto blauer wurde die Sohle und desto weiter entfernte sie sich. Sie schien zu fallen. Evelyne B. warf Glückspfennige in den Brunnen und zählte. Aber das Echo blieb aus. Die Sohle fiel und fiel, und Evelyne B. fiel mit ihr.

Sie legt die linke Hand auf seinen Oberarm, er nimmt die rechte, sie spürt seinen Atem auf der Stirn und die gelben Töne der Trompete, dunkelblaue Iris, große Pupillen, Rhythmus ...

Evelyne B. lag ausgestreckt auf einer Decke, um braun zu werden. Die Sonne war nicht mehr viel wert, schlapp war sie, ausgemergelt von den Ekstasen des Sommers. Aber sie machte es noch, sie tat so, als ob sie im Zenit stünde. Hier, wo sie nie im Zenit stand. Wo sie immer schräg und ein bißchen nebenbei auf das Land herunterblakte. Das kleine Land. Das kleine, ordentliche Land. Auf das ein riesiger, umgestürzter Brunnen gestülpt war mit einer blauen Sohle. Evelyne B. starrte hinunter in den schmalen, unheimlich tiefen Schacht und warf Glückspfennige und wartete und zählte, aber es kam kein Echo, nur Blau kam. Dunkelblau, und sie fiel und fiel und stürzte auf die Sohle zu.' Ibid., 11.

71 Bathrick, *The Powers of Speech*, 13.

72 Westgate, *Strategies under Surveillance.*

Chapter Three. Translating Revolution: Cuba and the 1960s Federal Republic

1 Dieter Kunzelmann, Christof Baldeney, Rudolphe Gasché, and Frank Böckelmann founded Subversiver Aktion, and Dutschke and Bernd Rabehl were members. Diederichsen, 'Persecution and Self-Persecution.' Gretchen Dutschke and Siegward Lönnendonker diverge somewhat on the attendees at the Pichelsdorf meeting. Rudi Dutschke, Rabehl, Wolfgang Lefèvre,

Urs Müller-Plantenberg, Christian Semler, and Rolf Stanzik were there, as were perhaps Peter Gäng and Peter Schneider. It is probable that the authors of *Der lange Marsch. Wege der Revolution in Lateinamerika* (Munich: Trikont Verlag, 1968) – T. Käsemann, R. Schöller, Gisela Mandel, and K.S. Karol – also shared these positions.

2 Some important exceptions are Balsen and Rössel, *Hoch die internationale Solidarität!*; Juchler, *Rebellische Subjektivität und Internationalismus*. Texts sometimes gesture towards the transhemispheric connections, while focusing on Germany, Europe, and/or the United States; see Koenen, *Das rote Jahrzehnt*; Schmidtke, 'Cultural Revolution or Cultural Shock?' For an overview of the literature, see Thomas, *Protest Movements in 1960s*.

3 For example, Dirke, *'All Power to the Imagination!'*

4 For example, Westad, *The Global Cold War*; Dubinsky et al., eds., *New World Coming*.

5 Banchoff, *The German Problem Transformed*.

6 Habermas, 'Staatsbürgerschaft und Nationale Identität.'

7 Chaussy, *Die Drei Leben des Rudi Dutschke*, 347.

8 Kraushaar, 'Rudi Dutschke und die Wiedervereinigung.'

9 Kraushaar, 'Rudi Dutschke und der bewaffnete Kampf.'

10 Thomas, *Protest Movements*, 163.

11 Hardt and Negri, *Empire*, 105.

12 Ibid., 105–6.

13 Sareika, *Die Dritte Welt in der westdeutschen Literatur der sechziger Jahre*, 27–63.

14 Fels, *Der Aufruhr der 68er*, 21.

15 Albrecht, *Der Sozialistische Deutsche Studentenbund (SDS)*; Juchler, *Die Studentenbewegungen in den Vereinigten Staaten und der Bundesrepublik Deutschland*.

16 For example, Dirke, 'All Power'; Lennox, 'Enzensberger, *Kursbuch*, and Third-Worldism'; Teraoka, *East, West, and Others*. My analysis of the Enzensberger-Weiss debate is particularly indebted to the latter two texts.

17 Consider also the recent focus on U.S.-FRG relations. For example, Klimke, *The Other Alliance*.

18 Karsunke and Michel, *Bewegung in der Republik, 1965–1984*.

19 Teraoka, *East, West, and Others*.

20 Such Eurocentric tendencies characterized much interest in the third world among left-leaning people in the FRG. Lennox, 'Enzensberger.'

21 Linke, *German Bodies*.

22 'Gerade die Beschäftigung mit internationalen Fragen war Resultat unserer widersprüchlichen Situation: Niemand von uns liebte die Mauer, nur

wenige hielten die DDR und die SED für wirklich sozialistisch, aber fast
alle haßten die heuchlerische Adenauer – "Republik" ... Dennoch sahen
wir in unserer eigenen Wirklichkeit keine Möglichkeiten für eine sinnvolle
politische Praxis.' Dutschke, 'Vom Antisemitismus zum Antikommunismus,' 62. (Translations of this article are mine.)

23 Ibid., 62, 65.
24 Thomas, *Protest Movements*, 72; Fels, *Der Aufruhr*, 26.
25 Kraushaar, 'Rudi Dutschke und der bewaffnete Kampf,' 33.
26 Dutschke, *Wir hatten ein barbarisches, schönes Leben*, 41, 52; Juchler, *Rebel-
    lische Subjektivität*, 15.
27 This statement was made by Klaus Wagenbach as a guest in a seminar
    on 1968 led by Professor Roland Berbig, Humboldt Universität, Berlin,
    2001–2. Ernesto Guevara's *Der Partisanenkrieg* (Berlin, 1962) was distrib-
    uted in the FRG in 1962 under license of the Militärverlag. Most West
    German editions were published in 1968: *Partisanenkrieg* (Cologne, 1966);
    Partisanenkrieg: Eine Methode (Munich, 1968); *Der Partisanenkrieg* (Hamburg,
    1968), reprinting of the 1962 GDR edition; Guevara, *Guerilla – Theorie und
    Methode* (Berlin, 1968).
28 Kraushaar, 'SED, Stasi und Studentenbewegung.'
29 Röhl, *So macht Kommunismus Spaß*.
30 SAPMO-BArch, DY 24, 6196.
31 On trans-Wall ties between authors, see Berbig, ed., *Stille Post*. The debate
    on the shooting of Benno Ohnesorg is a recent example. The question of
    whether the West Berlin police office Kurras who killed him was also a
    Stasi employee is vexed largely because of the controversial political mean-
    ings that inhere in its answer.
32 Fanon's influential *Les Damnés de la Terre* was available in 1961, its English
    translation *The Wretched of the Earth* in 1963, and its German translation *Die
    Verdammten dieser Erde* in 1966.
33 For an analysis of the relationship between the SDS and the SED, see
    Kraushaar, 'SED, Stasi und Studentenbewegung.'
34 Dutschke, 'Vom Antisemitismus,' 62–4.
35 Kraushaar, 'Editorial,' 13.
36 Marcuse, 'Das Problem der Gewalt in der Opposition.'
37 For a differentiated analysis of these events, see Holub, *Jürgen Habermas*.
38 Fanon, *The Wretched of the Earth*; Guevara, *Guerilla – Theorie und Methode*.
39 Juchler, *Rebellische Subjektivität*.
40 Kraushaar, 'Rudi Dutschke und der bewaffnete Kampf.'
41 'Wie und unter welchen Bedingungen kann sich der subjektive Faktor
    als objektiver Faktor in den geschichtlichen Prozeß eintragen? Guevaras

Antwort für Lateinamerika war, daß die Revolutionäre nicht immer auf die objektiven Bedingungen für die Revolution zu warten haben, sondern daß sie über den Focus, über die Revolution durch subjektive Tätigkeit schaffen können. Diese Frage stand in letzter Konsequenz auch hinter der Plakataktion, steht heute noch hinter jeder Aktion.' Dutschke, 'Vom Antisemitismus.' 69–70. Christian Semler and others point out the fluidity and multiplicity in the reception of various theories among non-Party leftists worldwide. Semler, personal discussion, September 2002; Siegward Lönnendonker, personal discussion, July 2002.

42 Dutschke, *Wir hatten*, 61; Guevara, 'Guerrillakrieg: Eine Methode,' 125.

43 Bartsch, 'Der Mythos der Che Guevara,' 387–97.

44 'Dort, wo eine Regierung auf mehr oder weniger demokratischem Wege an die Macht gelangt ist, mit oder ohne Wahlfälschungen, und wo wenigstens dem Anschein nach die verfassungsmäßige Gesetzlichkeit gewahrt wird, entsteht keine Guerillabewegung, weil die Möglichkeiten des legalen Kampfes noch nicht beseitigt sind.' Guevara, 'Guerrillakrieg: Eine Methode,' 24.

45 Szymanski, *Is the Red Flag Flying?* 191.

46 Juchler, *Rebellische Subjektivität*, 51.

47 For accounts of the OLAS conference see Elbaum, *Revolution in the Air*; Gerassi, 'Havana'; Juchler, *Rebellische Subjektivität*; Szymanski, *Is the Red Flag Flying?* See also Castro's closing speech: Castro, 'Waves of the Future.'

48 'Eine Strategie der Stadtguerilla wurde für einige Länder nicht von der Konferenz behandelt, aber auch nicht völlig ausgeschlossen. Die Entwicklung einer solchen Strategie scheint die Aufgabe der Revolutionäre der Länder, deren Bevölkerung zum größten Teil in der Stadt lebt, zu sein.' G., 'Cuba,' 9. The author may be Gisela Mandel or possibly Gaston Salvatore.

49 'Der beste Beitrag zur kontinentalen Revolution, der beste Ausdruck der Solidarität ist die Befreiung des eigenen Landes. "Der Imperialismus muß an jedem beliebigen Ort geschlagen werden." (Che).' Ibid., 9.

50 Dutschke, *Wir hatten*, 147; Slobodian, 'Radical Empathy.' The latter dissertation looks at the influence of Southern students on activism in the Federal Republic.

51 Guevara, 'Schaffen wir zwei, drei, viele Vietnam,' *Oberbaum Blatt*.

52 'Die Situation der Welt zeigt eine große Vielfalt an Aufgaben. Sogar die Länder des alten Europa warten noch auf die Aufgabe der Befreiung. Sie sind zwar genügend entwickelt, um alle Widersprüche des Kapitalismus fühlen zu können, aber zu schwach, um imperialistische Ziele verfolgen oder diesen Weg jetzt noch beschreiten zu können. In den nächsten Jahren werden dort die Widersprüche einen explosiven Charakter annehmen.

Ihre Probleme aber und darum letzten Endes auch deren Lösung sind
verschieden von denen unserer abhängigen und ökonomisch zurückge-
bliebenen Länder.' Guevara, 'Schaffen wir zwei, drei, viele Vietnam,' in
Guerilla, 147. I thank Christian Semler for his original copy of the essay in
pamphlet form, which came out in time for the Vietnam Conference and
was reprinted in Wagenbach Verlag's Rotbuch series. Different German
printings of Guevara's letter have significantly different messages. For
instance, the abridged version published on pages 43–53 of the August
1967 issue of *neue kritik* excises this paragraph.

53 'Sich steigernden politischen Kampf gegen "unsere" bestehende Ordnung,
die sich gerade durch die offenen und verdeckte Komplizenschaft mit den
USA auszeichnet, den vietnamesischen Befreiungskampf durch unseren
eigenen Emanzipationsprozeß konkret zu unterstützen.' Dutschke, 'Zum
Verhältnis von Organisation und Emanzipationsbewegung.' Kraushaar has
shown that the month printed on the issue (June) is not the month that it
was published (July).

54 Dutschke, *Wir hatten*, 143; Rabehl, 'Die Provokationselite,' 473.

55 Dutschke, *Wir hatten*, 143–4.

56 Enzensberger, 'Ein Gespräch über die Zukunft mit Rudi Dutschke, Bernd
Rabehl und Christian Semler.'

57 'Die NATO zerschlagen oder – in einer milderen Variante – aus ihr aus-
treten zu wollen, bedeutet ja wohl in bündnispolitischer Konsequenz,
einen Neutralitätskurs einzuschlagen, und dies wiederum, die verlorenge-
gangene nationale Souveränität zurückzugewinnen. Zu dieser Sichtweise
paßt es, daß Dutschke in seiner Rede auf dem Vietnamkongreß von der
"amerikanischen Besatzungsarmee" spricht. Vermutlich denkt er kom-
plementär dazu an eine sowjetische Besatzungsarmee und den Austritt
der DDR aus dem Warschauer Pakt. Dies jedoch 1968 in West-Berlin offen
auszusprechen, wäre nicht nur noch unrealistischer als die explizierte
Forderung gewesen, sonder zudem auch noch unter taktischen Gesich-
tspunkten unklug.' Kraushaar, 'Rudi Dutschke und die Wiedervereinigung,' 26.

58 Dutschke, 'Zum Verhältnis.'

59 For example, Castro, 'Zweite Deklaration von Havanna,' 365–98; Guevara,
Schaffen wir zwei, drei, viele Vietnam! Gaston Salvatore and Rudi Dutschke's
introduction to the latter also makes clear that they read independence as
Guevara's message.

60 'West-Berlin ist infolge seiner Abhängigkeit von der BRD besonders,
"gefährdet," gehen doch 75 Prozent der erzeugten Güter nach Westdeut-
schland.' Dutschke, 'Zum Verhältnis,' 4.

61 Freedman, *Kennedy's Wars.*
62 Enzensberger, 'Ein Gespräch,' 173.
63 Ibid., 173–4.
64 Dutschke, 'Zum Verhältnis,' 5.
65 'Die "Propaganda der Schüsse" (Che) in der "Dritten Welt" muss durch die "Propaganda der Tat" in den Metropolen vervollständigt werden, welche eine Urbanisierung ruraler Guerilla-Tätigkeit geschichtlich möglich macht.' Dutschke and Krahl, 'Organisationsreferat,' 290; Guevara, 'Der Guerillakrieg.'
66 'Ich weiß nicht, wie ich Euch nennen soll, alle Anreden sind von unseren Herren in Ost und West schon längst besetzt, es sei denn, Ihr akzeptiert den Begriff und die Anrede des Revolutionärs.' Dutschke, 'Zum Verhältnis,' 4.
67 Dutschke papers at the Archiv des Hamburger Instituts.
68 'El deber de todo revolucionario es hacer la revolución.' Juchler, *Rebellische Subjektivität*, 95.
69 Guevara, 'Der Guerillakrieg.'
70 Guevara, 'Der Sozialismus und der Mensch in Kuba.'
71 Bernd Rabehl, personal discussion, June 2002. See also Kraushaar, 'Rudi Dutschke und der bewaffnete Kampf.'
72 Rabehl makes little of this North-South connection. His aim is a different one. For example, Rabehl, *Rudi Dutschke.*

Chapter Four. Siting Trials: Cuba as Cipher for German Governance around the 1970s

1 Beyer, *Bockshorn*; Fries, 'Kubanische Kalenderblätter.'
2 Habermas, 'Der Golf-Krieg als Katalysator einer neuen Deutschen Normalität?' See also: http://de.wikipedia.org/wiki/Hans_Magnus_Enzensberger.
3 Lennox, 'Enzensberger, *Kursbuch*, and Third-Worldism.'
4 Lau, *Hans Magnus Enzensberger*, 230–1.
5 Grimm, 'Enzensberger, Kuba und La Cubana,' 487.
6 Lennox, 'Enzensberger,' 190.
7 Dietschreit and Heinze-Dietschriet, *Hans Magnus Enzensberger*, 65, 81; Enzensberger, ed., *Freisprüche.*
8 Enzensberger, 'Bildnis einer Partie. Vorgeschichte, Struktur und Ideologie der PCC.' 192–216.
9 Petersen, 'Das Floß der Medusa.' See also Henze and Labanyi, *Music and Politics*; Höller, ed., *Briefe einer Freundschaft*; Rickards, *Hindemith, Hartmann and Henz.*

10 http://de.wikipedia.org/wiki/Hans_Werner_Henze.

11 'Der Cimarrón ist nicht der "Neue Mensch": er trägt die Muttermale der alten Gesellschaft, sein Denken zeigt ihre Deformationen, ihre Schranken, ihre Mythen … Er begreift die Notwendigkeit des Volkskrieges, aber er sieht ihn nüchtern, frei von romantischer Hysterie. In seinen Augen finde ich nichts von dem ominösen Glanz jener, die sich einer Sache aufopfern, um ihr eigenes Leben zu vergessen. Der Cimarrón wehrt sich seiner Haut und kämpft um die seiner Brüder, in einem Atemzug … Lebt er noch? Ich sehe euch die Achseln zucken, und ich weiß, ihr glaubt mir nicht. Aber ich sage: "Ja er lebt."' Henneberg, ed., *El Cimarrón*, 38.

12 Cf. Sonntag, ed., *Che Guevara und die Revolution*; Later, Maschke, *Kritik des Guerillero*.

13 Enzensberger, *Das Verhör von Habana*, 255.

14 Thomas, *Cuba or the Pursuit of Freedom*, 1371.

15 Enzensberger, ed., *Das Verhör von Habana*.

16 Dutschke, 'Zum Verhältnis von Organisation und Emanzipationsbewegung'

17 Berghahn, 'Es genügt nicht die einfache Wahrheit'; Enzensberger, 'Bildnis einer Partie.'

18 Deutsches Historisches Museum exhibit, 'Flucht, Vertreibung, Integration, Heimat' (Berlin, 2006).

19 Stickler, 'Ostdeutsch heißt Gesamtdeutsch.'

20 Ibid., 267–8.

21 Ibid., 260.

22 E.g., Enzensberger, *Das Verhör von Habana*, 96–9.

23 Ibid., 97–100.

24 'Dies ist die Zeit des Apparats nicht mehr.' Braun, *Guevara oder der Sonnenstaat*, 49.

25 Mählert, *Kleine Geschichte der DDR*.

26 'Die Linke befand sich auch in Westeuropa auf dem Vormarsch. Diesseits wie jenseits des Eisernen Vorhanges dienten die Heroen der Befreiungskämpfe – allen voran Ernesto Che Guevara – als Identifikationsfigur. Die Revolutionsromantik eines Sozialismus unter Palmen ließ die Widersprüche im eigenen Alltag der DDR zeitweilig zurücktreten. Rückschläge wie der von den Vereinigten Staaten unterstützte Militärputsch 1973 in Chile sorgten innerhalb – wie auch außerhalb – des "Weltfriedenslagers" für ein Zusammenrücken, dem sich auch kritische Linke zeitweilig nicht entziehen konnten.' Ibid., 123.

27 For an elegant negotiation of this problematic, see Teraoka, *East, West, and Others*.

28 Aurelio Alonzo Tejada, personal interview with the author, February 2003.
29 See also Arnold, 'The Third World in the Work of Volker Braun and Heiner Müller.'
30 In a June 2003 telephone discussion with Volker Braun, Braun explained that he had originally been interested in continuing in this vein by writing about Max Höltz, a German anarchist who was responsible for many successful strikes, but that his interest in Cuba drew him to Guevara.
31 See also Bathrick, *The Powers of Speech*, 69–70.
32 Sevin, ed., *The Crisis of Youth and the Generation Gap in the GDR Novel of the Early Seventies*, 120.
33 Quoted in Marquardt, 'Nachbemerkung,' 66. Interestingly, this article suggests that the play was actually performed in 1977 in the GDR.
34 Volker Braun, telephone interview with the author, Berlin, June 2003.
35 Matthias Braun, 'Che Guevara – oder der Sonnenstaat.'
36 Ibid. Nadja Bunke and Raimund Krämer relate the story similarly.
37 Volker Braun, personal discussion with the author, Berlin, August 2006.
38 Hörnigk, 'Erinnerungen an Revolutionen.'
39 For example, Ibid.
40 'Zieht man in Betracht, dass die Demokratie der Volksversammlungen im "Sonnenstaat" nicht als real führende Kraft auftritt, dass das höchste Regierungsorgan im Grunde genommen sich selbst ergänzt, dann kann man den politischen Aufbau des "Sonnenstaat" als eine eigenartige Oligarchie der Intelligenz bei formaler Demokratie charakterisieren.' Wolgin, 'Campanellas Kommunistische Utopie,' 7, 11.
41 Guevara: … Die Revolution muss alle die Strukturen / Wenn sie jetzt dauern soll, infragestellen / Um brüderlich zu sein.
   Freund: Muß. Jetzt. Alle. / Das sind zu viele Worte für eine / Einfache Sache. Reicht dir nicht das Muß. / Das neue menschliche Wesen muß fressen / Und fragt nicht nach dem Besteck …
   Guevara: … Mach die Türe auf, da liegt Vietnam. / Blutend der Dreck unter den Füßen, da / Mit denen wir gehen unsre stolze Bahn / Des Wohlstands in dem sogenannten Frieden / Ost und West, das aber ist allein. / Geliefert nackt den mörderischen Yankees / Dicht neben unsrer Feigheit, fast verlassen / Und Gleichgültigkeit, mit der wir schwatzen / Von Solidarität. Der Widersinn / Schnürt mir die Kehle zu. Es wird keinen / Sozialismus geben, wenn wir uns nicht
   Freund: ändern / Und brüderlich statt alles festzuhalten / Was wir besitzen dieses Eigentum / Das wir uns retten das die Völker trennt / Dies Leben für uns selbst und Ungleichheit / Und fremd und sinnlos Handel zwischen uns / Wie zwischen Kapitalisten wir Komplizen / Der Ausbeu-

tung und Handel mit der Freundschaft / Erpressend auch den Freund
im Gleichgewicht / Der Blöcke Blöcke um unseren Hals / Und Vietnam
verblutet und wir sehn in die / Arena wie das Blut fließt dieses Spiel / Das
uns zum Äußersten treibt. Ich höre höre.
Guevara: Kuba, Hoffnung der Welt.
Freund: Schweig, Genosse.
Guevara: Alles ist wahr, kannst dus nicht hören, Freund / Was du dir
sagst.
Freund: So kannst du nicht reden.
Guevara: Ich kann es nicht, ahja, ich kann es nicht. / Dann ist der Kampf
unmöglich hier auch.
Freund: Wir / Kommen in Teufels Küche durch dein Reden / Die Hölle
des Kriegs vor Augen. Braun, *Guevara oder der Sonnenstaat*, 59–60.

42 See also Profitlich, *Volker Braun*, 16–17.

43 'Willst du ein Finanzwesen haben oder ein / Neues menschliches Wesen.
Nämlich wie / Die Produktion wichtig ist das Bewußtsein / Das sie
produziert. Den Sozialismus / Kannst du nicht mit den morschen Waffen
baun / Die der Kapitalismus liegenläßt.' Braun, *Guevara oder der Sonnen-*
staat, 59.

44 'Stillhaltend bricht der Haß mir aus dem Hals / Gegen den Zwang, der uns
an Drähten hält / In alter Zeit, und ich kenn mich nicht mehr.' Ibid., 62.

45 Debray first visited Cuba in 1959. Upon return to France, he explained the
Cuban project in: 'Le Castrisme: La Longue Marche de l'Amerique latine'
in *Les Temps Modernes* in January 1965. Voigt, *Aktivismus und Moralischer*
Rigorismus, 333.

46 Debray, *Révolution dans la Révolution?* In Cuba, Debray, *Revolución en la*
Revolución?

47 Cf. Huberman and Sweezy, *Regis Debray and the Latin American Revolution*,
5.

48 Monje: … und dein Fall / Ist nicht so neu, wie dir dein Tod sein wird./
Und alt sähen wir aus so angeführt / Und ohne Führung alle mit zwei
Führern / Und demoralisiert die Kraft, verwirrt / Des Volks. Das ist nicht
dein Tod nur, Guevara
packt ihn
Du liquidierst uns alle, die Partei / Wie sie jetzt lebt, indem du uns ins
Aus schlägst / Mit deinem Aufbruch und wir sehen zu / Wie Feiglinge
und können uns nicht helfen / Weil dir nicht mehr zu helfen ist.
Läßt ihn los.
Aber
Dein Heroismus ist nicht das Mistbeet / Der Revolutionen, und dein

Tod / Wird uns so wenig führen wie dein Leben.

Guevara *lacht*: Bau die Guerilla, und der Rest ergibt sich. / Und nur der Guerillero kann sie führen / Und nach dem Sieg auch er, der alles wagt / Er soll alles bekommen und nicht ihr / Die in den Städten zaudern, lustlos, Beamte / Und dienstbeflissen auf die Weisung warten.

Packt ihn:

Wie wird es mir gefallen an der Macht / Und sei es nur, um die Lakaien jeder / Sippschaft ans Licht zu ziehn und mit dem Rüssel / In ihre Schweinerei zu stoßen.

Läßt ihn los.

Genosse

Dies ist die Zeit des Apparats nicht mehr.

Monje: Wie soll ich das verstehen.

Guevara: Wie dus kannst.

Braun, *Guevara oder der Sonnenstaat*, 49.

49 Cosentino, 'Volker Brauns roter Empedokles'; Costabile-Heming, *Intertextual Exile*.

50 Subiotto, 'Volker Braun.'

51 An elegant exception is Klaus Schuhmann, 'Ich bin der Braun, den ihr kritisiert,' 132–3.

52 Quoted in Ibid., 133.

53 Braun, *Guevara oder der Sonnenstaat*.

54 For more on the trope of pyramids as power structures see Subiotto, 'Volker Braun.'

55 'Die Zukunft ist eine Mulattin.' Braun, 'La Rampa, Habana,' 16.

56 Zorach, 'From Grey East to Golden West,' 143. It would be interesting to discover whether Fries was writing in relation to Günter Maschke's 'Kubanisches Taschenkalender,' a highly critical piece produced in 1972 after Maschke visited the island that, published in *Kursbuch*, is credited with impacting FRG left public opinion of Cuba.

57 'Wenn man die Palmen und ein Getränk namens Mojito aus dem Spiel läßt. Alles andere sind Siebenmeilenstiefel, Jahrespläne, kubanische Wirtschaftswunder.' Fries, 'Kubanische Kalenderblätter,' 8.

58 '[D]ie utopische Mythologie der *Barbudos* (in den Köpfen der Zuschauer) darzustellen.'; 'Kommen wir, wenn es um Kuba geht, nicht ohne Zauber und Mythologie aus?' Ibid., 18.

59 'Morales, unser Betreuer, jung und gegenwärtig, kommt irgendwann, wer weiß warum, auf die Prostitution zu sprechen, die Kuba einmal zum Freudenhaus Lateinamerika's gemacht hatte. Die Prostituierten, sagt Morales, verschwanden mit dem letzten nordamerikanischen Touristen.' Ibid., 18.

60 'Dunkelhäutiges [Mädchen] in einem lichtblauen Kleid.' Ibid., 18.

61 'Immer wieder wird einer [der wartenden Männern], der scheinbar im Strom der anderen Getriebenen, von einem Hauseingang verschluckt … Die Haustüren zu ebener Erde scheinen eine magische Anziehungskraft zu haben, jäh lasse auch ich mich in ihre Tiefe fallen und befinde mich in einem von Negerinnen betriebenen Bordell. Ein lichtloser Flur, darin an den Wänden die schwarzen Gestalten. Die Jüngste hatte die Tür geöffnet. Später wird sie mich um Geld für ihre kranke Mutter bitten … wie in einer Szene aus dem schlechten Roman *Der Gringo*.' Ibid., 20.

62 'Sie sind ein Opfer der schwarzen Magie geworden, sagt K. [his mentor] … [Dieses Geschehnis] wird Ihnen Morales nicht abnehmen …' Ibid., 20.

63 '… Ich tauche in Blusen und Röcke, Tücher und Schals, zu Hause ausgebreitet, erwärmt von Frauenhaut, geschwellt von Weiblichkeit, werden sie mir Belegstücke für diese Reise sein.' Fries, 'Paris, doppel belichtet,' 136.

64 'Lieben Sie Frankreich nicht?'; '(Ich stürze mich in einen Liebesantrag, erkläre den kleinen Unterschied, Gott, sie ist wirklich naiv, rede mich heraus.)'; 'Entdecken dabei gemeinsame Geschmäcker.' Ibid., 137–8.

65 BA-FA, DR 1, MfK-HV Film: 115+B.

66 SAPMO-BArch, DR 117, BA 0015; SAPMO-BArch, DR 117, BA 1945.

67 Castro, 'Declaration of the First National Congress of Education and Culture (1971),' 134.

68 Seeba, 'Der Untergang der Utopie.'

69 For a recent work that treats Enzensberger's poetry in relation to its social and political concerns see: Melin, *Poetic Maneuvers*.

70 'Ich hätte das Buch aus Gründen, die leicht zu sehen sind, am liebsten in Kuba veröffentlicht, aber diese Möglichkeit stand mir nicht offen … Das Buch wäre nur im kubanischen Kontext, nicht aber in meinem eigenen konstruktiv gewesen.' Lau, *Hans Magnus Enzensberger*, 263.

71 Enzensberger, Hans Magnus. *The Sinking of the Titanic*, 9–10.

Wir suchten etwas, hatten etwas verloren
auf dieser tropischen Insel. Das Gras wuchs
über die abgewrackten Cadillacs. Wo war der Rum,
wo waren die Bananen geblieben? Etwas anderes
hatten wir dort zu suchen – schwer zu sagen,
was es eigentlich war –
doch wir fanden es nicht
in jener winzigen Neuen Welt,
wo alles vom Zucker sprach,
von der Befreiung, von einer Zukunft, reich
an Glühbirnen, Milchkühen, nagelneuen Maschinen.

Dort, wo mir die jungen Mulattinnen
mit der Maschinenpistole im Arm
zulächelten an den Straßenecken,
mir oder einem anderen, schrieb ich
und schrieb am *Untergang der Titanic.*
Es war nachts so warm, ich konnte nicht schlafen.
Jung war ich nicht – was heißt jung?
Ich wohnte am Meer – doch beinah zehn Jahre
Jünger als jetzt, und bleich vor Eifer.
Das muß im Juni gewesen sein, nein,
Anfang April, kurz vor Ostern war es,
wir gingen die Rampa hinunter,
es war ein Uhr vorbei, Maria Alexandrovna
sah mich aus zornig funkelnden Augen an,
Heberto Padilla rauchte, er saß noch nicht
im Gefängnis – aber wer dieser Padilla war,
weiß niemand mehr, weil er verloren ist, ein Freund,
ein verlorener Mann – und irgendein deutscher
Deserteur lachte unförmig – auch er
ist im Gefängnis gelandet, aber erst später,
und heute lebt er hier in der Nähe und trinkt
und treibt seine staatserhaltenden Forschungen,
und es ist komisch, dass ich ihn nicht
vergessen habe, nein, vergessen habe ich wenig.
Wir sprachen in einem Kauderwelsch,
Spanisch, Russisch und Deutsch,
von der fürchterlichen Zuckerernte
der Zehn Millionen, heute natürlich
spricht kein Mensch mehr davon. Was
geht mir der Zucker an, ich bin Tourist!
schrie der Deserteur, dann zitierte er
Horkheimer, ausgerechnet Horkheimer
in Habana! Wir sprachen auch von Stalin
und Dante, ich weiß nicht mehr warum,
was hatte Dante mit dem Zucker zu tun.(15–16)
Enzensberger, *Der Untergang der Titanic*

72 Maschke, 'Cubanischer Taschenkalender'; Maschke, 'Entfremdung.'
73 Especially: Maschke, *Kritik des Guerillero.*
74 http://www.jf-archiv.de/archiv/24aa7.htm.
75 Enzensberger, *The Sinking of the Titanic*, 10. 'Seine staatserhaltenden Forschungen.' Enzensberger, *Der Untergang der Titanic*, 16.

76 Preuße, *Der Politische Literat*, 137.

77 Wolf and Wolf, 'Wir haben uns natürlich immer beobachtet,' 81.

78 Enzensberger, *The Sinking of the Titanic*, 9.

> Damals dachte kaum einer an den Untergang,
> nicht einmal in Berlin, das den seinigen
> längst hinter sich hatte. Es schwankte
> die Insel Cuba nicht unter unsern Füßen.
> Es schien uns, als stünde etwas bevor,
> etwas von uns zu Erfindendes.
> Wir wußsten nicht, daß das Fest längst zu Ende,
> und alles Übrige eine Sache war
> für die Abteilungsleiter der Weltbank
> und die Genossen von der Staatssicherheit,
> genau wie bei uns und überall sonst auch.

Enzensberger, *Der Untergang der Titanic*, 15.

79 Enzensberger, *The Sinking of the Titanic*. 'Ich hoffe, … Sie können / müssen leben wie Che, mit dem Messer / der Sprache seinen Fall aufschneidend bis auf die Knochen dieses Jahrhunderts.' Enzensberger, *Der Untergang der Titanic*, Reprinted in the unnumbered back pages of the bound edition.

80 'Während Das Verhör seinen Lauf nimmt, geht in den Sümpfen der Zapata-Halbinsel, zweihundertfünfzig Kilometer vor den Türen des Theaters, der bewaffnete Kampf weiter. Hier wie dort wird um die gleiche Wahrheit gekämpft. Der diskursive Dialog vor dem Mikrophon setzt eine Begegnung anderer Art fort, die zur gleichen Stunde mit der Maschinepistole ausgetragen wird. Die Waffen der Kritik führen zu Ende, was die Kritik der Waffen begonnen hat. Jedes Wort, das hier fällt, lässt sich an einer materiellen Erfahrung messen. Aus ihr zieht Das Verhör seine Energie, sie prägt jeden Satz und jede Geste.' Enzensberger, *Der Untergang der Titanic*, 23.

Chapter Five. Touring Revolution and Resistance: Tamara Bunke and Che Guevara

1 Schumann, 'Grenzübertritte,' 41. The first jet of a travel agency that offered 'popularly priced' trips landed in Mallorca in 1962. Seven million flew in 1975. Thirteen million took charter flights to the island in 1995.

2 Stirken, 'Reisezeit,' 9.

3 Mahrad, 'Jugendpolitik in der DDR,' 208.

4 'Der Jugend Vertrauen und Verantwortung and Mit der Erziehung und Selbsterziehung der Jugend von heute das Gesicht der Gesellschaft von morgen prägen.' Friedrich, 'Die Jugendpolitik der SED,' 181.

5 'Friedliche Koexistenz,' in *Jugendlexikon*, 257; 'Nationale Befreiungsbewegung,' in *Jugendlexikon*, 488–9.

6 According to one survey of GDR students in the late 1960s, 34 per cent were familiar with Guevara and 22 per cent approved of him. This study (Student 69, JA-IZJ, B 6146, 67-75) is cited in Wierling, *Geboren im Jahr Eins*, 305.

7 It was first shown in the FRG in October 1970 and in the GDR in March 1973. My thanks to the reference librarians at the HFF Konrad Wolf for this information.

8 Merkel, 'Utopie und Bedürfnis. Die Geschichte der Konsumkultur in der DDR.'

9 'Das Blut Tausender Lateinamerikaner [floß] ... Es ist das Blut von Kommunisten und Kämpfern anderer Anschauungen, heute symbolisiert durch den Namen jenes großen Argentiniers, Kubaners und Lateinamerikaners – Ernesto Che Guevara' (Deklaration der Beratung der KP der Länder Lateinamerikas und des Karibischen Raumes [Declaration of the Advisory Committee of the Communist Party of the Nations of Latin American and Caribbean Region], Havanna, Juni 1975, APN-Verlag, Moskau 1975, s. 76). SAPMO-BArch, DR 1, 2389a.

10 *Forum: Zeitung der Studenten und der Jungen* Issue 3:9; Issue 4:9; Issue 9:9–11.

11 'Che Guevaras Taten dienten den verschiedenen Strömungen in der internationalen Arbeiter- und Jugendbewegung als Diskussionspunkt, vor allem seine Theorien über den Partisanenkrieg. Zeitweise wurde er wie ein Heiliger verehrt. Die "linke" Jugendbewegung trug seine Bilder in den Demonstrationen mit, und Plakate mit seinem Porträt waren überall in den Zimmern junger Menschen zu finden. Auch bei uns ist seine Gestalt bekannt. Er war zweimal in der DDR.' SAPMO-BArch, DR 1, 3547. Such reports (*Gutachten*) were part of the process of controlling publications in this centralized economy in which culture was an educational tool.

12 Guevara, *Bolivianisches Tagebuch*.

13 SAPMO-BArch, DR 1, 2389a.

14 Müller, 'Wie es ist, bleibt es nicht.' Quoted in Mann, *Untergrund, autonome Literatur und das Ende der DDR*, 92.

15 Krämer, 'Che Guevara und die DDR: Anmerkungen zu einem wechselvollen Verhältnis,' *Tranvia* 1997, 9.

16 Refrain: 'Uns bleibt, was gut war und klar war: / Daß man bei Dir immer durchsah / Und Liebe, Haß, doch nie Furcht sah / Comandante Che Guevara'; Stanzas: 'Sie fürchten dich, und wir lieben / dich vorn im Kampf, wo der Tod lacht, / wo das Volk Schluß mit der Not macht. / Nun bist du weg – und doch geblieben' (They fear you, and we love / you leading the

fight, where Death laughs / Where the people make an end of need / Now
you are gone – and yet remain). 'Und bist kein Bonze geworden / Kein
hohes Tier, das nach Geld schielt / Und vom Schreibtisch aus den Held
spielt / in feiner Kluft mit alten Orden Ja, grad die Armen der Erde, / die
brauchen mehr als zu fressen / und das hast du nie vergessen, / daß aus
Menschen Menschen werden' (Yes, precisely the poor of this world, / they
need more than to eat / and you never forgot that, / that men become of
men). 'Der rote Stern an der Jacke / Im schwarzen Bart die Zigarre / Jesus
Christus mit der Knarre – so führt Dein Bild uns zur Attacke.' Biermann,
'Comandante Che Guevara.' (My translations.)

Puebla's orginal refrain: 'Aquí se queda la clara, / La entrañable transpar-
encia / De tu querida presencia, / Comandante Che Guevara.' [The deep
(or beloved) transparency of your presence / became clear here / Commandante Che Guevara]; Puebla's original stanzas: Aprendimos a quer-
erte, / Desde la histórica altura, / Donde el sol de tu bravura / Le puso
cerco a la muerte' (We learned to love you / from the heights of history /
with the sun of your bravery / you laid siege to death). 'Vienes quemando
la brisa / con soles de primavera / para plantar la bandera / con la luz de
tu sonrisa' (You come burning the winds / with spring suns / to plant the
flag / with the light of your smile). 'Tu amor revolucionario / te conduce
a nueva empresa, / donde espera la firmeza / de tu brazo libertario' (Your
revolutionary love / leads you to a new undertaking / where they are
/ awaiting the firmness / of your liberating arm). 'Seguiremos adelante
/ como junto a ti seguimos / y con Fidel te decimos: / "¡Hasta siempre
Comandante!"' (We will carry on as we did along with you / and with
Fidel we say to you: Until Always, Commandante!) (English translation
from: http://www.marxists.org/subject/art/music/puebla-carlos/lyrics/
hasta-siempre.htm#english.)

17 SAPMO-BArch, DY 30, IV a 2/20/285. My thanks to Raimund Krämer for
apprising me of the relevance of this file; SAPMO-BArch, DR 117, 8525;
BStU, MfS – Gh – 99/78; BStU, MfS – Aim – 19049/63.

18 In addition to files at the SAPMO-BArch and the BStU, MfS, Nadja Bunke
bequeathed a collection of materials on her daughter to the Berlin chapter
of the solidarity organization Cuba Sí. Research here has yielded no new
information on these specific questions. One of the capable and helpful
researchers at the BStU, Frau Weiss, emphasized to me the influence of wil-
ful destruction on the BStU files concerning Latin America.

19 Ulises Estrada, *Tania*; Koenen, *Traumpfade der Weltrevolution*; Langelüddecke, 'So lebt Tania in uns weiter.' It has been impossible for me to obtain
Ms Langelüddecke's work, but Gerd Koenen refers to it positively.

20 Jorge Luis Acanda (professor of philosophy at University of Havana, who obtained his doctorate at the University of Leipzig) compares the GDR representation of Tamara to that of Rosa Luxemburg – heroic, but in many ways abstract. Personal interview with the author, Havana, March 2003.

21 SAPMO-BArch, DY 24, 6196.

22 SAPMO-BArch, DY 30, IV a 2/20/285.

23 Ibid.; Nadja Bunke, personal interview with the author, Berlin, September 2002. My thanks to Silke Dähmlow for putting me in touch with Nadja Bunke.

24 Julio A. García Oliveras, personal interview with the author, March 2003; see also Krämer, *Der alte Mann und die Insel*.

25 Informal interviews with East Germans, Berlin, 2002–5.

26 VEB F.A. Brockhaus, *Compañeros*.

27 Gries, 'Die Heldenbühne der DDR Zur Einführung.'

28 'Das Material [über Tamara Bunke] enthält eine Fülle von Anregungen, die richtig verarbeitet und auf der Grundlage einer klaren politischen Linie und Aussage entsprechend der Politik unserer Partei sehr gut für die patriotische und revolutionäre klassenmäßige [*sic*] Erziehung unserer Jugend verwertet werden können.' SAPMO-BArch, DY 30, IV a 2/20/285. At the time of writing it is believed that the records of the Militärverlag der Deutschen Demokratischen Republik that published *Tania la Guerrillera* were discarded when the press was taken over by the Dietz Verlag.

29 Ulises Estrada Lescaille, personal interview with the author, Havana, March 2003. Estrada fought with Castro and has worked in various prestigious official capacities. He trained Tamara, was romantically involved with her, and has published on her, including writing part of *Tania la Guerrillera Inolvidable* and the expanded English translation *Tania: Undercover with Che Guevara in Bolivia*. He is currently the editor of the journal *Tricontinental*.

30 SAPMO-BArch, DR 117, 8525; Letters between Bunke and various Cubans including Rojas, Rodríguez Calderón, and national liberation fighter and director of the Federation of Cuban Women Vilma Espin de Castro. Bunke Nachlass 4.1–7, 14, 16.

31 Wolfgang Kolhaase, personal communication with the author, Berlin, December 2005.

32 Bunke Nachlass 4.1–7, 14, 16; Nadja Bunke, interview.

33 SAPMO-BArch, DR 1, 2389a.

34 Nadja Bunke, interview; Eberhard Panitz, telephone interview with the author, Berlin, July 2002.

35 The weekend series began with Panitz, *Der Weg zum Rio Grande*; Rojas and Rodríguez Calderón, *Tania la Guerrillera*; Zimmerling, 'Tanja la Guerrillera.'

36 '[Das] Leben und Schicksal Tamara Bunkes sind außergewöhnlich und nicht wiederholbar. Warum soll dann aber gerade Tamara Vorbild und Beispiel für uns sein? Weil Tamara als Persönlichkeit Eigenschaften und Verhaltensweisen besaß, die in hohem Maße wertvoll und beispielgebend sind ... Weil Tamara uns vorgelebt hat, daß auch ein junger und moderner Mensch unserer Zeit vieles gleichzeitig sein kann: leidenschaftlich und tatkräftig als Kommunist und Revolutionär.' Tschierske, *Wir Ehren Tamara Bunke*, 21.

37 'Eine staatlich geprüfte Ulrike Meinhof hatten SED und FDJ aus der Leiche [von Tamara] gemacht, eine edle Buchheldin, eine Revolutionärin zum Anhimmeln, aber bloß nicht zum Nachmachen. Sei wie Tania, aber träum nicht, hau' nicht ab und lauf' nicht im Dschungel herum!' Schnibben, 'Tamara Bunke,' 124. Text originally published as 'Drei Leben in einer Haut' in *Der Spiegel* 39 (1996).

38 Tschierske, *Wir Ehren Tamara Bunke*, 26–7.

39 Bunke Nachlass 6.1; Wiesner, 'Mi Batalla por la Verdad.' Reprinted in Spanish translation in Rojas Rodríguez, Rodríguez Calderón, and Estrada Lescaille, *Tania la Guerrillera Inolvidable*, 206.

40 Research at the Deutsche Bibliothek and the Deutsche Bücherei revealed the following publishing history:
Tania la Guerrillera – 7 printings of 1 edition in the GDR and 1 printing of revised edition in united Germany: 1973 – 1st ed. (ten thousand); 1975 – 2nd printing (ten thousand); 1977 – 3rd printing (ten thousand); 1980 – 4th printing (ten thousand); 1982 – 5th printing (no quantity listed); 1985 – 6th printing (no quantity listed); 1989 – 7th printing (no quantity listed); 1998 – 2nd ed., revised and expanded, Dietz Verlag (no quantity listed).
Der Weg zum Rio Grande – 7 printings of 1 edition in the GDR and 2 licensed printings in the FRG, none with quantities listed: 1973 – 1st ed. & 1st licensed FRG printing; 1975 – 2nd printing; 1977 – 3rd printing; 1979 – 4th printing & 2nd licensed FRG printing at Weltkreis Verlag-GmbH; 1981 – 5th printing; 1989 – 6th printing.
Relying on the number and size of book printings to determine the popularity of a book in the GDR is not adequate. Siegfried Lokatis, a researcher specializing in GDR publishing history, points out that although these statistics are well documented, accessible, and generally accurate, they have limited meaning because political considerations significantly influenced printings. For example, because books were centrally distrib-

224 Notes to pages 156–7

uted, reading was popular, and paper was limited, nearly all books went out of print quickly and usually well before individual demand was satisfied. Moreover, quantity sometimes depended on politics as much as demand. This makes the use of such figures as difficult as in the FRG, although for different reasons; in the FRG and in other market-based nations, print runs are closely guarded trade secrets, except when they can be used to spur sales. Lokatis suggests that personal and professional opinions about the popularity of GDR texts are often the most useful sources of information. This caveat notwithstanding, in the cases of *Tania* and *Der Weg*, even the careful Lokatis agrees that the extremely high number and frequency of impressions evidence the popularity of the books. Siegfried Lokatis, personal discussion with the author, Berlin, May 2003.

41 On the former, see Bathrick, *The Powers of Speech.*

42 Köhler-Hausmann, *Literaturbetrieb in der DDR*, 92–3; Mann, *Untergrund, Autonome Literatur und das Ende der DDR*, 111.

43 Köhler-Hausmann, *Literaturbetrieb in der DDR*, 93.

44 Comments at the East German Summer Film Institute. Smith College, MA, July 2001.

45 Hille, 'Interessen von Jugendlichen,' 240.

46 See Stirken, 'Reisezeit,' 9.

47 As an unusual but telling example, an analysis of a cross section of Spanish textbooks from the FRG and GDR revealed, perhaps unsurprisingly, that each set reflects and forms the intents and demands of its audience. The FRG texts emphasize Spain, in the earliest books as a trading partner, then increasingly as tourist site. Latin America remains on the periphery; as a colonized land, its culture and language are less 'authentic' and less significant. GDR textbooks emphasize Cuba, and focus on educational and professional exchange. Socialist Cuba is presented more positively – more beautiful, less ridden with social problems, more progressive – than capitalist Spain. Cuba's positioning as a socialist brotherland is emphasized, rather than its revolution and revolutionary ideals. Discussions with GDR professors who taught Spanish language and linguistics at the University of Rostock also support this contention. Hildtrud Mielke, telephone interview with the author, Berlin, September 2002; Svend Plesch, personal communication with the author, Havana, February 2003.

48 I have been unable to consider the production circumstances and the reception of *Tania la Guerrillera inolvidable* in Cuba, or the international distribution plans for the book from the Cuban perspective. The topic of Guevara and Bunke remains politically sensitive for the government. The

documentary film-maker Heidi Specogna has had some success in gathering relevant information on Tamara Bunke in Cuba. Specogna, *Tania la Guerrillera*.

49 'Hier ist ein echtes Vorbild für unsere Jugend entstanden, die sich mit dem revolutionären Patriotismus, dem Mut, der Zielstrebigkeit und der Opferbereitschaft der Partisanin und Kundschafterin Tanja identifizieren kann.' SAPMO-BArch, DR 1, 3546a.

50 Brecht, *Gesammelte Werke*, 1024. This reading was inspired by a discussion with Matthew Miller.

51 'In den ersten Tagen besuchte ich, wie es sich für eine Touristin gehörte, Museen und Ausstellungen, dabei lernte ich im archäologischen Museum Tiahuanacu den Maler Moísés Chile Barrientos kennen, einen Verwandten des bolivianischen Präsidenten.' Panitz, *Der Weg zum Rio Grande*, 119.

52 Reid, *Writing without Taboos*.

53 Panitz, *Der Weg zum Rio Grande*, 124; Rojas and Rodríguez Calderón, *Tania la Guerrillera*, 156.

54 'Ich beobachtete [Tania und ihren Verlobten] beim Verlassen des Kinos, sie gingen zu Fuß in Richtung ihres Hauses; während dieses Weges war sie sichtlich die Aktive. Bestimmende. –Am 7. Januar verließ sie um 8.30 Uhr das Haus.' Panitz, *Der Weg zum Rio Grande*, 131.

55 Stephan, *Für die Liebe noch zu mager?* This film is available for viewing in VHS form at the DEFA Film Library, University of Massachusetts.

56 SAPMO-BArch, DR 117, BA 3118.

57 Poss, *DEFA 50 Gespräche aus Acht Filmnächten Protokolle*, 74; Löser, 'Dokumentarfilme an der Babelsberger Filmhochschule,' 353.

58 The film was a box-office hit by GDR standards. SAPMO-BArch, DR 117, BA 3118; Poss, *DEFA 50*.

59 Ironically, this openness towards more alternative cultures later haunted the film; when Renft defected the film was pulled from circulation pro forma. Poss, *DEFA 50*, 67. My thanks also to Ed Larkey.

60 The GDR press nearly ignored these elements, while such mention was not unusual in the FRG-press reviews. Media reception folders on the film at the HFF Konrad Wolf. Since the GDR reviewers emphasized the politically appropriate aspects of the film, while the FRG emphasized the socially critical aspects, it is probable that GDR journalists also saw links between the use of these extra-national elements and social critique.

61 *Für die Liebe noch zu mager?* is no exception; indeed, the film includes intriguing overtly pedagogical discussions of female sexual practices. I have considered these themes in a paper entitled 'Fathers Apples and

Good Socialist Girls: The Political Pedagogy of Reproduction in DEFA's *Für die Liebe noch zu mager?'* presented at the German Studies Association Conference in New Orleans in 2003.

62 This scene also links sexual deviance to Western consumerism. See Kramer, 'Blauhemd und Blue Jeans in Filmen der DEFA.'

63 Cf. Dölling, 'We all Love Paula but Paul is More Important to Us.' (A case study of the DEFA film *Die Legende von Paul und Paula*.)

64 Köck, 'Mit dem Finger auf der Landkarte: Abenteuerurlaub für Alle,' 60.

65 *Spinner* is a colloquialism that translates approximately as 'freak' or 'fool.' In direct contrast, Susanne is a textile technician who constructively spins (threads) for the needs of society.

66 Nearly all GDR reviews take this perspective, while many more FRG reviews read Lutz as a rebel. (Media reception folders on the film at the BA-FA and the HFF Konrad Wolf.) A GDR HFF master's thesis on the film justifies Lutz's nonconformity in this manner and by emphasizing that perfect heroes are not effective among young audiences. Bohnenstengel, 'Besonderheiten der Regiekonzeptionen von Filmen für das jugendliche Publikum.' Reader reports emphasize that Susanna likes Lutz simply because he does not seek to take advantage of her. (HV folder on the film at the BA-FA.)

67 Wisst ihr wieviel Grad es in Kuba sind? 40 Grad in Schatten. Mensch, von Schweiß Salzflecken auf dem Hemd und Durst, *viehischen* Durst. Aber der zweite Tag ist entscheidend. Wenn ihr da nicht umfällt, Leute, dann ...
Daisy: Olle Spinner.
Lutz: Ernsthaft, die ZEMA baut dort eine Zuckerfabrik.
Susanne: Seid wann bist du denn bei der ZEMA?
Lutz: Abwarten, bis so eine Fabrik steht, dass dauert ewig. Da fehlt mal das, und mal das und dann müssen sie wieder auf den nächsten Dampfer warten. Kuba ist weit.
Susanne: Kleine Abkühlung bei 40 Grad im Schatten?

68 1957 Freier Deutscher Gewerkschaftsbund, Abteilung Feriendienst und Kuren (hg). 'Urlaub, Erholung, Genesung durch den Freien Deutschen Gewerkschaftsbund.' Cited in Selbach, 'Reise Nach Plan,' 70. A 1976 *Der Augenzeuge* report thematizes both GDR and Cuban construction workers enjoying a well-deserved vacation on Cuban beaches and the large cement factory built in Cienfuegos as GDR solidarity work that benefits the social-ist bloc as well as Cuba. DEFA-Wochenschau, *Der Augenzeuge*.

69 Rolf: Am Tiefpaßfilter stimmt was nicht
Susanne: Wer ist denn das da auf dem Bild?
Rolf: Sag bloss du kennst ihn wirklich nicht. Gib mal die Zange!

Susanne: Fidel Castro

Rolf: Beinah richtig. Hör mal, Schlagzeug. Das Grün kommt nicht. Du kennst ihn wirklich nicht? Nie was von Che Guevara gehört? Jetzt schon wieder zu wenig Grün.

70 Susanne: Wie kommt denn so ein Mädchen von der DDR nach Bolivien?

Martin: Sie war zuerst in Kuba.

Susanne: Ob sie ihn geliebt hat, den Bärtigen auf dem Bild?

Martin: Vielleicht, aber nicht so.

Susanne: Bestimmt, ganz bestimmt. Mensch, von der DDR nach Bolivien. Die hat sich was getraut, unter so viel Männern als Partisanin.

Martin: Sie wollten über den Fluss; sie hatten Verwundete und Kranke mit. Und als sie durch's Wasser gingen, schossen die Soldaten. Es war ein Hinterhalt.

71 Various sources record different versions of the song lyrics. This reflects changes during project development, in part due to censorship. My understanding of the soundtrack is as follows: 'Ist mein Auge grau am Morgen? Ist die Stadt im meinem Fenster grau, Fenster grau, Fenster grau? Sag ich meinem Mund: Sei freundlich! Alles hat die Stadt, ein Lächeln fehlt. Lächeln fehlt, Lächeln fehlt. Lächelt hell mein Mund am Morgen? Geht die Stadt vorbei und wird nicht hell, wird nicht hell, wird nicht hell. Braucht die Stadt nur meine Hände? Braucht denn diese Stadt nicht meinen Mut? Meinen Mut? Meinen Mut? Lächele du, schnell mal probiert, fotografiert. Seht mich nicht an. Augen zu. Bin im Blitzlicht. Ich ein Witz nicht. Augen zu, man!' 'Seht mal her! [unintelligible] Schmeckt mir die Wut. Seht mich an. Neu ist mal gut. Wut steht mir gut. Wach doch auf, man!'

72 I would also like to take this opportunity to express my regret that I was not able to treat the 1960s film *Liebe, usw* in this project. The Bayerische Rundfunk, which owns the rights and (to my knowledge) the only publicly available copy of the film, did not support my multiple research requests.

73 My thanks to Barbara Kosta for pointing out to me the use of the poster in this film.

74 This idea stems from a discussion with Christian Schertz, the Bunke family's lawyer.

75 For example, Schnibben, 'Tamara Bunke'; Varchmin, 'Tania, eine Frau unter Männern.'

76 Calder, *Heroes: from Byron to Guevara*, 196.

77 An exception to this is the small West Berlin medical solidarity group, Tamara Bunke, that worked in Nicaragua in the 1980s. Balsen and Rössel, *Hoch die Internationale Solidarität!*, 451, 600.

78 Scheer, 'Die Partisanin.'

79 'Die durch die Ost-West-Spannungen veranlaßte wirtschaftliche Begünstigung der Bundesrepublik Deutschland ermöglicht breiten Schichten relativen Wohlstand; Tourismus ist ein Wohlstandsphänomen.' Bauschinger, 'Wie die Deutschen zu Reiseweltmeistern werden,' 29.

80 For example, Enloe, *Bananas, Beaches and Bases.*

81 Häußermann, 'Das Berliner Milieu und die Stadtforschung,' 46.

82 'Der junge Guevara durchstreifte Lateinamerika, nicht um Länder und Sehenswürdigkeiten "abzuhaken," sondern er unterzog sich der Mühe, nicht nur die Lage der armen und ärmsten Menschen zu ergründen, sondern auch Denkweise und Selbstverständnis der Menschen zu hinterfragen.'Gross, 'Vorwort,' 7.

83 Lartéguy, 'Auch Christus hätte zum Gewehr gegriffen.'

84 Ibid., 62.

85 'Guerilla-Führer Guevara "Alles große entsteht aus dem Chaos."' Ibid., 40.

86 Ibid., 45.

87 'Tourist Guevara, Premier Chruschtschow "Die Revolution der Russen"'and 'Tourist Guevara, Parteichef Mao … ist der größte Betrug aller Zeiten.' Ibid., 66–7.

88 'Guevara-Partisanen am Rio Grande: "Landesfremde Abenteurer aus Kuba."' Ibid., 54.

Epilogue

1 Knauth, 'Fragen zu Kuba und Internationalismus.'

2 Wright, *Three Nights in Havana*, 65.

3 Kirk and McKenna, *Canada-Cuba Relations*, Wright and Wylie, eds., *Our Place in the Sun*. My thanks to Karen Dubinsky for her discussion with me on this topic.

4 The lecture was held at 100 34th Ave, Lincoln Park, on 2 July 2004. Further information at: http://artdecosociety.biz/about/events/images/artdecoflyer.pdf.

Works Cited

Adelson, Leslie. 'Imagining Migrants' Literature.' In *The Imperialist Imagination: German Colonialism and Its Legacy*, edited by Sara Friedrichsmeyer, Sara Lennox, and Susanne Zantop, 265–80. Ann Arbor: University of Michigan Press, 2001.

Agneskirchner, Alice. 'Gespräch mit Uli Gaulke.' In a publicity brochure for *Havanna mi amor*, 8–11. Potsdam-Babelsberg: Flying Moon Filmproduktion, 2000.

Ahbe, Thomas. 'Der Dammbruch.' *Freitag*, 29 August 2003, 11.

Albrecht, Willy. *Der Sozialistische Deutsche Studentenbund (SDS). Vom parteikonformen Studentenverband zum Repräsentanten der Neuen Linken*. Bonn: J.H.W. Dietz Nachfolger, 1994.

Alea, Tomás Gutiérrez. '¿Que es lo moderno en el arte?' *Cine Cubano* 3, no. 9 (1962): 31–49.

Amin, Samir. *Obsolescent Capitalism: Contemporary Politics and Global Disorder*. Translated by Patrick Camiller. London & New York: Zed Books, 2003.

Anderson, Benedict. *Imagined Communities: Reflections on the Origin and Spread of Nationalism*, rev. and extended ed. London: Verso, 1991.

Appadurai, Arjun. 'Putting Hierarchy in Its Place.' *Cultural Anthropology* 3, no. 1 (1988): 36–49.

Arnold, Herbert A. 'The Third World in the Work of Volker Braun and Heiner Müller.' *Seminar* 28, no. 2 (1992): 148–58.

Ashcroft, Bill, Gareth Griffiths, and Helen Tiffin. *The Post-Colonial Studies Reader*. London: Routledge, 1995.

'Autobiographical Travel Reports.' http://www.worldsexguide.org.

BA-FA, DR 1, MfK-HV Film: 203.

BA-FA, DR 1, MfK-HV Film: 115+B.

BA-FA, 17552.

Balsen, Werner, and Karl Rössel. *Hoch die internationale Solidarität! Zur Geschichte der Dritte Welt-Bewegung in der Bundesrepublik.* Cologne: Kölner Volksblatt, 1986.

Bammer, Angelika. *Partial Visions: Feminism and Utopianism in the 1970s.* London: Routledge, 1991.

– 'Sozialistische Feminismen. Irmtraud Morgner und amerikanische Feministinnen in den Siebziger Jahren.' In *Zwischen Gestern und Morgen. Schriftstellerinnen der DDR aus amerikanischer Sicht,* edited by Ute Brandes, 237–47. Berlin: Peter Lang, 1992.

Banchoff, Thomas. *The German Problem Transformed: Institutions, Politics and Foreign Policy, 1945–1995.* Ann Arbor: University of Michigan Press, 1999.

Barck, Simone *'Jedes Buch Ein Abenteuer'. Zensur-System und literarische Öffentlichkeiten in der DDR bis Ende der Sechziger Jahre.* Berlin: Akademie Verlag 1997.

Bartsch, Günter. 'Der Mythos der Che Guevara. Wenn der Mensch zum höchsten Wesen für den Mensch wird.' *Neue politische Literatur* 14, no. 3 (1969): 387–97.

Bathrick, David. *The Powers of Speech: The Politics of Culture in the GDR.* Modern German Culture and Literature. Lincoln: University of Nebraska Press, 1995.

Bauschinger, Hermann. 'Wie die Deutschen zu Reiseweltmeistern werden.' In *Endlich Urlaub! Die Deutschen reisen,* edited by Hermann Schäfer, 25–32. Cologne: Stiftung Haus der Geschichte der Bundesrepublik Deutschland – Dumont, 1996.

Bauschinger, Sigrid, and Susan Cocalis, eds. *'Neue Welt'/'Dritte Welt'. Interkulturelle Beziehungen Deutschlands zu Lateinamerika und der Karibik.* Tübingen: Francke Verlag, 1994.

Beck, Evelyn Torton. 'Frauen, Neger und Proleten. Die Stiefkinder der Utopie.' In *Deutsches utopisches Denken im 20. Jahrhundert,* edited by Reinhold Grimm, Jost Hermand, and Student Collective of University of Wisconsin, 30–50. Stuttgart: Kohlhammer, 1974.

Behar, Ruth. 'While Waiting for the Ferry to Cuba.' *Michigan Quarterly Review* 41, no. 4 (2002): 651–67.

Beier, Birgit. 'Tourismus als wirtschaftlicher und gesellschaftlicher Faktor.' In *Kuba Heute: Politik, Wirtschaft, Kultur,* edited by Ottmar Ette and Martin Franzbach, 371–84. Frankfurt/Main: Vervuert, 2001.

Benn Michaels, Walter. 'Race into Culture: A Critical Genealogy of Cultural Identity.' In *Identities,* edited by Henry Louis Gates and Kwame Anthony Appiah, 32–62. Chicago: University of Chicago Press, 1995.

Berbig, Roland, ed. *Stille Post. Inoffizielle Schriftstellerkontakte zwischen West und Ost*. Berlin: Ch. Links Verlag, 2005.

Berghahn, Klaus L. 'Es genügt nicht die einfache Wahrheit. Hans Magnus Enzensbergers "Verhör Von Habana" als Dokumentation und als Theaterstück.' In *Hans Magnus Enzensberger*, edited by Reinhold Grimm, 279–93. Frankfurt/Main: Suhrkamp, 1984.

Berman, Nina. *Orientalismus, Kolonialismus und Moderne. Zum Bild des Orients in der deutschsprachigen Kultur um 1900*. Stuttgart: M & P Verlag für Wissenschaft und Forschung, 1997.

Beyer, Frank. *Bockshorn*. DEFA / ICAIC, 1983.

Biermann, Wolf. 'Comandante Che Guevara.' In *Es gibt ein Leben vor dem Tod*. Hamburg: Wolf Biermann Lieder Produktion, original recording 1976.

Blunk, Harry. 'The Concept of "Heimat-GDR" in DEFA Feature Films.' In *DEFA: East German Cinema, 1946–1992*, edited by Sean Allan and John Sandford. New York: Berghahn, 1999.

Boa, Elizabeth, and Rachel Palfreyman. *Heimat – A German Dream: Regional Loyalties and National Identity in German Culture 1890–1990*. Oxford: Oxford University Press, 2000.

Bohnenstengel, Peter. 'Besonderheiten der Regiekonzeptionen von Filmen für das jugendliche Publikum, Untersucht an den DEFA-Produktionen: "Für die Liebe noch zu mager?" "Liebe mit 16."' Master's thesis, HFF der DDR (now Konrad Wolf), 1976.

Bordo, Susan. *Unbearable Weight: Feminism, Western Culture, and the Body*. Berkeley: University of California Press, 1993.

Borris, Maria. 'Sonne und Amore.' *Neue Sammlung* 5, no. 3 (1965): 231–42.

Boyer, Dominic. 'Ostalgie and the Politics of the Future in Eastern Germany.' *Public Culture* 18, no. 2 (2006): 361–81.

Braun, Matthias. '"Che Guevara – oder der Sonnenstaat" Bedenken hatten nicht nur die kubanischen Genossen.' In *Volker Braun*, edited by Frank Hörnigk, 123–7. Berlin: Theater der Zeit und Literaturforum im Brecht-Haus, 1999.

Braun, Volker. *Guevara oder der Sonnenstaat*. Leipzig: Philipp Reclam, 1983.

– 'La Rampa, Habana.' In *Training des aufrechten Ganges*, 16. Halle: Mitteldeutscher Verlag, 1979.

Brecht, Bertolt. *Gesammelte Werke*, vol. 17. Frankfurt/Main: Suhrkamp, 1968.

Breger, Claudia. '"Meine Herren, spielt in meinem Gesicht ein Affe?" Strategien der Mimikry in Texten von Emine S. Özdamar und Yoko Tawada.' In *Aufbrüche. Kulturelle Produktionen von Migrantinnen, Schwarzen und jüdischen Frauen in Deutschland*, edited by Cathy Gelbin, Kader Konuk, and Peggy Piesche, 30–59. Königstein: Ulrike Helmer Verlag, 1999.

Bremme, Bettina. 'Havanna Mi Amor. Eine Glotze geht auf Reisen.' *Latein-amerika Nachrichten* 308 (February 2000): 42–3.

Brockmann, Stephen. *Literature and German Reunification*. Cambridge Studies in German. Cambridge: Cambridge University Press, 1999.

Brunner, Horst. *Die poetische Insel. Inseln und Inselverstellungen in der Deutschen Literatur*. Stuttgart: J.B. Metzlersche Verlagsbuchhandlung, 1967.

BStU, MfS – Aim – 19049/63.

BStU, MfS – Gh – 99/78.

Bunke Nachlass, Cuba Si solidarity group, Berlin, Germany, 4.1–7, 14, 16; 6.1.

Bussmann, Rudolf. 'Die Utopie schlägt den Takt. Rumba auf einen Herbst und seine Geschichte ein Nachwort.' In *Rumba auf einen Herbst*, 321–34. Munich: DTV, 1995.

Butler, Judith. *The Psychic Life of Power: Theories in Subjection*. Stanford: Stanford University Press, 1997.

– *Bodies That Matter: On the Discursive Limits of 'Sex.'* New York: Routledge, 1993.

Butler, Richard W. 'Tourism Development in Small Islands.' In *The Development Process in Small Island States*, edited by Douglas G. Lockhart, David Drakakis-Smith, and John Schembri, 71–91. London: Routledge, 1993.

Cabezas, Amalia Lucia. 'Discourses of Prostitution: The Case of Cuba.' In *Global Sex Workers: Rights, Resistance, and Redefinition*, edited by Kamala Kempadoo and Jo Doezema, 79–86. New York: Routledge, 1998.

Calder, Jenni. *Heroes: From Byron to Guevara*. London: Hamilton, 1977.

Cardinal, Agnès. 'Irmtraud Morgner's *Rumba auf einen Herbst.' German Monitor: Retrospective and Review. Aspects of the Literature of the GDR 1976–1990* 40 (1994): 141–53.

Carstens-Wickham, Belinda. 'Gender in Cartoons of German Unification.' *Journal of Women's History* 10, no. 1 (1998): 127–56.

Castro, Fidel. 'Declaration of the First National Congress of Education and Culture (1971).' In *The Case of the Cuban Poet Heberto Padilla: Introduction, Selections and Translations*, edited by Scott Johnson, 95–134. New York: Gordon Press, 1977.

– 'Waves of the Future.' In *Latin American Radicalism*, edited by Irving Louis Horowitz, Josué de Castro, and John Gerassi, 543–79. New York: Random House, 1967.

– 'Zweite Deklaration von Havanna.' In *Fanal Kuba. Reden und Schriften 1960–1962. Mit einem Dokumentenanhang und einer Chronologie*, 365–98. Berlin: Dietz, 1963.

Chanan, Michael. *Cuban Cinema*. Minneapolis: University of Minnesota Press, 2004.

Chaussy, Ulrich. *Die drei Leben des Rudi Dutschke. Eine Biographie.* Berlin: Links, 1993.

Christian, Barbara. 'The Race for Theory.' In *Contemporary Postcolonial Theory: A Reader*, edited by Padmini Mongia, 148–57. London: Arnold, 1996.

Conlin, Michael, and Tom Baum. 'Introduction.' In *Island Tourism Management Principles and Practice*, edited by Michael Conlin and Tom Baum. New York: John Wiley and Sons, 1995.

Cosentino, Christine. 'Volker Brauns roter Empedokles. Guevara oder der Sonnenstaat.' *Monatsheft* 71 (1979): 41–8.

Costabile-Heming, Carol Anne. *Intertextual Exile: Volker Braun's Dramatic Re-Vision of GDR Society.* Hildesheim: Georg Olms Verlag, 1997.

Crew, David F., ed. *Consuming Germany in the Cold War.* Oxford: Berg, 2003.

'Cuba: Arrivals of Non-Resident Visitors at National Borders, by Country of Residence.' Madrid: World Tourism Organization, 1999.

Dahlke, Birgit. *Papierboot. Autorinnen aus der DDR – inoffiziell publiziert.* Würzburg: Königshausen & Neumann, 1997.

Debray, Régis. *Revolución en la Revolución?* Havana: Casa de las Américas, 1967.

– *Révolution dans la Révolution? Et Autres Essais.* Paris: Maspero, 1972.

DEFA-Wochenschau. *Der Augenzeuge – 1974–1976.* Berlin: Icestorm, 2001. VHS.

Diederichsen, Diedrich. 'Persecution and Self-Persecution: The Spur Group and Its Texts: The Neo-Avant-Garde in the Province of Postfascism.' *Grey Room*, no. 26 (Winter 2007): 56–71.

Diemer, Susanne. *Patriarchalismus in der DDR.* Opladen: Leske und Budrich, 1994.

Dietschreit, Frank, and Barbara Heinze-Dietschriet. *Hans Magnus Enzensberger.* Stuttgart: Metzler, 1986.

Dirke, Sabine Von. *'All Power to the Imagination!' The West German Counterculture from the Student Movement to the Greens.* Modern German Culture and Literature. Lincoln: University of Nebraska Press, 1997.

Dölling, Irene. '"We All Love Paula but Paul Is More Important to Us": Constructing a "Socialist Person" Using the "Femininity" of a Working Woman.' *New German Critique* 82 (Winter 2001): 77–90.

– '"Wir alle lieben Paula, aber uns liegt an Paul". Wie über die "Weiblichkeit" einer Arbeiterin der "Sozialistische Mensch" konstruiert wird.' *Potsdamer Studien zur Frauen- und Geschlechterforschung* 2 (1997).

Dubinsky, Karen, Catherine Krull, Susan Lord, Sean Mills, and Scott Rutherford, eds. *New World Coming: The Sixties and the Shaping of Global Consciousness.* Toronto: Between the Lines, 2009.

Dueck, Cheryl. 'Gendered Germanies: The Fetters of a Metaphorical Marriage.' *German Life and Letters* 54, no. 4 (2001): 366–76.

Dümcke, Wolfgang, and Fritz Vilmar. *Kolonialisierung der DDR. Kritische Analysen und Alternativen des Einigungsprozesses*, 3rd ed. Münster: Agenda, 1996.

Dutschke, Gretchen. *Wir hatten ein barbarisches, schönes Leben. Rudi Dutschke eine Biographie.* Cologne: Kiepenheuer und Witsch, 1996.

Dutschke, Rudi. 'Vom Antisemitismus zum Antikommunismus.' In *Rebellion der Studenten oder die neue Opposition*, edited by Uwe Bergmann, Rudi Dutschke, Wolfgang Lefèvre, and Bernd Rabehl. Reinbeck: Rowohlt, 1968.

Dutschke, Rudi [R.S., pseud.]. 'Zum Verhältnis von Organisation und Emanzipationsbewegung – Zum Besuch Herbert Marcuses.' *Oberbaum Blatt* (12 July [labelled June] 1967): 1, 4–6.

Dutschke, Rudi, and Hans-Jürgen Krahl. 'Organisationsreferat.' In *Frankfurter Schule und Studentenbewegung von der Flaschenpost zum Molotowcocktail 1946 bis 1995*, edited by Wolfgang Kraushaar, 287–90. Hamburg: Rogner and Bernhard, 1967.

Eason, Jeff. 'Ry Cooder's Buena Vista Project Scuttled by Cuba Policy: Cultural Exchanges under Fire from Bush Administration.' *The Mountain Times*, 27 February 2003.

Edmond, Rod, and Vanessa Smith, eds. *Islands in History and Representation.* London: Routledge, 2003.

Elbaum, Max. *Revolution in the Air: Sixties Radicals Turn to Lenin, Mao and Che.* London: Verso, 2002.

Elliott, Robert. *The Shape of Utopia: Studies in a Literary Genre.* Chicago: University of Chicago Press, 1970.

Emde, Silke von der. 'Irmtraud Morgner's Postmodern Feminism: A Question of Politics.' *Women in German Yearbook* 10 (1994): 117–42.

Enloe, Cynthia. *Bananas, Beaches and Bases: Making Feminist Sense of International Politics.* Berkeley: University of California Press, 1990.

Enzensberger, Hans Magnus. 'Bildnis einer Partie. Vorgeschichte, Struktur und Ideologie der PCC.' *Kursbuch* 18 (1969): 192–216.

– ed. *Das Verhör von Habana.* Berlin: Schaubühne am Halleschen Ufer, 1970–1.

– *Das Verhör von Habana.* Frankfurt/Main: Suhrkamp, 1972.

– *Der Untergang der Titanic.* Frankfurt/Main: Suhrkamp, 1978.

– 'Ein Gespräch über die Zukunft mit Rudi Dutschke, Bernd Rabehl und Christian Semler.' *Kursbuch* 14 (1968): 146–74.

– *Freisprüche. Revolutionäre vor Gericht.* Frankfurt/Main: Suhrkamp, 1970.

– *The Sinking of the Titanic.* Translated by Hans Magnus Enzensberger. Boston: Houghton Mifflin Company, 1980.

Estrada, Ulises. *Tania: Undercover with Che Guevara in Bolivia.* Melbourne: Ocean Press, 2005.

Ette, Ottmar. 'Einleitung. Kuba – Insel der Inseln.' In *Kuba heute. Politik, Wirt-*

schaft, Kultur, edited by Ottmar Ette and Martin Franzbach, 9–28. Frankfurt/
Main: Vervuert, 2001.

Fachinger, Petra. *Rewriting Germany from the Margins: Other German Literature
of the 1980s and 1990s*. Kingston: McGill-Queen's University Press, 2001.

Fanon, Frantz. *The Wretched of the Earth*. Translated by Constance Farrington.
Harmondsworth: Penguin Books, 1973.

Feinstein, Joshua. *The Triumph of the Ordinary: Depictions of Everyday Life in East
German Cinema 1949–1989*. Chapel Hill: University of North Carolina Press,
2002.

Fels, Gerhard. *Der Aufruhr der 68er. Zu den geistigen Grundlagen der Studentenbewegung und der RAF*. Bonn: Bouvier, 1998.

Ferns, Chris. *Narrating Utopia: Ideology, Gender, Form in Utopian Literature*. Liverpool: Liverpool University Press, 1999.

Foucault, Michel. 'Of Other Spaces.' *Diacritics* 16, no. 1 (1986): 22–7.

Freedman, Lawrence. *Kennedy's Wars: Berlin, Cuba, Laos, and Vietnam*. New
York: Oxford University Press, 2000.

'Friedliche Koexistenz.' In *Jugendlexikon*, edited by Gerhard Butzmann, Jonny
Gottschalg, Günter Gurst, and Annelies Müller-Hegemann, 257. Leipzig:
VEB Bibliographisches Institut Leipzig, 1981.

Friedrich, Paul. 'Die Jugendpolitik der SED – Ein schöpferischer Beitrag zur
Lehre des Marxismus-Leninismus.' *Wissenschaftliche Zeitschrift der Karl-
Marx-Universität Leipzig* 15, no. 1 (1966).

Friedrichsmeyer, Sara, Sara Lennox, and Susanne Zantop, eds. *The Imperialist
Imagination: German Colonialism and Its Legacy*. Social History, Popular Culture,
and Politics in Germany. Ann Arbor: University of Michigan Press, 2001.

– 'Introduction.' In *The Imperialist Imagination: German Colonialism and Its
Legacy*, edited by Sara Friedrichsmeyer, Sara Lennox, and Susanne Zantop,
1–29. Ann Arbor: University of Michigan Press, 2001.

Fries, Fritz Rudolf. 'Kubanische Kalenderblätter.' In *Alle meine Hotel Leben*,
7–27. Berlin: Aufbau, 1980.

– 'Paris, doppel belichtet.' In *Alle meine Hotel Leben*, 125–45. Berlin: Aufbau,
1980.

Fusco, Coco. 'Hustling for Dollars: Jineterismo in Cuba.' In *Global Sex Workers: Rights, Resistance, and Redefinition*, edited by Kamala Kempadoo and Jo
Doezema, 151–67. New York: Routledge, 1998.

G. 'Cuba: Die OLAS und die lateinamerikanische Revolution.' *Oberbaum Blatt*,
14 November 1967, 5, 9.

Gaulke, Uli. *Havanna mi amor*. Berlin: Salzgeber, 2000. DVD.

Gaulke, Uli, and Jeannette Eggert. *Heirate mich!* Berlin: Flying Moon Filmproduktion, 2003. DVD.

Gemünden, Gerd. 'Nostalgia for the Nation: Intellectuals and National Identity in Unified Germany.' In *Acts of Memory: Cultural Recall in the Present*, edited by Mieke Bal, Jonathan Crewe, and Leo Spitzer, 120–33. Hanover: University Press of New England, 1999.

Gerassi, John. 'Havana: A New International Is Born.' In *Latin American Radicalism: A Documentary Report on Left and Nationalist Movements*, edited by Irving Louis Horowitz, John Gerassi, and Josué de Castro, 532–42. New York: Random House, 1969.

Ghosh, Jayati. 'The Many Uses of Jazz.' *Frontline* 17, no. 2 (2000). http://www.frontlineonnet.com/fl1702/17021050.htm.

Gjelten, Tom. *Bacardi and the Long Fight for Cuba*. New York: Viking, 2008.

Glissant, Edouard. *Poetics of Relation*. Translated by Betsy Wing. Ann Arbor: University of Michigan Press, 1997.

Göckeritz, Heinz. 'Die Bundesbürger entdecken die Urlaubsreise.' In *Entlich Urlaub! Die Deutschen reisen*, edited by Hermann Schäfer, 43–50. Cologne: Stiftung Haus der Geschichte – DuMont, 1996.

Grass, Günter. *Ein Weites Feld*, 3rd ed. Munich: DTV, 1999.

Gries, Rainer. 'Die Heldenbühne der DDR zur Einführung.' In *Sozialistische Helden eine Kulturgeschichte von Propagandafiguren in Osteuropa und der DDR*, edited by Silke Satjukow and Rainer Gries, 84–100. Berlin: Links, 2002.

Grimm, Reinhold. 'Enzensberger, Kuba und La Cubana.' In *Texturen. Essays und Anderes zu Hans Magnus Enzensberger*, 65–77. New York: Peter Lang, 1984.

Gross, Horst-Eckart. 'Vorwort.' In *Ernesto Che Guevara. Schriften zum Internationalismus*, edited by Horst-Eckart Gross, 7–11. Dortmund: Weltkreis Verlag, 1989.

Guevara, Che. 'Der Guerillakrieg.' In *Guerilla – Theorie und Methode*, edited by Klaus Wagenbach, 20–98. Berlin: Wagenbach, 1968.

– 'Der Sozialismus und der Mensch in Kuba.' In *Ernesto Che Guevara: Der Neue Mensch*, edited by Horst-Eckart Gross, 14–36. Bonn: Pahl-Rugenstein, 1997.

– *Guerilla – Theorie und Methode*. Edited by Klaus Wagenbach. Berlin: Wagenbach/Rotbuch, 1968.

– 'Guerillakrieg: Eine Methode.' In *Guerilla – Theorie und Methode*, edited by Klaus Wagenbach, 124–42. Berlin: Wagenbach/Rotbuch, 1968.

– *Schaffen wir zwei, drei, viele Vietnam!* Translated by Rudi Dutschke and Gaston Salvatore. Berlin: Oberbaumpresse Berlin, 1967.

– 'Schaffen wir zwei, drei, viele Vietnam.' *Oberbaum Blatt* (1967): 1.

– 'Schaffen wir zwei, drei, viele Vietnam.' In *Guerilla – Theorie und Methode*, edited by Klaus Wagenbach, 143–58. Berlin: Wagenbach/Rotbuch, 1968.

Guevara, Ernesto Che. *Bolivianisches Tagebuch*. Translated by Klaus Laabs. Berlin: Verlag Volk und Welt, 1987.

H.A. 'Abenteuer in der Schweinebucht.' *Nationalzeitung*, 22 March 1964.

Habermas, Jürgen. 'Der Golf-Krieg als Katalysator einer neuen Deutschen Normalität?' In *Vergangenheit als Zukunft? Das alte Deutschland im neuen Europa*, edited by Jürgen Habermas. Munich: Piper, 1993.

– *Die nachholende Revolution*. Frankfurt/Main: Suhrkamp, 1990.

– *Die Normalität einer Berliner Republik*. Frankfurt/Main: Suhrkamp, 1995.

– 'Staatsbürgerschaft und nationale Identität.' In *Faktizität und Geltung*, edited by Jürgen Habermas. Frankfurt/Main: Suhrkamp, 1992.

Halle, Randall. *German Film after Germany: Toward a Transnational Aesthetic*. Urbana-Champaign: University of Illinois Press, 2008.

Hanel, Stephanie. *Literarischer Widerstand zwischen Phantastischem und Alltäglichem. Das Romanwerk Irmtraud Morgners.* Pfaffenweiler: Centaurus-Verlagsgesellschaft, 1995.

Hardt, Michael, and Antonio Negri. *Empire*. Cambridge: Harvard University Press, 2001.

Harvey, David. *Spaces of Hope*. Edinburgh: Edinburgh University Press, 2000.

Hau'ofa, E. 'Our Sea of Islands.' In *A New Oceania: Rediscovering Our Sea of Islands*, edited by E. Waddell, V. Naidu, and E. Hau'ofa. Suva: University of the South Pacific, 1993.

Häußermann, Hartmut. 'Das Berliner Milieu und die Stadtforschung.' In *Radikalisierte Aufklärung*, edited by Heinz Bude and Martin Kohli, 43–70. Weinheim: Juventa, 1989.

Hein, Jakob. *Mein erstes T-Shirt*. Munich: Piper, 2005.

Henneberg, Claus H., ed. *El Cimarrón: Ein Werkbericht von Hans Magnus Enzensberger, Hans Werner Henze, William Pearson, Karlheinz Zöller, Leo Brouwer, Tsutomu Yamash'ta*. Mainz: B. Schott's Söhne, 1971.

Hensel, Jana. *Zonenkinder*, 3rd ed. Reinbek: Rowohlt, 2002.

Hentzi, Gary. 'Buena Vista Social Club.' *Film Quarterly* 53, no. 4 (2000): 47–50.

Henze, Hans Werner, and Peter Labanyi. *Music and Politics: Collected Writings, 1953–81*. Ithaca: Cornell University Press, 1982.

Herzka, Alfred. *Kuba, Abschied vom Kommandanten?* Frankfurt/Main: Suhrkamp, 1998.

Herzog, Dagmar. '"Pleasure, Sex, and Politics Belong Together": Post-Holocaust Memory and the Sexual Revolution in West Germany.' *Critical Inquiry* 24 (Winter 1998): 393–444.

Hille, Barbara. 'Interessen von Jugendlichen im interkulturellen Vergleich zwischen der Bundesrepublik Deutschland und der DDR.' In *Jugend im doppelten Deutschland*, edited by Walter Jaide and Barbara Hille, 226–49. Opladen: Westdeutscher Verlag, 1977.

Hobsbawm, E.J. *The Age of Extremes*. New York: Vintage, 1996.

- *Nations and Nationalism since 1780: Programme, Myth, Reality*. Cambridge: Cambridge University Press, 1990.

Hobsbawm, E.J., and T. Ranger, eds. *The Invention of Tradition*. Cambridge: Cambridge University Press, 1983.

Hohendahl, P.U. 'Von der Rothaut zum Edelmenschen. Karl Mays Amerikaromane.' In *Amerika in der deutschen Literatur: Neue Welt – Nordamerika – USA*, edited by Sigrid Bauschinger, Horst Denkler, and Wilfried Malsch, 229–45. Stuttgart: Reclam, 1975.

Hollander, Paul. 'Political Tourism in Cuba and Nicaragua.' *Society* 23, no. 4 (1986): 28–37.

Höller, Hans, ed. *Briefe einer Freundschaft. Ingeborg Bachmann, Hans Werner Henze*. Munich: Piper, 2004.

Holub, Robert. *Jürgen Habermas: Critic in the Public Sphere*. London: Routledge, 1991.

Hong, Young-Sun. 'Remarks at the Round Table on Transnationalism.' Paper presented at the German Studies Association meeting, Pittsburgh, 1 October 2006.

Hörnigk, Frank. 'Erinnerungen an Revolutionen. Zu Entwicklungstendenzen in der Dramatik Heiner Muellers, Peter Hacks und Volker Brauns Ende der Siebziger Jahre.' In *Tendenzen und Beispiele: Zur DDR-Literatur in den Siebziger Jahren*, edited by Hans Kaufmann, 148–84. Leipzig: Reclam, 1981.

Hosek, Jennifer Ruth. 'Postcommunist Spectacle: Germany, Commodity, Comedy.' In *Postcommunism, Postmodernism, and the Global Imaginary*, edited by Christian Moraru, 169–92. New York: Columbia University Press, 2009.

- 'Whose Culture, Whose Feminism: A Consideration of "Feminist" Perspectives in Texts by Gloria Naylor and Kerstin Hensel.' In *Northeast Modern Languages Association Conference*. Pittsburgh, 1999.

Huberman, Leo, and Sweezy Paul M. *Regis Debray and the Latin American Revolution*. New York: Monthly Review, 1968.

Jacoby, Russell. *The End of Utopia: Politics and Culture in an Age of Apathy*. New York: Basic Books, 1999.

Jameson, Fredric. 'Of Islands and Trenches: Naturalization and the Production of Utopian Discourse.' *Diacritics* 2 (1977): 2–21.

Jiménez, García. 'La Economía del turismo en Cuba.' *Estudios y Perspectivas en Turismo* 8, no. 3/4 (1999): 213–31.

Juchler, Ingo. *Die Studentenbewegungen in den Vereinigten Staaten und der Bundesrepublik Deutschland der Sechziger Jahre. Eine Untersuchung hinsichtlich ihrer Beeinflussung durch Befreiungsbewegungen und -theorien aus der Dritten Welt*. Beiträge zur Politischen Wissenschaft. Berlin: Duncker & Humblot, 1994.

– Rebellische Subjektivität und Internationalismus. Der Einfluß Herbert Marcuse und der nationalen Befreiungsbewegung in der sog. Dritten Welt auf die Studentenbewegung in der BRD. Marburg: Verlag Arbeiterbewegung und Gesellschaftswissenschaft, 1989.

Just-drinks.com, editorial. 'Cuba: Havana Club Extends Global Ad Campaign.' http://www.just-drinks.com/article.aspx?id=94414.

Kacandes, Irene. 'From Deconstruction to Postcolonialism, 1980 to the Present.' In German Studies in the United States: A Historical Handbook, edited by P.U. Hohendahl, 243–58. New York: The Modern Language Association of America, 2003.

Kapcia, Antoni. Cuba: Island of Dreams. Oxford: Berg, 2000.

Kaplan, Caren, and Inderpal Grewal. 'Transnational Feminist Cultural Studies: Beyond the Marxism/Poststructuralism/Feminism Divides.' In Between Woman and Nation: Nationalisms, Transnational Feminisms, and the State, edited by Norma Alarcón, Caren Kaplan, and Minoo Moallem, 349–63. Durham: Duke University Press, 1999.

Karsunke, Ingrid, and Karl Markus Michel. Bewegung in der Republik, 1965–1984. Eine Kursbuch-Chronik. 2 vols. Basisbücher, 8–9. Frankfurt/Main: Büchergilde Gutenberg, 1985.

Kaufmann, Eva. 'Interview mit Irmtraud Morgner.' Weimarer Beiträge 30, no. 9 (1984): 1494–532.

Kempadoo, Kamala. 'The Migrant Tightrope: Experiences from the Caribbean.' In Global Sex Workers: Rights, Resistance, and Redefinition, edited by Kamala Kempadoo and Jo Doezema, 124–38. New York: Routledge, 1998.

Kirk, John, and Peter McKenna. Canada-Cuba Relations: The Other Good Neighbor Policy. Gainesville: University Press of Florida, 1997.

Klimke, Martin. The Other Alliance: Student Protest in West Germany and the United States in the Global Sixties: Princeton University Press, 2009.

Knauth, Christopher. 'Fragen zu Kuba und Internationalismus.' Blätter des iz3w 101 (May 1982): 47–58.

Köck, Christoph. 'Mit dem Finger auf der Landkarte: Abenteuerurlaub für Alle.' In Endlich Urlaub! Die Deutschen reisen, edited by Hermann Schäfer, 59–64. Cologne: Stiftung Haus der Geschichte – DuMont, 1996.

Koenen, Gerd. Das rote Jahrzehnt. Cologne: Kiepenheuer & Witsch, 2001.

– Traumpfade der Weltrevolution – Das Guevara-Projekt. Cologne: Kiepenheuer & Witsch, 2008.

Köhler-Hausmann, Reinhild. Literaturbetrieb in der DDR. Schriftsteller und Literaturinstanzen. Stuttgart: Metzler, 1984.

Kolker, Robert Phillip, and Peter Beicken. The Films of Wim Wenders: Cinema as Vision and Desire. Cambridge: Cambridge University Press, 1993.

Kontje, Todd. *German Orientalisms*. Ann Arbor: University of Michigan Press, 2004.

Kramer, Karen Ruoff. 'Blauhemd und Blue Jeans in Filmen der DEFA.' In *Jeans, Rock and Vietnam. Amerikanische Kultur in der DDR*, edited by Theresa Hoernigk, 129–51. Berlin: Theater der Zeit/Literaturforum im Brecht-Haus, 2002.

Krämer, Raimund. 'Che Guevara und die DDR. Anmerkungen zu einem wechselvollen Verhältnis.' *Tranvia* (1997): 5–10.

– *Der alte Mann und die Insel. Essays zu Politik und Gesellschaft in Kuba*. Berlin: Berliner Debatte Wissenschaftsverlag, 1998.

Kraushaar, Wolfgang. 'Editorial.' In *Frankfurter Schule und Studentenbewegung. Von der Flaschenpost zum Molotowcocktail 1946–1995*, edited by Wolfgang Kraushaar, 13–15. Hamburg: Rogner & Bernhard, 1998.

– 'Rudi Dutschke und der bewaffnete Kampf.' In *Rudi Dutschke, Andreas Baader und die RAF*, edited by Wolfgang Kraushaar, Karin Wieland, and Jan Philipp Reemtsma, 13–50. Hamburg: Hamburger Edition, 2005.

– 'Rudi Dutschke und die Wiedervereinigung: Zur heimlichen Dialektik von Internationalismus und Nationalismus.' *Mittelweg 36*, no. 2 (1992): 12–47.

– 'SED, Stasi und Studentenbewegung.' In *1968 als Mythos, Chiffre und Zäsur*, edited by Wolfgang Kraushaar, 139–62. Hamburg: Hamburger Edition, 2000.

LaCapra, Dominick. *Representing the Holocaust: History, Memory, Trauma*. Ithaca: Cornell University Press, 1994.

Laclau, Ernesto, and Chantal Mouffe. *Hegemony and Socialist Strategy: Towards a Radical Democratic Politics*. London: Verso, 1985.

Lange, Günter. *Heimat: Realität und Aufgabe. Zur marxistischen Auffassung des Heimatbegriffs*. Berlin: Akademie Verlag, 1975.

Langelüddecke, Ines. '"So lebt Tania in uns weiter." Tamara Bunke und die Konstruktion eines politischen Mythos in der DDR.' Master's thesis, Humboldt Universität, 2003.

Larsen, Neil. *Reading North by South: On Latin American Literature, Culture and Politics*. Minneapolis: University of Minnesota Press, 1995.

Lartéguy, Jean. '"Auch Christus hätte zum Gewehr gegriffen." Che Guevara und Revolution in Lateinamerika.' *Der Spiegel*, 1968, 40–72.

Lau, Jörg. *Hans Magnus Enzensberger. Ein öffentliches Leben*. Berlin: Alexander Fest Verlag, 1999.

Le Bel, Pierre-Mathieu. *La réhabilitation de la vieille Havane: Le local dans le global en milieu socialiste*. Montreal: Crises, 2005.

Lennox, Sara. 'Enzensberger, *Kursbuch*, and Third-Worldism.' In *'Neue Welt'/'Dritte Welt'. interkuturelle Beziehungen Deutschlands zu Lateinamerika und der Karibik*, edited by Sigrid Bauschinger and Susan Cocalis, 185–200. Tübingen: Franke, 1994.

Letz, Malte. 'Im Osten nichts Neues? Ostdeutsche Solidaritätsgruppen vor und nach der Wende.' *Forschungsjournal neue soziale Bewegungen* 7, no. 3 (1994): 49–62.

Levine, Art. 'Viva *Buena Vista Social Club*.' http://www.salon.com/entertainment/music/feature/1999/03/09feature.html.

Lindner, Bernd. *Die demokratische Revolution in der DDR 1989/90*. Bonn: Bundeszentrale für Politische Bildung, 1998.

Linke, Uli. *German Bodies: Race and Representation after Hitler*. New York: Routledge, 1999.

Linklater, Beth. *'Und immer zügelloser wird die Lust.' Constructions of Sexuality in East German Literatures*. Bern: Lang, 1997.

Lionnet, Françoise, and Shu-mei Shih. 'Introduction.' In *Minor Transnationalism*, edited by Françoise Lionnet and Shu-mei Shih, 1–22. Durham: Duke University Press, 2005.

Löser, Claus. 'Dokumentarfilme an der Babelsberger Filmhochschule.' In *Schwarzweiß und Farbe: DEFA-Dokumentarfilme 1946–92*, edited by Filmmuseum Potsdam, 342–55. Berlin: Filmmuseum Potsdam, 2000.

Maase, Kaspar. *BRAVO Amerika. Erkundungen zur Jugendkultur der Bundesrepublik in den Fünfziger Jahren*. Schriftenreihe des Hamburger Instituts für Sozialforschung. Hamburg: Junius, 1992.

MacCannell, Dean. *Empty Meeting Grounds: The Tourist Papers*. London: Routledge, 1992.

Maetzig, Kurt, and Wolfgang Schreyer. *Preludio 11*. Berlin: ICAIC & DEFA, 1963.

Mählert, Ulrich. *Kleine Geschichte der DDR*. Munich: Beck, 1998.

Mahrad, Christa. 'Jugendpolitik in der DDR.' In *Jugend im doppelten Deutschland*, edited by Barbara Hille and Walter Jaide, 195–226. Opladen: Westdeutscher Verlag, 1977.

Mann, Ekkehard. *Untergrund, autonome Literatur und das Ende der DDR*, edited by Paul Gerhard Klussmann. Vol. 4, *Schriften zur Europa- und Deutschlandforschung*. Frankfurt/Main: Lang, 1996.

Mannheim, Karl. *Ideology and Utopia: An Introduction to the Sociology of Knowledge*. New York: Harcourt Brace, 1936.

Marcuse, Herbert. 'Das Problem der Gewalt in der Opposition.' In *Das Ende der Utopie. Vorträge und Diskussionen in Westberlin 1967*, 44–58. Frankfurt/Main, 1980.

Marquardt, Hans. 'Nachbemerkung.' In *Guevara oder der Sonnenstaat*, 65–7. Leipzig: Philipp Reclam, 1983.

Marquardt, Nancy, and Otto Marquardt. *Report aus Havanna*. Leipzig: VEB F.A. Brockhaus Verlag, 1971.

Maschke, Günter. 'Cubanischer Taschenkalender.' *Kursbuch* 30 (December 1972): 129–54.

– 'Entfremdung – Herrschaft-Produzenten-Demokratie. Bemerkungen zum Problem der Übergangsperiode.' *Kursbuch* 23 (1973): 85–95.

– *Kritik des Guerillero*. Frankfurt/Main: Fischer, 1973.

McClintock, Anne. 'The Angel of Progress: Pitfalls of the Term "Post-Colonialism."' In *Colonial Discourse and Post-Colonial Theory: A Reader*, edited by Patrick Williams and Laura Chrisman, 291–304. New York: Columbia University Press, 1994.

– *Imperial Leather: Race, Gender and Sexuality in the Colonial Contest*. New York: Routledge, 1995.

Melin, Charlotte Ann. *Poetic Maneuvers: Hans Magnus Enzensberger and the Lyric Genre*. Evanston: Northwestern University Press, 2003.

Melin, Charlotte, and Cecile Cazort Zorach. 'Cuba as Paradise, Paradigm, and Paradox.' *Monatshefte* 78, no. 4 (1986): 480–99.

Merkel, Ina. 'Utopie und Bedürfnis. Die Geschichte der Konsumkultur in der DDR.' In *Jeans, Rock und Vietnam. Amerikanische Kultur in der DDR*. Berlin: Literaturforum im Brecht-Haus, 2002.

Mesa, Vladimir Smith. 'Kino Cuban: The Significance of Soviet and East European Cinemas for the Cuban Moving Image.' PhD diss., University of London, 2011.

Moltke, Johannes von. *No Place Like Home: Locations of Heimat in German Cinema*. Berkeley: University California Press, 2005.

Morgenthaler. 'Zwischen Rum und Revolution. Die Barcardis.' Germany: MDR, 2006.

Morgner, Irmtraud. *The Life and Adventures of Trobadora Beatrice as Chronicled by Her Minstrel Laura*. Translated by Jeanette Clausen. Lincoln: University of Nebraska Press, 1992.

– *Rumba auf einen Herbst*, 2nd ed. Munich: DTV, 1995.

Müller, Heiner. '"Wie es ist, bleibt es nicht." Zu Thomas Brasch "Kargo."' *Der Spiegel*, 12 September 1977, 212.

Nachbar, Herbert. *Die gestohlene Insel. Eine Robinsonade*. Berlin: Aufbau, 1976.

'Nationale Befreiungsbewegung.' In *Jugendlexikon*, edited by Gerhard Butzmann, Jonny Gottschalg, Günter Gurst, and Annelies Müller-Hegemann, 488–9. Leipzig: VEB Bibliographisches Institut Leipzig, 1981.

Naughton, Leonie. *That Was the Wild East: Film Culture, Unification, and the 'New' Germany*. Ann Arbor: University of Michigan Press, 2002.

Nielsen, Henrik Kaare. 'Aspekte der Faschismuskritik der antiautoritären Bewegung.' In *Antifaschismus in deutscher und skandinavischer Literatur*, edited by Jens Peter Lund Nielson, 141–50. Aarhus: Arkona, 1983.

Obeyesekere, Gananath. '"British Cannibals": Contemplation of an Event in the Death and Resurrection of James Cook, Explorer.' In *Identities*, edited by Henry Louis Gates and Kwame Anthony Appiah, 7–31. Chicago: University of Chicago Press, 1995.

Opaschowski, Horst W. *Jugendauslandsreisen. Geschichtliche, soziale und pädagogische Aspekte*. Darmstadt and Berlin: Luchterhand, 1970.

Ospina, Hernando Calvo. *Bacardi: The Hidden War*. London: Pluto Press, 2000.

Oteri, Frank. 'Tania León Interview.' http://www.newmusicbox.org/firstperson/aug99/interview2.html.

Otto, Herbert. *Republik Der Leidenschaft*. Berlin: Volk und Welt, 1964.

Palmowski, Jan. 'Building an East German Nation: The Construction of a Socialist Heimat 1945–1961.' *Central European History* 37, no. 3 (2004): 365–99.

Panitz, Eberhard. *Der Weg zum Rio Grande: Ein biographischer Bericht über Tamara Bunke*. Berlin: Verlag Neues Leben, 1973.

– *Kubaskizzen*. [Citation information incomplete on photocopy.]

Parkes, Stuart. 'Postmodern Polemics: Recent Intelle ctual Debates in Germany.' In *The New Germany Literature and Society after Unification*, edited by Osman Durrani, Colin H. Good, and Kevin Hilliard, 92–101. Sheffield: Sheffield Academic Press, 1995.

Petersen, Peter. 'Das Floß der Medusa – Mehr als ein Konzertskandal.' In *Hans Werner Henze. Ein politischer Musiker. Zwölf Vorlesungen*, 101–9. Hamburg: Argument, 1988.

Poss, Ingrid. *DEFA 50 Gespräche aus acht Filmnächten. Protokolle*. Brandenburg: Brandenburgische Landeszentrale für Politische Bildung, 1997.

Pratt, Mary Louise. *Imperial Eyes: Travel Writing and Transculturation*. London: Routledge, 1992.

Preuße, Holger-Heinrich. *Der politische Literat. Hans Magnus Enzensberger*. Frankfurt/Main: Peter Lang, 1989.

Profitlich, Ulrich. *Volker Braun*. Munich: Fink Verlag, 1985.

Rabehl, Bernd. 'Die Provokationselite. Aufbruch und Scheitern der subversiven Rebellion in den Sechziger Jahren.' In *Die antiautoritäre Revolte: der Sozialistische Deutsche Studentenbund nach der Trennung von der SPD*, edited by Siegward Lönnendonker, Bernd Rabehl, and Jochen Staadt, 401–512. Wiesbaden: Westdeutscher Verlag, 2002.

– *Rudi Dutschke: Revolutionär im geteilten Deutschland*. Dresden: Edition Antaios, 2004.

Reichardt, Achim. *Nie vergessen,Solidarität üben! Die Solidaritätsbewegung in der DDR*. Berlin: Kai Homilius Verlag, 2006.

Reid, J.H. *Writing without Taboos: The New East German Literature*. New York: Oswald Wolff Books, 1990.

Renan, Ernest. 'What Is a Nation?' In *Becoming National: A Reader*, edited by Geoff Eley and Ronald Grigor Suny, 42–56. Oxford: Oxford University Press, 1996.

Retamar, Roberto Fernández. 'The Enormity of Cuba.' *Boundary 2* 23, no. 3 (1996): 165–90.

Rickards, Guy. *Hindemith, Hartmann and Henz*. London: Phaidon, 1995.

Rinke, Andrea. 'From Motzki to Trotzki: Representations of East and West German Cultural Identities on German Television after Unification.' In *The New Germany: Literature and Society after Unification*, edited by Osman Durrani, Colin H. Good, and Kevin Hilliard, 231–51. Sheffield: Sheffield Academic Press, 1995.

Röhl, Bettina. *So macht Kommunismus Spaß. Ulrike Meinhof, Klaus Rainer Röhl und die Akte Konkret*. Hamburg: Europäische Verlagsanstalt, 2006.

Rojas, Marta, and Mirta Rodríguez Calderón. *Tania la Guerrillera*. Berlin: Militärverlag der Deutschen Demokratischen Republik, 1973.

Rojas Rodríguez, Marta, Mirta Rodríguez Calderón, and Ulises Estrada Lescaille. *Tania la guerrillera inolvidable*, 2nd (rev. and expanded) ed. Havana: Editorial de Ciencias Sociales, 2001.

Roth, Ursula. 'Der erste Schnee, die erste Rolle für Aurora.' *Brandenburgische Neueste Nachrichten*, 8 February 1963.

Rubinstein, Hilde. 'Meine kubanische Reise.' *Sinn und Form* 4 (1981).

Rusch, Claudia. *Meine Freie Deutsche Jugend*, 4th ed. Frankfurt/Main: Fischer, 2003.

Santana Castillo, Joaquin. Unpublished manuscript. Havana, 2002.

SAPMO-BArch, DR 1, 2389a.

SAPMO-BArch, DR 1, 3546a.

SAPMO-BArch, DR 1, 3547.

SAPMO-BArch, DR 117, 8525.

SAPMO-BArch, DR 117, BA 0015.

SAPMO-BArch, DR 117, BA 1945.

SAPMO-BArch, DR 117, BA 1948.

SAPMO-BArch, DR 117, BA 3118.

SAPMO-BArch, DY 24, 6196.

SAPMO-BArch, DY 24, 6954.

SAPMO-BArch, DY 30, IV a 2/20.

SAPMO-BArch, DY 30, IV a 2/20/185.

SAPMO-BArch, DY 30, IV a 2/20/285.

Sareika, Rüdiger. *Die Dritte Welt in der westdeutschen Literatur der sechziger Jahre*. Saarbrücker Beiträge zur Literaturwissenschaft. Frankfurt/Main: Rita G. Fischer, 1980.

Scheer, Maximilian. *Von Afrika nach Kuba*. Berlin: Verlag der Nation, 1961.

Scheer, Regina. 'Die Partisanin.' In *Wild Women: Furien, Flittchen, Flintenweiber*, edited by Baerbel Becker, 131–5. Berlin: Elefanten Press, 1992.

Schieber, Elke. 'Im Dämmerlicht der Perestroika 1980 bis 1989.' In *Schwarzweiß und Farbe: DEFA-Dokumentarfilme 1946–92*, edited by Günter Jordan and Ralf Schenk, 180–233. Berlin: Filmmuseum Potsdam, 2000.

Schmidtke, Michael A. 'Cultural Revolution or Cultural Shock? Student Radicalism and 1968 in Germany.' *South Central Review* 16, no. 4 (1999–2000): 77–89.

Schnibben, Cordt. 'Tamara Bunke.' In *Rebellinnen. Leben als Aufstand*, edited by Michaela Adelberger and Maren Lübbke, 123–44. Mannheim: Bollmann, 1997.

Schölzel, Arnold. 'Warum drehen Sie Filme über Kuba?' *Die junge Welt*, 18 July 2000.

Schubert, Hans-Gert. *Rote Insel im Atlantik*, 2nd ed. Berlin: Neues Leben, 1979.

Schuhmann, Klaus. *'Ich bin der Braun, den ihr kritisiert': Wege zu und mit Volker Brauns literarischem Werk*. Leipzig: Leipziger Universitäts-Verlag, 2004.

Schumann, Kerstin. 'Grenzübertritte – Das "Deutsche" Mittelmeer.' In *Endlich Urlaub! Die Deutschen reisen*, edited by Hermann Schäfer, 33–43. Cologne: Stiftung Haus der Geschichte der Bundesrepublik Deutschland – DuMont, 1996.

Schwarzer, Alice. 'Jetzt oder nie! Die Frauen sind die Hälfte des Volkes!' *Emma* (1990): 32–8.

Seeba, Hinrich C. 'Der Untergang der Utopie: Ein Schiffbruch in der Gegenwartsliteratur.' *German Studies Review* 4, no. 2 (1981): 281–98.

Selbach, Claus-Ulrich. 'Reise nach Plan: Der Feriendienst des Freien Deutschen Gewerkschaftsbundes.' In *Endlich Urlaub! Die Deutschen reisen*, edited by Hermann Schäfer, 65–76. Cologne: Stiftung Haus der Geschichte – DuMont, 1996.

Sevin, Dieter, ed. *The Crisis of Youth and the Generation Gap in the GDR Novel of the Early Seventies*. Studies in GDR Culture and Society 3. Lanham, MD: University Press of America, 1983.

Sieg, Katrin. *Ethnic Drag: Performing Race, Nation, Sexuality in West Germany*. Ann Arbor: University of Michigan Press, 2002.

Simon, Jana. *Denn wir sind anders*. Berlin: Rowohlt, 2002.

Skulski, Gudrun. 'Sechs Mann in einem Boot.' *Die Neue Zeit*, 28 February 1963.

Slobodian, Quinn. 'Radical Empathy: The Third World and the New Left in 1960s West Germany.' PhD diss., New York University, 2009.

Soden, Kristine von. 'Sexualität als Produktivkraft?' In *Irmtraud Morgners hexische Weltfahrt. Eine Zeitmontage*, edited by Kristine von Soden, 101–8. Berlin: Elefanten Press, 1991.

Sonntag, Heinz Rudolf, ed. *Che Guevara und die Revolution*. Frankfurt/Main: Fischer, 1968.

Speck, Ulrich. 'Deutsche Interessen. Eine Kritik der Rot-Grünen Außenpolitik.' *Merkur* 58, no. 2 (2004): 1–11.

Specogna, Heidi. *Tania la Guerrillera*. Switzerland and FRG: FAMA Film Produktion and ZDF, 1991.

Spode, Hasso. '"Reif für die Insel." Prolegomena zu einer historischen Anthropologie des Tourismus.' In *Arbeit, Freizeit, Reisen. Die feinen Unterschiede im Alltag*, edited by Christiane Cantauw, 105–22. Münster: Waxmann, 1995.

Stephan, Bernhard. *Für die Liebe noch zu mager?* DEFA, 1973.

Stephanson, Anders. 'Cold War Origins.' In *Encyclopedia of American Foreign Policy*, edited by The Gale Group Inc., 2002. http://www.answers.com/topic/cold-war-origins (accessed 7 July 2009).

Stickler, Matthias. *'Ostdeutsch heißt gesamtdeutsch.' Organisation, Selbstverständnis und heimatpolitische Zielsetzungen der deutschen Vertriebenenverbände 1949–1972*. Düsseldorf: Droste.

Stirken, Angela. 'Reisezeit – Zeitreise. Ziel, Konzept und Realisierung der Ausstellung.' In *Endlich Urlaub! Die Deutschen reisen*, edited by Hermann Schäfer, 9–12. Cologne: Stiftung Haus der Geschichte der Bundesrepublik Deutschland, 1996.

Subiotto, Arrigo. 'Volker Braun: Literary Metaphors and the Travails of Socialism.' In *Socialism and the Literary Imagination: Essays on East German Writers*, edited by Martin Kane, 195–212. New York, Oxford: Berg, 1991.

Szymanski, Albert. *Is the Red Flag Flying? The Political Economy of the Soviet Union*. London: Zed, 1979.

Taussig, Michael. *Mimesis and Alterity: A Particular History of the Senses*. New York: Routledge, 1993.

Teraoka, Arlene. *East, West, and Others*. Lincoln: University of Nebraska Press, 1996.

Thomas, Hugh. *Cuba or the Pursuit of Freedom* New York: Da Capo, 1990.

Thomas, Nick. *Protest Movements in 1960s: West Germany a Social History of Dissent and Democracy*. Oxford: Berg, 2003.

Tschierske, Gottfried. *Wir ehren Tamara Bunke*. Edited by Betriebsschule 'Tamara Bunke' VEB Bandtex Pulsnitz. Radeberg: Polydruck, 1980.

Varchmin, Ulla. 'Tania, eine Frau unter Männern.' *Tranvia* 47 (December 1997): 11–13.

VEB F.A. Brockhaus. *Compañeros im sozialistischen Amerika. Freundschaftsbesuch der Partei- und Regierungsdelegation der DDR unter Leitung des Ersten Sekretärs des ZK der SED, Erich Honecker, in der Republik Kuba*. Leipzig: Brockhaus Verlag, 1974.

Viett, Inge. *Cuba Libre bittersüß*, 2nd ed. Hamburg: Nautilus, 2000.

Villain, Jean. *Frühling auf Kuba*. Berlin: Verlag Volk und Welt, 1971.

Vogel, Frank. 'Heisses Pflaster Havanna.' *Filmspiegel*, no. 25 (1962).

Voigt, Lothar. *Aktivismus und moralischer Rigorismus*. Wiesbaden: Deutscher Universitäts-Verlag, 1991.

Voss, Ursula A. *Die Bacardis. Der Kuba-Clan zwischen Rum und Revolution*. Frankfurt/Main: Campus, 2005.

Wallerstein, Immanuel. *Utopistics: Or, Historical Choices of the Twenty-First Century*. New York: The New Press, 1998.

Wedel, Mathias. 'Jetzt seid ihr alle Spreewaldgurken.' *Freitag*, 29 August 2003, 1.

Wenders, Wim. *Buena Vista Social Club*. Road Movies Filmproduktion, 1999. DVD.

Westad, Odd Arne. *The Global Cold War*. Cambridge: Cambridge University Press, 2005.

Westgate, Geoffrey. *Strategies under Surveillance: Reading Irmtraud Morgner as a GDR Writer*. Amsterdam: Rodopi, 2002.

Wickham, Christopher J. *Constructing Heimat in Postwar Germany: Longing and Belonging*. New York: Edwin Mellen Press, 1999.

Wierling, Dorothee. *Geboren im Jahr Eins. Der Jahrgang 1949 in der DDR. Versuch einer Kollektivbiographie*. Berlin: Links, 2002.

Wiesner, Christoph. 'Mi Batalla por la Verdad.' *Die junge Welt*, 7–8 March 1998.

Wikipedia. 'Hans Werner Henze.' http://de.wikipedia.org/wiki/Hans_Werner_Henze.

Wildenthal, Lora. 'Notes on a History of "Imperial Turns" in Modern Germany.' In *After the Imperial Turn*, edited by Antoinette Burton, 144–56. Durham: Duke University Press, 2003.

Wolf, Christa, and Gerhard Wolf. 'Wir haben uns natürlich immer beobachtet.' Interview in *Stille Post. Inoffizielle Schriftstellerkontakte zwischen West und Ost*, edited by Roland Berbig. Berlin: Ch. Links, 2005.

Wolgin, W.P. 'Campanellas Kommunistische Utopie.' In *Der Sonnenstaat*, 5–13. Berlin: Akademie Verlag, 1955.

Wright, Robert. *Three Nights in Havana: Pierre Trudeau, Fidel Castro and the Cold War World*. Toronto: Harper Collins, 2007.

Wright, Robert, and Lana Wylie, eds. *Our Place in the Sun: Canada and Cuba in the Castro Era*. Toronto: University of Toronto Press, 2009.

Zantop, Susanne. *Colonial Fantasies: Conquest, Family, and Nation in Precolonial Germany 1770–1870*. Durham: Duke University Press, 1997.

Zimmerling, Zeno. 'Tanja la Guerrillera.' *Die junge Welt*, 8–9 March 1969, 1, 6.

Zimmermann, Peter. 'Der Dokumentarfilm der DEFA. Zwischen Propaganda,

Alltagbeobachtung und subversiver Rezeption.' In *Deutschlandbilder Ost. Dokumentarfilme der DEFA von der Nachkriegszeit bis zur Wiedervereinigung*, edited by Peter Zimmermann, 9–27. Constance: UVK-Medien/Ölschläger, 1995.

Zorach, Cecile Cazort. 'From Grey East to Golden West: Fritz Rudolf Fries and GDR Travel Literature.' *Studies in GDR Culture and Society* 4 (1984): 137–52.

Index

GERMAN AND EUROPEAN STUDIES

General Editor: Rebecca Wittmann